PRACTICAL GRAMMAR

A CANADIAN WRITER'S RESOURCE

MAXINE RUVINSKY

OXFORD
UNIVERSITY PRESS

OXFORD
UNIVERSITY PRESS

70 Wynford Drive, Don Mills, Ontario M3C 1J9
www.oup.com/ca

Oxford University Press is a department of the University of Oxford.
It furthers the University's objective of excellence in research, scholarship,
and education by publishing worldwide in

Oxford   New York

Auckland   Cape Town   Dar es Salaam   Hong Kong   Karachi
Kuala Lumpur   Madrid   Melbourne   Mexico City   Nairobi
New Delhi   Shanghai   Taipei   Toronto

With offices in

Argentina   Austria   Brazil   Chile   Czech Republic   France   Greece
Guatemala   Hungary   Italy   Japan   Poland   Portugal   Singapore
South Korea   Switzerland   Thailand   Turkey   Ukraine   Vietnam

Oxford is a trade mark of Oxford University Press
in the UK and in certain other countries

Published in Canada
by Oxford University Press

Library and Archives Canada Cataloguing in Publication

Ruvinsky, Maxine, 1950–

Practical grammar : a Canadian writer's resource / Maxine Ruvinsky.

Includes bibliographical references and index.

ISBN-13: 978-0-19-542324-2
ISBN-10: 0-19-542324-0

1. English language—Grammar—Textbooks. I. Title.

PE1112.R89 2006   428.2   C2005-906953-8

3 4 – 09 08 07

Cover Design: Brett J. Miller

This book is printed on paper which contains 60% pre-consumer
recycled fibre and 40% post-consumer waste ✪.

Printed in Canada

PRACTICAL
GRAMMAR

Contents

A Note to the Reader

This book is intended to give you just enough grammar to make you a better writer. It's not about parsing sentences, although that remains, of course, an excellent way to study how sentences work. But many students—maybe most—have long since abandoned hope of making sense of the rules of grammar and rely solely on their ears to judge what is correct. Since they are often right anyway, without knowing why, their dislike and mistrust of grammar are reinforced. Why bother with long, complicated explanations, they reason, if you can get it right most of the time going with what "sounds right"?

They have a point.

This book began as an attempt to reconcile my students at the Thompson Rivers University School of Journalism—many of whom had never heard of parts of speech—to the bottom-line need to master grammar, and to persuade them that mastering grammar is indeed possible. Many were not only convinced that grammar is ultimately indecipherable but also deeply suspicious of attempts to undermine that position. It was as if they assumed that grammar is something to be suffered, not understood, or much less mastered. Some even imagined that good grammar has nothing to do with good writing and that one can become a competent writer without mastering basic grammar. This is a tragic misconception, for while many aspects of good writing do defy analysis and instruction, grammar isn't one of them.

The good news is that grammar does make sense, and with patient practice in the service of a larger goal (good writing), it can be mastered. For various reasons—bad teaching, stop-and-start efforts, the veritable jungle of grammatical terminology, warring experts—most students hate grammar and long ago gave up trying to de-mystify it. In a thicket of confusion, they adopted guessing as the most suitable strategy for achieving grammatical correctness. If this sounds like you, help is at hand.

The purpose of this book is to encourage you to abandon the strategy of guessing, and take one last kick at the grammar can. The text offers a simplified but comprehensive overview of the basics of English grammar. Supplemented by in-chapter drills and end-of-chapter exercises, it is meant to serve as a complete, "one-stop" grammar resource, for use in writing classes or as a personal reference guide kept close at hand. The drills and exercises are meant to help you develop an "operational" knowledge of grammar rather than one that is merely descriptive or prescriptive. The difference is that with prescriptive knowledge you can recite the rules; with operational knowledge, you can understand and apply them.

I have tried to use a minimum—but not *the* minimum—of grammatical terminology. I've also tried to adopt the simplest possible terminology without over-simplifying or misleading. You should be aware, though, that grammarians differ widely—and passionately—in their choice of terminology and in the range of their tolerance for different terminologies; perfect agreement in these matters is rare. Whatever system of labels you adopt, whether it's the one used here, an alternative offered by your instructor, or some other one, you will have to do a certain amount of "drill" work to learn the vocabulary of grammar, just as you would to learn any new vocabulary.

If you master the material in this book—and the material is designed to lead you step by step to mastery—your writing is guaranteed to improve, but not only because it will be grammatically correct. A genuine understanding of grammar can help you analyze your own work by giving you the terminology you need to discuss it; that in turn can build your confidence, allowing you to write with more pleasure and more power. The study of grammar, by helping you refine your grasp of the language, can also broaden your capacity for creativity and risk-taking. After all, in order to break rules for artistic or intellectual effect, you have first to understand and command those rules; to break the rules because you don't know them is nothing more illustrious than simple ignorance.

This book is divided into four parts comprising ten chapters. *Part I: Grammar Basics* is concerned with the most basic grammatical terms and concepts. Most students have avoided grappling with grammar for so long that becoming fluent in its lexicon is the first hurdle. Because familiarity with these terms is a prerequisite for success, the first two chapters concentrate on basic terminology. Chapter 1 introduces the eight parts of speech; it's crucial that you master these before proceeding to Chapter 2, which addresses the essentials of sentence structure, including subjects and predicates, phrases and clauses, and sentence types and patterns.

Once you have assimilated the names for things, you can begin to distinguish consistently between grammatical *forms* (the variations of a word, for example *whom* and *whose*, from *who*) and grammatical *functions* (what the words do in a given context). This is a distinction made throughout the text, but especially in Chapter 2, which shows, for instance, how *amazed* and *amazing*, both forms of the verb *amaze*, can function as adjectives, as well as how phrases and clauses can function as single parts of speech.

Chapter 3 covers the major qualities and aspects of the verb, including person, number, tense, mood, and voice. It describes the verb's principal parts and three participles, and it discusses different kinds of verbs, such as auxiliary verbs, finite and non-finite verbs, action and linking verbs, and transitive and intransitive verbs. It also explains the difference between active and passive voice. The end-of-chapter exercises should help you cement your grasp of the grammatical principles introduced here.

Part 2: Elementary Errors is designed to help you build operational as opposed to theoretical knowledge by introducing the most common errors and ways to detect and fix them. Chapter 4 covers the rules of subject–verb agreement and Chapter 5, those of clear pronoun reference, pronoun–antecedent agreement, and pronoun case. Chapter 6 considers faulty diction, dangling or misplaced modifiers, and how to recognize and fix both.

Part 3: Points of Style pans out, in Chapter 7, to the higher-order errors of bad logic resulting from lack of parallelism and faulty constructions. Chapter 8 tackles punctuation, noting that the conventions of North American punctuation differ slightly from those of British punctuation, and that even within countries, stylistic preferences may vary from one organization to the next. Stylistic conventions in general, including those of punctuation, vary widely and can change quickly, unlike grammatical terms and rules, which are based on logic rather than convention and change only slowly.

Part 4: Writing Essentials presents a brief overview of basic writing techniques and ends with a collection of 12 tips. Finally, Chapter 10, provides a quick study of different documentation styles, highlighting three styles (the MLA, APA, and Chicago styles). Differing style guidelines exist simultaneously for various English-speaking countries, for various trades, professions, and scholarly disciplines; they also change by region and over time. All style guides should be impeccably logical, but in the real world, the only practical point of style guides is to help you maintain consistency. Once you've learned to use one style guide, you've learned enough to use them all.

A Note to the Teacher

This text is meant to be used to complement the grammar component of introductory college and university writing classes. Although it is also suitable as a basic introduction or review for self-directed learners, special procedures aimed at meshing the grammar and writing aspects and exercises of the course apply for instructors using it in the classroom.

Studies have repeatedly shown that a straightforward "drill" approach to teaching and learning grammar doesn't work to improve student writing. Studies also show that students write better—with greater coherence, livelier style, truer voice, *and* fewer errors of all kinds—when they are focused on critical thinking and self-expression rather than on avoiding error.

Thus, this text is meant to be used in a "workshop" manner. Students, in groups of four or five, should complete the grammar exercises together after having prepared for that day's lesson. Once the groups have had a chance to discuss and debate the correct answers, the whole class reconvenes to have answered any outstanding questions and resolve any lingering confusion.

These grammar exercises should be balanced with writing exercises (see, for example, Gabrielle Rico's "clustering," Peter Elbow's "direct writing process," and Julia Cameron's "morning pages," among others detailed in books referenced in the *Resources List*). But in addition to mixing straight grammar with more expressive writing exercises, the instructor can invent simple writing-based exercises to supplement the grammar exercises. For example, for the class that covers Chapter 1, which deals with learning to recognize the parts of speech, the instructor, having addressed any outstanding questions or issues related to the review exercises, could have students write short pieces (one or two paragraphs at most), applying certain restrictions that flex the newly acquired grammatical language; have them write 200 words about their morning, but limit the number of nouns in the piece to 20.

Trying to find the best ways to teach traditional classroom grammar has shown me two things about the (according to some, doomed) effort. First, the practice of having students reason together in small peer groups on the exercises and issues of the day is critical and indispensable to success. But second, as genuine understanding begins to replace fear and loathing in their quest for the Holy Grail of grammatical proficiency, students can be heard on occasion to discuss these issues outside the classroom, often arguing their various points with a certain style and verve. That students can come to think critically about the grammar that once tied their tongues tight is a gratifying indication of the possibilities.

Part I

Grammar Basics

Chapter 1

Parts of Speech

Every word in a sentence can be categorized as one of eight parts of speech depending on its *function*—what it does—in that sentence. The following are the eight parts of speech:

- **Nouns** name people (*Jared*, *doctor*), animals (*Fido*, *dog*), places (*Paris*, *home*), and things, both concrete things such as objects or substances (*houses*, *air*) and abstract things such as qualities or concepts (*sorrow*, *intelligence*), measures (*inches*, *years*), and actions (*reading*, *writing*).

- **Pronouns** substitute for nouns, so that instead of having to write, "Francine got Francine's hair cut, but Francine didn't get Francine's hair coloured, and Francine also didn't get Francine's hair permed," you can write: "Francine got *her* hair cut, but *she* didn't get *it* coloured, and *she* also didn't get *it* permed."

- **Verbs** assert something, showing either action or state of being. The verb is the single most important word in a sentence, since it alone can say what the subject of the sentence does, has, or is (*she sings, she has fun, she is happy*). The basic form of the verb is the infinitive (the form usually preceded by the word *to*: *to sing, to be*).

- **Adjectives** describe or modify nouns and pronouns (*stucco house, lucky lady*). The words *the*, *a*, and *an* are regarded as special kinds of adjectives, called articles. *The* is the definite article; *a* and *an* are the indefinite articles.

- **Adverbs** describe or modify verbs (*ran quickly*), adjectives (*very tall girl*), or other adverbs (*ran too quickly*). Adverbs usually tell where, when, why, how, or in what way something is done or experienced.

- **Prepositions** introduce objects—the nouns or pronouns that follow them—and together the preposition and its object form a prepositional phrase. (A phrase is a group of words without a subject-and-verb combination. A group of words with a subject-and-verb combination is called a clause.) The prepositions are underlined in the following examples: <u>up</u> the hill, <u>down</u> the road, <u>into</u> the house, <u>before</u> the party, <u>after</u> the show, <u>in</u> Montreal, <u>at</u> home. Prepositions that consist of more than one word are called compound prepositions (*along with, in regard to*).

- **Conjunctions** connect or join words or groups of words in a sentence. A co-ordinating conjunction (such as *and, but, or, for, nor, yet*) is used to join sentence elements of equal rank (for example, two single nouns to each other, as in *apples and oranges*). A subordinating conjunction (such as *because, as, while, if, that, unless*) is used to join subordinate (or "dependent") clauses to the main or "independent" one. In the following examples, the independent clause is in plain type, and the subordinate clause, beginning with its subordinating conjunction, is in italics.

  ○ She went home *because she was tired.*
  ○ I read *while I waited.*
  ○ They decided to go out *unless it rained.*

- **Interjections** are words or short phrases that are grammatically independent of the other words in the sentence. They serve no grammatical function within the sentence, but instead "interrupt" it, expressing surprise or strong feeling. (*Hey! Oh no! Ouch! Gee!*)

Words are categorized as one or another part of speech on the basis not of their form (or spelling), but of their function (the work they do). Notice how, in the examples below, the same word can function as different parts of speech.

○ noun: I found my *key* on the front lawn.
○ verb: They *key* the list of answers to the workbook questions.
○ adjective: He suggested the *key* concept for the conference.

○ noun: The audience listened intently to the *talk*.
○ verb: The two sisters *talk* on the phone every day.
○ adjective: We tuned in to our favourite *talk* show.

Nouns

Nouns are words that name things:

- People: *Jeremiah, colleague, francophone*
- Animals: *dogs, cats, horses*
- Places: *Montreal, New York, Milan*
- Objects: *chairs, tables, inkwells*
- Substances: *water, earth, air*
- Qualities or ideas: *strength, courage, compassion*
- Measures: *years, inches, metres*
- Actions: *dancing, jumping, talking*

The italicized words in the following sentence are all nouns:

> ○ When *Marybeth* returned from the *market* in *St. John's*, her *mother* had good *news* for her; an acceptance *letter* had arrived from the *university*.

Marybeth is a person; *market* is a place; *St. John's* is a place; *mother* is a person; *news* is a concept; *letter* is an object; and *university* is a place.

Exercise 1.1

Identify the following nouns by type: person, animal, place, object, substance, quality or idea, measure, action.

1. saucer _____
2. bushel _____
3. dancing _____
4. camel _____
5. home _____
6. talent _____
7. Montreal _____
8. client _____
9. magazine _____
10. year _____
11. tree _____
12. humour _____
13. mountain _____
14. pilot _____

Exercise 1.1 – *continued*

15. Canada   _____

16. month   _____

17. talking   _____

18. steel   _____

19. playing   _____

20. performer   _____

Exercise 1.2

Underline all the nouns in the following sentences.

1. Mordecai bought a used guitar from his friend.

2. Editors are looking for certain kinds of writing.

3. The staff at the plant signed a petition.

4. The book contains examples of feature writing.

5. The teacher had patience and skill.

6. The young musician played his flute in class.

7. A car sped down the quiet street at noon.

8. Oranges and lemons are grown in Israel.

9. Despite predictions, TV has not replaced the book.

10. Pina and her friends went to the festival.

We've seen that nouns name people, animals, places, and things—both concrete things such as objects and substances, and abstract things such as qualities and concepts, measures and actions. Concrete nouns name things that can be grasped by the senses, for example seen or touched (*cat, mouse, hail*); abstract nouns name ideas and other "things" that must be grasped by the mind (*truth, justice, beauty*). (Some grammars classify nouns as countable or uncountable rather than as concrete or abstract.)

In addition to being classed as concrete or abstract, nouns may also be classed as proper (beginning with a capital letter) or common (beginning with a lowercase letter). Proper nouns are capitalized because they name specific people, places, and things (*Yoko Ono, Montreal, Queen Elizabeth Hotel*). All other nouns are common nouns and begin with lowercase letters (*spatula, house, loyalty*).

Nouns that refer to a group rather than an individual (*team, herd, family*) are called collective nouns. Nouns made up of two or more words (*Parliament Buildings, father-in-law*) are called compound nouns. The words of a compound noun can be joined (*homework*), or separate (*ice cream*), or hyphenated (*mother-in-law*). Compound nouns change over time, often evolving from two words to a hyphenated word to a single word without hyphens. When in doubt about the correct form, consult the appropriate style guide (see Chapter 10 on style and documentation).

Exercise 1.3

Identify the italicized nouns as concrete or abstract, and common or proper; also identify any collective or compound nouns.

1. Never is an awfully long *time*. _____

2. An old saying has it that *beauty* is in the eye of the beholder. _____

3. My *sister-in-law* is performing at the café tonight. _____

4. I thoroughly enjoyed reading Joy Kogawa's book, *Obasan.* _____

5. The *Parliament Buildings* are located in the capital city of Ottawa. _____

6. My best friend and I really treasure our *relationship*. _____

7. The *truth* is I won't come to the event because I disapprove of it. _____

8. I hope the *Blue Birds* won the relay race. _____

9. A *gaggle* of geese could be seen in the distance. _____

10. I know that middle-aged *couple*; they live on Battle Street. _____

Remember that a word is a noun if you can make it plural or possessive (or both). Take the noun couple. You can make that noun plural (*two <u>couples</u>*) and possessive (*the <u>couple's</u> house*). A word is also a noun if you can put before it one of the articles, *a*, *an*, or *the* (*<u>a</u> house, <u>an</u> orange, <u>the</u> party*), or a possessive noun or pronoun (*<u>Tom's</u> house, <u>his</u> house*).

Exercise 1.4

Underline all the nouns in the following sentences.

1. The dog dug a hole under the fence.

2. Our mother graduated this year.

3. Maps were distributed among the students in the class.

4. The captain congratulated the winners.

5. The leader had vision and talent.

6. Singing and dancing are her favourite activities.

7. Bernard bought a new home in Westmount.

8. Our class was interrupted by the student.

9. Sky-diving is a dangerous sport.

10. Books and magazines lay scattered around the room.

11. Jeremy hoped to take lessons in swimming.

12. Flour and sugar are useful ingredients.

13. The school made many changes.

14. The doctor prescribed rest for her exhausted patient.

15. The train leaves the station in an hour.

16. That student has initiative.

17. Two friends just returned from a trip to Boston.

18. Her bracelet fell into the water.

19. Heat from the fireplace warmed the room.

20. Caviar and champagne were served at the event.

Pronouns

Pronouns take the place of nouns and allow us to avoid the awkward writing that would result from having to repeat them, so that instead of having to write "Zelda forgot Zelda's keys; Zelda left the keys at Zelda's office," we can write "Zelda forgot *her* keys; *she* left *them* at *her* office."

There are six main kinds of pronoun: personal, relative, demonstrative, indefinite, interrogative, and reflexive.

Personal pronouns

There are six forms of personal pronoun, as shown in the following chart.

First person means the person or people speaking (singular *I*, or plural *we*). **Second person** means the person or people spoken to (*you* for both singular and plural); and **third person** means the person or people or thing(s) spoken about (singular *he*, *she*, *it*, and plural *they*).

	Singular	Plural
First person *(person/s speaking)*	I	we
Second person *(person/s spoken to)*	you	you
Third person *(person/s spoken about)*	he, she, it	they

Relative pronouns

These are used to link less important ideas to the main idea of a sentence. They include *that*, *which*, and *who* (also *whom* and *whose*). The relative pronoun thus performs two jobs at once: it joins a less important (or subordinate) clause to a main clause, and also refers back to its antecedent, the noun it substitutes for. The following examples show the relative pronoun in boldface type and the antecedent of the pronoun in italics:

- Here's the *book* **that** I promised you.
- She took the *train*, **which** was late.
- I met a *guy* **who** sells sailboats.

Demonstrative pronouns

These point out or indicate specific things. There are only four demonstrative pronouns: *this*, and its plural form, *these*; and *that*, and its plural form, *those*.

Indefinite pronouns

These are numerous; like all pronouns, indefinite pronouns refer to persons, animals, places, and things, but not specific or particular ones. The following list shows commonly used indefinite pronouns: *all, any, anybody, anyone, anything, both, each, either, enough, everybody, everyone, everything, few, less, many, more, most, much, neither, nobody, none, no one, nothing, one(s), other(s), several, some, somebody, someone, something.*

Interrogative pronouns

These are easy to recognize because they ask questions. They include the following: *what, where, when, which, why, how,* and *who* (also *whom* and *whose*). The interrogative pronouns in the following examples are in italic type.

- *What* did he say? *Where* is my toothbrush?
- *When* did she call? *Which* way did they go?
- *Why* bother? *How* do you know? *Who* is at the door?

Reflexive pronouns

These refer back to the subject and are also easy to recognize because they always end in *self* or *selves* (*myself, yourself, himself, herself, itself, ourselves, yourselves* and *themselves*). Reflexive pronouns are used when the subject and object of a verb are one and the same, as in this sentence:

- *She* cut *herself.*

Reflexive pronouns are also used for emphasis:

- I *myself* saw the deed done.

When possessive pronouns are used as adjectives, they are called possessive adjectives. In the following examples the possessive adjectives are italicized: We took off *our* coats and hung them in the closet. Allie put *her* boots in the mud room and Armand left *his* umbrella by the door. That's *my* book. Where is yours? Notice that the word "yours" in the last example is not a possessive adjective, but a possessive pronoun (it doesn't describe a noun; it takes the place of one).

Exercise 1.5

Identify the pronouns in the following sentences.

1. Valarie has been busy; she won't be at the party tonight._____

2. The books are on the desk. Please take them. _____

3. George and Kit are coming to visit; they will stay a week. _____

4. I looked for the car but couldn't find it. _____

Exercise 1.5 – *continued*

5. A society owes much to its writers. _____

6. The couple entered the contest and won it. _____

7. Yingqing invited people to dinner but they didn't show. _____

8. All the students attended and some stayed on to ask questions. _____

9. Each of the contestants paid a fee, which was refundable. _____

10. I overheard them discussing your plans. _____

11. I ate all the cookies that you made; they were delicious. _____

12. He gave the money to a charity; he kept none. _____

13. We have pets whom we consider part of the family. _____

14. It is the thing that matters most to me. _____

15. Those are my daffodils; hand them over. _____

16. Anybody may join the club, but he must obey its rules. _____

17. Many attended the concert and few forgot it. _____

18. They say you catch more flies with honey. _____

19. Why would you want to catch them? _____

20. Among the reviewers, several mentioned it. _____

21. The child who was missing returned. _____

22. These are my papers. _____

23. They asked her to show them to me. _____

24. We went to Montreal with them. _____

25. Eileen will not tell her why I quit. _____

26. He objected to the procedure, and the committee amended it. _____

27. Anyone can apply for the job. _____

28. That is the meal they served. _____

Exercise 1.5 – *continued*

29. The dress that you wore was admired by others. _____

30. Although I questioned her, she did provide much information. _____

31. These are on reserve, but those are not._____

32. She held the baby in her arms. _____

33. The meal was excellent and it was consumed heartily. _____

34. That is the movie I told you about. _____

35. He didn't wait for them as they had instructed him to do. _____

36. That was the story that I heard from them. _____

37. Years passed and many forgot the tale, but some remembered._____

38. The horses seemed uneasy when we entered the barn. _____

39. Each brought his or her resumé and work samples. _____

40. She can tell you where the others have gone with their friends. _____

Exercise 1.6

Identify the nouns with a capital N and the pronouns with a capital P.

1. He found it behind the sofa.

2. The crowd cheered the home team.

3. Some got overtime pay but others got nothing.

4. All the teenage girls bought jeans at the same store.

5. She looked for the textbook but couldn't find it.

6. He wore an expensive suit that was made in London.

7. Only the federal government can make criminal law.

8. He found a seat at the back of the bus and sat down.

9. Those were the literary works that she most enjoyed.

10. All of us decided to help her.

Verbs

The verb expresses action or state of being. It is the single most important part of speech since every sentence must have at least one verb, telling what the subject—the person, animal, place, or thing that the sentence is about—is doing, having, or being.

To tell whether a word is a verb, see if you can change its tense without turning the sentence into nonsense or dramatically altering its meaning. For instance, "They chair the meeting" can become "They chaired the meeting" because *chair* in these clauses is a verb. In the next example, *chair* is not a verb but a noun:

○ He put his bag on the chair.

It would make no sense to write: *He put his bag on the chaired.*

There are two main kinds of verbs: action verbs and linking verbs. Most are action verbs, those that express actions (though not necessarily physical ones; for example, *to think* is a kind of action verb). Linking verbs express something about the subject, either identifying the subject (*she is the singer*) or describing it (*she is talented*). The most common linking verb is *to be* (in all forms: *I am, you are, he/she/it is, we are, you are, they are, I was, you were,* etc.). Other linking verbs include *appear, become, feel, grow, keep, look, prove, remain, seem, smell, sound, stand, stay, taste,* and *turn*. Most of these can be used as either action or linking verbs, as in the following examples:

○ Tamara appeared [action verb] in the doorway.
○ Tamara appeared [linking verb] happy.

Exercise 1.7

Identify the verbs in the following sentences as action or linking verbs.

1. The bicycle swerved off the road. _____

2. Parents usually know their children well. _____

3. Snowflakes fell for hours. _____

4. You put your coat on the couch. _____

5. The kittens meowed at her. _____

Exercise 1.7 – *continued*

6. The weather was cold. _____

7. He leapt over the barriers. _____

8. The companies merged. _____

9. Kinga went to graduate school in London. _____

10. Allie won an essay contest at school. _____

11. They travelled to Maine for a vacation. _____

12. We stopped the car. _____

13. The temperature is just right. _____

14. They complained about poor writing skills. _____

15. She read the novel three times. _____

16. The incident provoked controversy. _____

17. The sun shone brightly that day. _____

18. Jenny met her future husband in college. _____

19. Slowly, the conductor turned to the audience. _____

20. My associate is a true scholar. _____

Don't confuse a noun that names an action (*dancing is fun*) with an action verb, which expresses an action carried out by a subject (*he was dancing, they were dancing*, etc.).

The verb in a sentence may consist of a single word (*she sings*), but it may also consist of more than one word (*six months have passed, a week will have passed*). When the sentence verb is a phrase instead of a single word then the last word—the one that tells what's happening—is the main (or principal) verb; all the preceding words are auxiliary (or helping) verbs.

If I write *I go*, I have a verb made up of a single word, *go*. If I write *I have gone*, I have a verb phrase made up of the auxiliary verb *have* and the principal verb *gone*. The rule holds regardless of the number of auxiliaries. In the verb phrase *must have been leaving*, the principal verb is *leaving*, and all the other words (*must, have,* and *been*) are auxiliaries.

In addition to the verbs *be, have,* and *will,* which are used routinely to form certain tenses (*I am going, I have gone, I will go*), the following verbs are also commonly used. They are called modal auxiliaries: *do, must, ought, let, used, need, shall* and *should, will* and *would, can* and *could,* and *may* and *might.*

Exercise 1.8

Identify the verbs (V) and verb phrases (VP) in the following sentences.

1. The accident affected his vision, but he still drives.
2. The rain had been falling for hours.
3. Movies are a popular form of entertainment.
4. You broke it; you should fix it.
5. The new journalism school is attracting students.
6. After we arrived, we began unpacking.
7. Felicity was studying for her final exam.
8. Nanette will drive to Vancouver on Saturday.
9. The children were growing fast.
10. You must have left the keys in the car.

Exercise 1.9

Identify the principal verbs (P) and auxiliary verbs (A) in the verb phrases.

1. He would live to regret that decision.
2. All the details had been finalized by friends.
3. I was walking the dog down Main Street.
4. We did object to the plan.
5. They will decide later whether to attend.
6. The first storm clouds had been seen.
7. The policy does allow returns.
8. Billy had grown a lot in the last year.
9. Hiroshi was named a bureau chief of the Canadian Press.
10. She is creating the sets for the play.
11. The twins were saving their allowance.
12. The signs of a struggle were noted in his police report.
13. The curtains were blowing lazily beside the open window.
14. She had been sleeping when the phone rang.
15. It had never been done before.

When a verb or verb phrase is stated in the negative (*they did not go, we were not thinking*), the word *not* (or the equivalent word that makes the meaning negative) is considered an adverb. This is because its task is to modify the verb or verb phrase, not to be part of it.

Adjectives

An adjective describes or modifies a noun or pronoun (*a white house, a cool drink*), adding more information to make the meaning of the noun or pronoun more vivid, clear or precise. The adjective can add information (*a red hat, a large house, a beautiful picture*), or it can limit the meaning to show which, whose, or how many (*this hat, Tanya's house, five pictures*). The words *the, a, an*—the definite and indefinite articles—are special kinds of adjectives. They belong in a category of words called **determiners** or **markers**, which indicate that a particular part of speech will follow. Most adjectives can be compared, as in the following examples: *nice, nicer, nicest; kind, kinder, kindest; intelligent, more intelligent, most intelligent.*

⚬ His *sympathetic* eyes made my heart melt.

(*Sympathetic* is an adjective that modifies or describes the noun *eyes*.)

⚬ She was *thin* and *pale*.

(*Pale* and *thin* are adjectives modifying the pronoun *she*.)

⚬ One large white house stood on the hill.

(The adjectives *one, large* and *white* modify the noun *hill*.)

A word is usually an adjective if it can be applied before the noun or pronoun it modifies without changing the meaning. For example:

⚬ George Szanto's novel, *The Condesa of M,* is brilliant.

The adjective brilliant can be placed directly before the noun it modifies—novel—with no change in intended meaning: brilliant novel.

Exercise 1.10

Identify the adjectives and the nouns they modify.

1. A dozen roses were delivered. _____
2. The spare room was converted into a study. _____
3. The accountant gave a short speech. _____
4. They swam in the deep end of the pool. _____
5. A new scholarship was offered to the candidate. _____
6. Many famous actors live in Hollywood. _____
7. The pouring rain soaked my clothes. _____
8. Ten students attended the free concert. _____
9. The dress has bright sequins. _____
10. He found the wet towels in the kitchen. _____
11. They gave her a gold watch. _____
12. Teenagers like the company of other teenagers. _____
13. I tried to revise the second draft. _____
14. The teacher assigned a critical reading. _____
15. She tried to butter the fresh bread. _____
16. Bright panels were added to the display. _____
17. He gave a provocative lecture on journalism. _____
18. The excited puppies raced around the yard. _____
19. Cold drinks were served to the clients. _____
20. The house was hidden by large trees. _____
21. The clean glasses gleamed. _____
22. Sufficient food was provided for the event. _____
23. What a lovely sight! _____
24. I interviewed a former boxer. _____
25. Aline lives in a small city. _____
26. The school has an innovative approach. _____
27. A colourful poster was made for the march. _____

Exercise 1.10 – *continued*

28. A trio of senior officials introduced the show. _____

29. Anne is a respected historian. _____

30. She sang sweet lullabies to the baby. _____

31. He overcame so many obstacles. _____

32. We climbed to the highest peak. _____

33. Tiny raindrops began to fall. _____

34. Nutritious food helps build health. _____

35. The storyteller related a sad tale. _____

Possessive words can function as nouns (*that one is Emanuel's*), pronouns (*this one is hers*), or adjectives (*Emanuel's coat, his coat*). When possessives are used as adjectives, telling to whom or to what something belongs, they are called possessive adjectives.

Notice that possessive nouns (*that is Jinny's, this is the boy's*) do not change form when they are used as adjectives (*Jinny's strike, the boy's hat*), but most possessive pronouns do: the coat is *mine,* but that's *my* coat, and so on (*yours/your, hers/her, ours/our, theirs/their*).

In this next example, the possessive adjective *your* in the first part of the sentence and the possessive pronoun *yours* in the second part illustrate the difference:

○ *Your* jacket is on the couch; *yours* is in the closet.

In the first part, *your* is an adjective because it has a noun to modify (*jacket*); in the second part, *yours* is a pronoun, taking the place of a noun.

Exercise 1.11

Identify the possessive words—i.e. the ones that show to what or to whom something belongs—and decide whether each is functioning as an adjective, noun, or pronoun. Note that a noun takes an apostrophe (') to indicate possession, while a pronoun does not.

1. Her dress was the colour of lilacs. _____

2. Auren gave Fred his notes. _____

3. He made a call on his cell phone. _____

Exercise 1.11 – *continued*

4. Audrey gave Fred's notes to Scott. _____

5. Your keys are on the shelf; mine are in my purse. _____

6. Tanya's are the wrong size; try mine. _____

7. His father will call Steve's friend tomorrow. _____

8. We helped get her keys out of the lock. _____

9. They stopped at his place for the gifts. _____

10. I carried the baby in my arms and rocked her. _____

11. Our boots are here; theirs are in the closet. _____

12. She gave hers to Fritz and kept Joannie's. _____

13. Brenda drove Shawn to his office. _____

14. His essays are good; hers are brilliant. _____

15. We read their names from Henry's list. _____

16. Cristina wrote her essay on censorship and its ills. _____

17. Dani's internship at the newspaper went well. _____

18. Their houses blended; his stood out. _____

19. I loved her sense of fairness and her honesty. _____

20. The box fell and its contents tumbled to the floor. _____

Adverbs

An adverb can describe a verb, an adjective, or another adverb; it can also describe a whole sentence or clause. When an adverb describes a verb, it shows when (time), where (place), or how (manner) something is done. When it describes an adjective or another adverb, it illustrates the extent or degree of some quality or condition. As noted above, when a verb is stated in the negative, the *not* is an adverb.

  ○ That performer dances *beautifully.*
  (*Beautifully* is an adverb modifying the verb *dances*; it shows manner, how the performer danced.)

° He has an *extremely* aggressive dog.
(*Extremely* is an adverb modifying the adjective *aggressive*; it shows the degree to which the dog is aggressive.)

° I work *too hard*.
(*Too* is an adverb modifying another adverb, *hard*.)

° *Strangely*, the room was empty.
(*Strangely* is an adverb that modifies or describes the whole clause, *the room was empty*.)

Adjectives and adverbs are useful but for a strong style avoid excessive use of them. Before using an adjective or adverb, especially one grown anemic from overuse (such as *good, interesting, rather, very*), try the sentence without modifiers to see whether they are even necessary.

Paradoxically, a phrase or clause is often stronger without the modifier. For example, compare these two sentences:

° I was really very scared.
° I was scared.

Somehow, the addition of the adverbs *really very* in the first sentence actually detracts from the sentence, weakening its sense and impact. When a phrase or sentence seems to lack emphasis, don't pile on the modifiers; instead, think about what you need to say, and find better, more precise nouns and verbs to make the modifiers unnecessary.

Exercise 1.12

Identify the adverbs, and indicate what each expresses: time, place, manner, or degree.

1. The paper was delivered daily. _____

2. I seldom have a chance to read novels._____

3. Ross can throw the ball farther._____

4. Five years have passed since she moved here. _____

5. They went everywhere to collect donations._____

Exercise 1.12 – *continued*

6. The wounded bird soon grew stronger. _____

7. Quietly, he left the room. _____

8. She plays that piece beautifully. _____

9. She said she had to leave now. _____

10. The weeds grew fast. _____

11. The lost earring could be anywhere. _____

12. Spending was sharply reduced. _____

13. I see him occasionally. _____

14. She wants to speak to you privately. _____

15. Sometimes we go to the farmers' market. _____

16. I've been staying at home lately. _____

17. Kimberly is slowly but surely recuperating. _____

18. The little girl cautiously opened the jar. _____

19. They often take that route to work. _____

20. I waited impatiently in line. _____

Exercise 1.13

Identify the italicized words as adjectives or adverbs.

1. We were *tired* and *hungry* after our journey. _____

2. I am *appalled* at your behaviour! _____

3. I had a *really good* time at your party. _____

4. I found a *gold* ring in my living room. _____

5. I was *never good* at public speaking. _____

6. I *very nearly* lost control of the car just then. _____

7. *Yesterday*, I dreamed I saw a *giant* lobster. _____

8. I had *two* cream puffs for lunch. _____

9. You look *ill*. _____

10. We painted the *small* bedroom *midnight* blue. _____

Prepositions

A preposition is used to introduce a phrase. (Recall that a phrase is a group of words without a subject-and-verb combination.) The main noun or pronoun in the phrase is called the object of the preposition. Here are examples of such phrases, with the prepositions in italics and the objects underlined:

- *up* the hill
- *down* the road
- *into* their house
- *before* the party.

Prepositions don't modify words (only adjectives and adverbs do that), but in linking the words of the phrase to the rest of a sentence, prepositions show important relationships. For example, notice how the meaning varies when different prepositions are used with the same object:

- *on* the chair
- *beside* the chair
- *below* the chair
- *to* the chair.

Recall that the noun or pronoun following a preposition is called the object. A prepositional phrase consists of a preposition and its object, often with an article between them. The previous examples contain the definite article, *the*, which along with the indefinite articles *a* and *an* is considered a special kind of adjective, since it always modifies a noun or pronoun. The phrase may also contain modifiers (*on the comfortable chair*). The whole structure—the preposition (*on*), the article (*the*), any modifiers of the object (*comfortable*), and the object noun or pronoun itself (*chair*)— is called a prepositional phrase.

Additional words between the preposition and its object do not change the grammatical relationship: the preposition and its object form the backbone of the prepositional phrase. For example:

- The house *in the once-green valley* was destroyed *by a raging fire.*

In the first phrase, *in* is the preposition, and *valley* is the object of the preposition; *the* is the definite article and *once green* is an adjective modifying the noun *valley*. In the second phrase, *by* is the preposition, *fire* is the object of the preposition, *a* is the indefinite article, and *raging* is an adjective modifying the noun *fire*. The whole prepositional phrase includes the preposition, its object, plus any modifiers.

Compound prepositions usually consist of two words, and sometimes three. The following are common examples:

> ∘ ahead of, away from, inside of, together with, apart from, because of, instead of, up at, as for, belonging to, out of, up on, contrary to, owing to, up to, aside from, due to, rather than, with reference to, with regard to, on account of, in spite of, for the sake of.

A particle is a special kind of preposition that functions as part of a verb, forming something called a verb–particle composite. Here are two examples:

> ∘ He was so drunk that he *passed out.*
> ∘ She *ran across* an old friend.

Notice that the verb in such verb-particle composites has a different meaning from that of the verb by itself: Drunken people who "pass out" don't necessarily "pass out" anything. And "running across" an old friend is not the same as "running over" him.

Exercise 1.14

Identify the prepositions and the phrases they introduce. _____

1. They will vote on the motion at this meeting. _____

2. We found his wallet on the back seat. _____

3. We found your pocketbook in the house. _____

4. Flowers were planted along the path. _____

5. His birthmark looked like a large plum. _____

6. The author read from his new novel._____

7. We copied those pages from the book. _____

8. The doctor walked into the room. _____

9. A large box sat beside the main door. _____

10. The lovers walked along the beach. _____

11. The lilacs in the yard smell wonderful. _____

12. Rumours began to spread throughout the town._____

13. My cousin moved to Boston with her husband. _____

14. She was tutored by a college student. _____

15. He wrote a play about Canadian politicians. _____

Conjunctions

Conjunctions connect words or groups of words in a sentence. The two kinds are co-ordinating conjunctions (such as *and*, *yet*, *but*, *for*, *nor*, *or*, *either*, *neither*, *yet*), which join elements of equal rank in a sentence (single words to single words, phrases to phrases, and clauses to clauses), and subordinating conjunctions (such as *if*, *since*, *because*, *that*, *while*, *unless*, *although*), which join subordinate clauses to independent ones.

Conjunctions are indispensable but they are often misused or treated carelessly. They help to express the logical connections between ideas, so be careful to use the right one. Different conjunctions can radically change meaning:

- *Because* she loved him, she had to leave.
- *Although* she loved him, she had to leave.

Co-ordinating conjunctions

These connect elements of equal rank. The following examples illustrate co-ordinate elements, with the conjunctions in italic type:

- I love apples *and* blueberries.
- She looked in the closet *and* under the bed.
- No one else was at home, *and* I answered the phone.

The first conjunction joins two nouns (*apples, blueberries*); the second joins two phrases (*in the closet, under the bed*); the third joins two independent clauses (*No one else was at home, I answered the phone*).

Subordinating conjunctions

These connect subordinate clauses to independent ones. They show that one idea, expressed in the subordinate clause, leans on another idea, expressed in the independent clause. The following example illustrates:

- I answered the phone because no one else would.

Because no one else would is a subordinate clause. Unlike the independent clause, *I answered the phone*, it does not make sense by itself; it needs to be joined to the independent clause to have meaning. *Because* is the subordinating conjunction that does the job.

Correlative conjunctions

These come in pairs (*both . . . and; neither . . . nor; either . . . or; not only . . . but also*), with each half of the pair introducing one of the two things being joined:

- I love ice cream, *both* vanilla *and* chocolate.
- I enjoy *neither* doing the laundry *nor* cleaning the house.
- I want *not only* to live well *but also* to act honourably.

Recall that a relative pronoun (*who, which, that*) can do the work of a subordinating conjunction, and introduce a subordinate clause. Example:

- Here is the book *that* I promised to lend you.

When *that* is used to join a subordinate clause to a main clause in a sentence, it is either a subordinating conjunction or a relative pronoun. Here's how to tell the difference: A relative pronoun has an antecedent; a conjunction just joins. In the following example, *that* is a subordinating conjunction:

- Lienne called to let me know that she would arrive on Wednesday.

The *that* has no antecedent; it just joins the subordinate clause *that she would arrive on Wednesday* to the independent clause *Lienne called to let me know.*

In this next example, *that* is a relative pronoun:

- Ram forgot the suitcase *that* he wanted to borrow.

The *that* has an antecedent, *suitcase.*

Conjunctive adverbs

A conjunctive adverb is one that also performs the work of a conjunction, joining sentence elements. It can be used to join two independent clauses. Words used as conjunctive adverbs include the following: *however, thus, indeed, moreover, consequently, also, anyhow, besides, furthermore, nevertheless.*

Exercise 1.15

Identify the co-ordinating conjunctions and the words they join.

1. They wore long coats and fur hats. _____

2. The girls baked cakes and cookies for the sale. _____

3. I can bring the drinks or the salad to the party. _____

4. Anne and I prefer the same kinds of books. _____

Exercise 1.15 – *continued*

5. She left the room and closed the door behind her. _____

6. The erosion occurred slowly but surely. _____

7. He and I are planning the convocation events. _____

8. Lienne writes movie scripts and TV shows. _____

9. The boutique sold no tams or berets._____

10. The bed was covered with papers and clothes. _____

11. Every Saturday, I visit my friends Lu and Morris._____

12. The doctor ordered her to eat well and get some rest. _____

13. Singing and dancing are both fun._____

14. I like pasta, but I don't like pesto._____

15. The tired but happy couple returned home._____

Interjections

Interjections are used to express strong emotion and have no grammatical relation to the rest of the sentence. Some words are always used as interjections (*Hey! Wow! Ouch!*). Other words, although generally used as other parts of speech, may also be used as interjections. (*Great! Oh no! Too bad!*)

Exercise 1.16

Identify the conjunctions and the interjections.

1. The boy loved hiking and swimming._____

2. Wow! That was invigorating. _____

3. Call back this evening or tomorrow morning._____

4. Cristine and Danielle worked together. _____

5. I felt happy but tired. _____

6. The dinner was elaborate and delicious. _____

7. Oh no! I left the keys in my other bag. _____

8. They discussed profits and losses. _____

Exercise 1.16 – *continued*

9. Oh boy! That was the day from hell. _____

10. She must decide on one or the other_____

11. The hotel was lovely but expensive. _____

12. Sweat bathed his arms and chest. _____

13. They liked the resort yet decided to leave early._____

14. They wanted to vacation in Paris or London. _____

15. He ordered soup and salad._____

Review Exercises

Remember as you complete the following exercises this critical fact about parts of speech: A word may serve as different parts of speech in different sentences or contexts. What functions as a noun in one context can serve as an adjective in another; or a verb in one phrase may perform as a noun in another. It is the function performed by the word in a given context (and not its form or spelling) that determines its part of speech.

When you ask yourself what *function* each word performs in the sentences below, remember that nouns and pronouns name, verbs assert, adjectives and adverbs describe or modify, prepositions and conjunctions join, and interjections exclaim or interrupt.

Exercise 1.A

Identify the part of speech of each of the italicized words as noun, pronoun, verb, adjective, adverb, conjunction, preposition, or interjection. Notice in the first example that the word *sand*, usually a noun, is used differently in order to modify the noun *castle*.

1. We built a *sand* castle *on* the beach. _____

2. *Joi* plays the piano *well*. _____

3. The cleaning lady *removed* her *jacket*. _____

4. She *told* the tale to *all* of her friends. _____

5. *They* grew *cherries* and apricots. _____

6. *Everyone* loved to hear the *old* stories. _____

7. *She* loved her first experience of *Montreal*. _____

Exercise 1.A – *continued*

8. *Oh*, what a *beautiful* view!_____

9. They *were* a *greedy* lot. _____

10. She *was waiting* at the *school*. _____

11. Lailani was driving slowly *down* the *road*._____

12. I *recently* changed *jobs*. _____

13. You *can call* today *or* tomorrow. _____

14. Her *scholarly* specialty was *wolves*. _____

15. *Music* is an *engaging* pastime. _____

16. Lienne *has* a *beautiful* face._____

17. *Nobody* likes the *new* schedule. _____

18. *He* spent most of his free time *with* her. _____

19. The plumber *has been repairing* the *pipe*. _____

20. Chris *takes* the dog for a walk every *day*. _____

21. *Carolyn and* I waited for you at the airport. _____

22. *Gee*, look at *that*. _____

23. Walk *quickly* when you *go* past that place._____

24. Anne's bathrobe was worn *to threads*. _____

25. I *scraped* my elbow *badly* when I fell. _____

26. A thick *layer* of jam *now* covered the bread. _____

27. I was feeling *better*, *so* I went for a walk. _____

28. The *excited* children played in the *yard*._____

29. I *love* taking my *niece* to the zoo. _____

30. Kate has *two* top grades *on* her report card. _____

31. *Health* food *has become* popular here. _____

32. The *massive* wave *suddenly* crested. _____

33. The Canadian dollar *has reached* a new *low*. _____

34. She walked away with *her* cat *under* her arm._____

35. Leaving *home* was *heartbreaking*._____

Exercise 1.A – *continued*

36. *Many* people *complain* about the weather._____

37. Frannie went out, *but* Eddie stayed at *home.* _____

38. *Experts* are predicting a *very* flat market. _____

39. *Wow*, that pie is *really* delicious! _____

40. *Ray* was one of the guitarists *who* performed. _____

41. *If* you're afraid, don't look *down.* _____

42. The *team* picked up a first *down.* _____

43. A parade led *by* the mayor *marched* past. _____

44. The *conductor* gave the group a *down* signal. _____

45. The *opposition* rallied in the last *round.*_____

46. The *little* boy found a *shiny* penny. _____

47. *When* you *round* the next corner, look up. _____

48. The *young* girl finally ended her *fast.* _____

49. The truck *was travelling* much too *fast.* _____

50. Some people *like* the *fast* trains better._____

51. The brain is a *part* of the nervous *system.* _____

52. *Those* are my memories of *her.*_____

53. When *I* was little, I heard *many* stories. _____

54. *Most* of our friends urged *us* to visit. _____

55. If *anyone* phones, say I'm *busy.* _____

Exercise 1.B

Name the part of speech of each word in the following examples, except for the articles *a*, *an*, and *the*. Use these labels: N for noun; P for pronoun; V for verb or verb phrase; ADJ for adjective; ADV for adverb; CON for conjunction; PRP for preposition and INT for interjection.

1. The editor followed the story closely.

2. I found a great pair of boots at the mall.

3. He has brought two extra chairs to the table.

4. Eileen is a talented photographer.

5. Bad weather led to a cancelled flight.

6. Ouch! That was my big toe.

7. Books and papers were everywhere.

8. The story was read aloud by the teacher.

9. He wrote a letter to the Attorney General.

10. A mysterious stranger came to town.

Exercise 1.C

Identify the parts of speech of the italicized words. _____

1. He watched *proudly* as his son accepted the *top* award. _____

2. The baby *was crying* throughout that long *night*. _____

3. They *should have placed* salt on the *icy* road. _____

4. Have *they* made all the *appropriate* arrangements? _____

5. *By* the riverside, he waited *among* tall grasses. _____

6. *Around* the statue grew *multi-coloured* flowers. _____

7. Her library *includes* many books *on* philosophy. _____

8. *Look* at that wonderful sunset; the colours *are* wild. _____

9. His *troubles* were weighing heavily on *him*. _____

10. I *felt* the material; it was *soft*. _____

Exercise 1.D

Identify the parts of speech of the italicized words. _____

1. He watched proudly *as* his *son* accepted the top award. _____

2. The baby was crying *throughout* that *long* night._____

3. They should have placed *salt* on the icy *road*. _____

4. Have *they* made all the appropriate *arrangements*?_____

5. By the *riverside*, he *waited* among tall grasses. _____

6. Around the statue *grew* multi-coloured *flowers*._____

7. Her library includes *many* books on *philosophy*. _____

8. Look at that *wonderful* sunset; the colours are *wild*._____

9. *His* troubles were weighing *heavily* on him. _____

10. *I* felt the material; *it* was soft. _____

Exercise 1.E

Identify the parts of speech of the italicized words. _____

1. He *watched* proudly as his son *accepted* the top award. _____

2. The *sick* baby was crying throughout that *long* night._____

3. *They* should have placed salt *on* the icy road. _____

4. *Have* they *made* all the *appropriate* arrangements?_____

5. By the riverside, he waited among *tall grasses*. _____

6. Around the *statue grew* multi-coloured flowers._____

7. *Her* library includes many *books* on philosophy. _____

8. Look at *that* wonderful sunset; the colours *are* wild._____

9. His troubles *were weighing* heavily *on* him. _____

10. I felt the *material*; it *was* soft. _____

Chapter 2

Sentence Structure

Subjects and Predicates

A sentence is a group of words that expresses a complete thought and has two main parts: a subject (the noun or pronoun that the sentence is about) and a predicate (the verb or verb phrase that says something about the subject). You can form a sentence with only two words—for example: "Birds fly." Those two words fulfil the definition of a sentence because they make sense by themselves and contain both a subject (the noun *birds*) and a predicate (the verb *fly*).

Subject

The simple subject is the main noun or pronoun; the complete subject includes that noun or pronoun plus all the words that describe or go with it. Example:

    ◦ *Birds* of many colours are flying high in a blue and cloudless sky.

The simple subject is still *birds*; the complete subject is *birds of many colours*.

    A sentence can have a compound subject, with two or more nouns or pronouns joined by a conjunction like *and*. Example:

    ◦ *Jack and Jill* went up the hill.

Jack and *Jill* form the simple subject—in this case, a compound subject.

    To find the subject, first find the verb, and then ask "Who?" (or "What?") before it. In the example above, the verb is *went*. Who went? Jack and Jill went, so *Jack and Jill* is the compound subject. When normal sentence order (first the subject, then the verb, then the object) is reversed, and the verb comes before the subject (*Up the hill went Jack and Jill*), the grammatical subject remains *Jack and Jill*.

Predicate

The predicate tells what the subject does, has, or is. The simple predicate is the verb or verb phrase (the principal verb with any auxiliaries). The complete predicate includes the verb along with all the words that describe, complete, or go with it. Example:

○ Birds of many colours *are flying* high in a blue and cloudless sky.

The simple predicate is the verb phrase *are flying* (which consists of the main verb, *flying*, and the auxiliary verb, *are*). The complete predicate is *are flying high in a blue and cloudless sky*.

Like the subject, the predicate may be compound, with two or more verbs joined by a conjunction. (Jack *went* up the hill and *looked* around for Jill.) The two verbs, *went* and *looked*, are joined by the conjunction *and*, forming a compound predicate. Here's another example of a compound predicate, with four verbs: Birds *flew* from the roof, *circled* the yard, *swooped* down again, and finally *soared* away.

In the following table of examples, the left-hand side of the table gives the complete subject in boldface type and the complete predicate in italics. The simple subject(s) and simple predicate(s) are given in the right-hand column.

Table 2.1

Many birds *flew above us and squawked incessantly.*	Birds; flew, squawked
The wolf *is a loyal and beautiful animal.*	Wolf; is
Mom and Dad *lost their way driving to our place.*	Mom, Dad; lost
Among the large weeds grew **some lovely wildflowers**.	Wildflowers, grew
Running with scissors in your hand *could prove deadly.*	Running; could prove
The spring-cleaning task *grew more difficult with delay.*	Task; grew
Worried about his driving, I *swore never to ride with him again.*	I; swore
The alien *wore a cape and claimed to have come from Mars.*	Alien; wore, claimed
There but for fortune, go **you and I**.	You, I; go
The lovely strains of guitar music *could be heard in the distance.*	Strains; could be heard

Exercise 2.1

Identify the simple subjects and the simple predicates, including any compound subjects and predicates.

1. The young woman suspected her sources. _____

2. The little boy has a new tricycle painted bright red. _____

3. He ran to the house and answered the ringing phone. _____

Exercise 2.1 – *continued*

4. Wanda brought the textbook to class. _____

5. Soraya left the class with all her books. _____

6. She had taught at colleges in England and Canada. _____

7. Many avoided the noisy demonstration. _____

8. He put the slides on the table beside the projector. _____

9. The audience clapped enthusiastically for the first number. _____

10. Pierre and I ran down the road and waved our hands. _____

Exercise 2.2

Identify the simple subject and the simple predicate, including any compound subjects and predicates.

1. The woman set the platter on the table and sat down. _____

2. My mother entered the room and said hello. _____

3. The darkest hour and the dawn are not far apart. _____

4. Karisa stopped the car and rolled down the window. _____

5. Boris and Natasha went into town for groceries. _____

6. She and I have been close friends for years. _____

7. They travelled to Europe and then returned home. _____

8. Germs and colds travel and spread like wildfire. _____

9. The teacher and her students eyed the newcomer. _____

10. We wrapped the present and mailed it on Tuesday. _____

Phrases and Clauses

We've seen that phrases and clauses refer to groups of words rather than to single words.

A **phrase** is a group of related words with no subject/verb combination:

- up the mountain
- with great feeling
- down by the riverside

- along the pier
- at season's end

Adding more descriptive words to a phrase cannot make the phrase into a sentence, as long as it is still lacking a subject and a verb. The following examples are still phrases, even though they contain more information (by means of modifying words) than the initial examples:

- up the lush green mountain
- with great feeling and sensitivity
- down by the mud-strewn riverside
- along the old meandering pier
- at season's sweet but somewhat sad end

A **clause** is a group of related words that does contain a subject/verb combination:

- he climbed
- she sang
- they wept
- we walked
- he arrived

Remember that it takes only a two-word clause—a noun or pronoun to act as the simple subject, and a verb to act as the simple predicate—to construct a sentence. Most sentences, however, contain more than these bare essentials and use both clauses and phrases. In the examples that follow, the clauses are in plain type, the phrases in italics:

- He climbed *up the hill.*
- She sang *with great feeling.*
- They wept *down by the riverside.*
- We walked *along the pier.*
- He arrived *at season's end.*

Phrases

Phrases in sentences can perform the work of certain parts of speech: nouns, adjectives, and adverbs. In terms of their form, rather than their function, phrases can be classified as one of five basic types: prepositional (with which we are now familiar from our study of prepositions in Chapter 1), participial, gerund, infinitive, and absolute. Although phrases generally can function as nouns, adjectives, and adverbs, not all forms of phrases can serve all three functions:

- The prepositional phrase can function as an adjective or adverb, but not as a noun.
- The gerund phrase always functions as a noun.
- The participial phrase always functions as an adjective.
- The infinitive phrase can function as a noun, adjective, or adverb.
- The absolute phrase does not function as a part of speech; it describes or refers to the sentence as a whole.

A **prepositional phrase** opens with a preposition and ends with the object of the preposition—a noun or pronoun. This kind of phrase can function in a sentence as an adjective or adverb, but not as a noun. In the examples that follow, ask yourself what the phrase modifies (i.e. what it refers to or describes).

○ I ordered a burger *with fries.*

(What was ordered *with fries*? A burger. Thus the prepositional phrase—made of the preposition *with* and its object, *fries*—is working as an adjective to modify the noun *burger*.)

○ The child hid *in the closet.*

(To what does the phrase *in the closet* refer? Answer: to where the child hid. Thus the prepositional phrase *in the closet* is working as an adverb to modify the verb *hid*.)

A **participial phrase** contains a present, past, or perfect participle. We'll deal with participles in the next chapter, but the following definition will serve for now: a participle is a word form derived from a verb. Take the verb *to talk*. When I write or say I *have talked* or I *am talking*, both forms of the verb—*talked* and *talking*—are participles. In terms of function, a participial phrase always works as an adjective to modify or describe a noun or pronoun.

○ *Holding the tiny baby,* Mother entered the room.

Who was holding the tiny baby? Mother. This phrase uses the present participle, *holding*, to modify the noun *Mother*.

○ *Beautifully restored,* the ship was ready to sail.

What was beautifully restored? The ship. This phrase uses the past participle, *restored*, to modify the noun *ship*.

○ *Having eaten,* we declined their offer of lunch.

Who has eaten? Answer: we. This phrase uses the perfect participle, *having eaten,* to modify the pronoun *we.*

A **gerund phrase** contains a gerund, which is a present participle (the one that ends in *−ing*) used as a noun. Like the gerund itself, the gerund phrase always functions as a noun; it acts, as a noun does, in one of three ways: as a subject (of a clause or sentence), as an object (of a verb or preposition), or as a predicate noun following a linking verb and completing its meaning. A gerund phrase may be introduced by a preposition; in that case, the whole phrase is the object of the preposition.

○ *Lying about it* is no way to deal with the problem.

The phrase begins with the gerund, *lying,* and the whole gerund phrase, *lying about it,* functions as the subject of the sentence.

○ The teacher recommended *studying parts of speech carefully.*

The phrase begins with the gerund, *studying;* the whole gerund phrase *studying parts of speech carefully* functions as the object of the verb, *recommended.*

○ Her goal was *winning the creative writing award.*

The gerund phrase *winning the creative writing award* functions as the predicate noun that follows the linking verb *was* and completes its meaning.

○ We lost points *by failing in the first round.*

The gerund phrase *failing in the first round* functions as the object of the preposition *by.*

○ *After brushing my teeth,* I went to bed.

The gerund phrase here works as the object of the preposition *after.*

An **infinitive phrase** contains the infinitive form of the verb (*to sing*), and can function as a noun, an adjective, or an adverb.

○ The students plan *to organize soon.*

The infinitive phrase *to organize soon* functions as a noun, the object of the verb *plan.*

○ *To attend McGill University* was her most ardent wish.

The infinitive phrase *To attend McGill University* functions as a noun, the subject of the verb *was*.

○ He chose a book *to read*.

The infinitive phrase works as an adjective, modifying the noun *book*.

○ Mark performed *to please his father*.

The infinitive phrase functions as an adverb, modifying the verb *performed*.

An **absolute phrase** usually consists of a noun or noun substitute followed by an adjective or participle. The phrase refers to the rest of the clause or sentence but isn't joined to it by the preposition *with* or by a subordinating conjunction:

○ *First light dawning*, the birds began to sing.

By contrast, if this were written as "*With first light dawning*, the birds began to sing," the phrase would be prepositional, not absolute. The construction "*As first light was dawning*, the birds began to sing" does not begin with a phrase at all; it is instead a subordinate clause introduced by the subordinating conjunction *as*.

More examples of absolute phrases:

○ *Her face flushed with emotion*, she ran from the room.
○ *The rain pouring down*, we blew off our usual morning walk.
○ *My exam completed*, I left the classroom.
○ *Our flight cancelled*, we missed the wedding.
○ There he sat, *his mouth gaping*.

Exercise 2.3

Identify the phrases, indicating in each case whether the phrase is prepositional, participial, gerund, infinitive, or absolute.

1. He wanted to become an expert in the field._____

2. After acing the exam, Alain celebrated. _____

3. The flower beds along the path need watering._____

4. The teacher received an award for her work._____

Exercise 2.3 – *continued*

5. Helping the neighbours was an all-day affair._____

6. Three women stood in the line before me. _____

7. Raising the phone to her ear, she said hello. _____

8. We had fun at the lake last weekend. _____

9. His favourite activity was going cross-country skiing._____

10. Lisa drove to the store for milk, bread, and butter. _____

11. Hoping for the best helps to raise flagging spirits._____

12. We gave them a plaque honouring their contribution. _____

13. To learn a skill requires consistent practice._____

14. Holding her teddy bear, Sarah entered the room. _____

15. The sun shining brightly, she left the house without
    her umbrella._____

Clauses

Recall that a clause is a group of words that contains a subject/verb combination. Clauses are either independent or subordinate (also called dependent). An independent clause is a group of words that includes both a subject and a verb and that expresses a complete thought able to stand alone. (*Birds fly. Flowers bloom. She loves blueberries.*) Written in this way, an independent clause is also a sentence.

A subordinate (or dependent) clause also has a subject and a verb, but it needs to be joined to an independent clause to make sense; it cannot stand alone. The following are subordinate clauses: *while birds fly; if flowers bloom; who loved blueberries*. Notice that the only difference between the examples of independent and subordinate clauses is the addition of a conjunction.

Clauses are joined to the other words in a sentence by conjunctions. Co-ordinating conjunctions join independent clauses (and other elements of equal rank; for example, phrases to phrases and single words to single words). Subordinating conjunctions join subordinate clauses to independent ones.

○ I woke up, *but* I wasn't very hungry.

Two independent clauses are joined here by the co-ordinating conjunction, *but*. Both clauses are independent because they could stand alone and make sense by themselves. In fact, they could be written as two separate sentences: *I woke up. But I wasn't very hungry.* Each sentence delivers a complete thought.

  ○ When I wake up, I am not very hungry.

In this example, a subordinate clause begins the sentence. The independent clause—*I am not very hungry*—forms a complete thought that makes sense by itself. The subordinate clause, with its subordinating conjunction *when*, is *when I wake up.* It does not form a complete thought; it makes sense only in relation to the independent clause. Notice how the subordinate clause seems to cry out for completion.

Subordinate clauses are like phrases in that they can function as three parts of speech: nouns, adjectives, or adverbs.

Noun clause
A noun clause works as a noun, naming a person, animal, place, or thing as the subject of a sentence, the object or complement of a verb, or the object of a preposition. In the examples below, the noun clauses are in italic type.

  ○ *What I dreamt last night* actually happened today.

What I dreamt last night is a subordinate clause functioning as a noun, the subject of the sentence.

  ○ She decided *that she would take her vacation in June.*

This noun clause functions as the object of the verb *decided.*

  ○ One point in her favour is *that she graduated at the top of her class.*

This noun clause functions as the complement—the predicate noun—of the linking verb *is.*

  ○ Give the documents to *whoever opens the door.*

This noun clause functions as the object of the preposition *to.*

Adjective clause
This is also called a "relative" clause. It does the work of an adjective, modifying a noun or pronoun.

○ The book's narrator was a woman *who believed in divine justice*.

This adjective clause modifies the noun *woman*. *Who* is the subject of the clause, and *believed* is the verb. *Who* is also a relative pronoun, rather than a subordinating conjunction; while *who* serves the way a conjunction does to join the clause to the rest of the sentence, it also has an antecedent, the word *woman*.

○ Monday is the day *that we receive our first assignment*.

This adjective clause modifies the noun *day*. You can omit a relative pronoun that introduces an adjective clause if the meaning is clear without it. In this example, the relative pronoun *that* can be omitted without changing or obscuring the meaning of the sentence.

○ The dog ate the cake, *which was meant for Sita's birthday party*.

This adjective clause modifies the noun *cake*. It is joined to the independent clause by means of the relative pronoun *which*. Notice that in this example the relative pronoun *which* could not be omitted.

Adverb clause
An adverb clause modifies a verb, an adjective or another adverb.

○ I was attending university *while my sister worked in a law office*.

This adverb clause modifies the verb *was attending* in the independent clause. *Sister* is the subject of the adverb clause; *worked* is the verb. *While* is a subordinating conjunction joining the adverb clause, *while my sister worked in a law office*, to the independent clause, *I was attending university*.

○ The children were happy *until they moved*.

The adverb clause, *until they moved*, modifies the adjective *happy* in the independent clause, *The children were happy*.

○ Martin works faster *than David does*.

The adverb clause, *than David does*, modifies the adverb *faster* in the independent clause, *Martin works faster*.

Exercise 2.4

Identify the subordinate clauses and indicate whether each is a noun clause, an adjective (or relative) clause, or an adverb clause.

1. Suzanne is the student whom I would choose._____

2. Everyone knows how he can get to the arena quickly. _____

3. Even though she dislikes crowds, Bena will attend the show. _____

4. Does anyone know if the coach is in his office?_____

5. After I finished washing the dishes, I went out. _____

6. The gift that she returned was bought only a week ago. _____

7. Ask him where the school auditorium is located. _____

8. They enjoyed the film that a friend had recommended._____

9. They say that all six passengers were injured in the accident. _____

10. She visited Mina in the hospital after she finished the shopping._____

11. Tell your mother what happened in the mall today._____

12. He always went to Schwartz's when he visited Montreal. _____

13. The guitar was a Fender that had seen better days. _____

14. Emanuel had a clear idea of where he wanted to work._____

15. I was so nervous that my hands were trembling. _____

That, which, and *who*

As we've seen, the words *that, which,* and *who* may serve as relative pronouns and be used to introduce adjective clauses. Most North American writers use *that* and *which* interchangeably, and some contemporary stylists and critics argue there's nothing wrong with so using them. I agree, however, with the authors of the classic *Elements of Style*, who insist there remains an important difference between *that* and *which*, one that ought to be preserved. Here's the distinction: *that* is for restrictive clauses (a clause is restrictive when it is essential to the meaning of the sentence, when it identifies the noun or pronoun it refers to); *which* is for non-restrictive clauses (merely supplying additional information about the noun and so not essential to the meaning of the sentence). Restrictive clauses don't need commas; non-restrictive clauses do.

- Restrictive: The vacuum cleaner *that is in the closet* works well.

The clause requires *that* rather than *which* to introduce it because the information is essential to the meaning of the sentence. The clause identifies the vacuum cleaner we mean; it says there is one in the closet that works well—perhaps there's another in the shed that doesn't.

- Non-restrictive: The vacuum cleaner, *which is in the closet*, works well.

Here the implication is that there is only one vacuum cleaner, which happens to work well. The meaning would not change if we removed the non-restrictive clause altogether: *The vacuum cleaner works well.* It's easy to see the difference in the following example:

- We decided not to celebrate our wedding anniversary, *which* is in June.
- We decided not to celebrate our wedding anniversary *that* is in June.

Since by most accounts "we" have a single wedding anniversary, the second sentence makes no sense; the restrictive "that" is incorrect.

The distinction between restrictive and non-restrictive clauses applies as well to adjective clauses introduced by the pronoun *who*, making the use of the comma particularly important:

- The store is run by women who are disorganized.
- The store is run by women, who are disorganized.

In the first sentence, the adjective clause is restrictive; it defines the particular women referred to as disorganized. In the second sentence, the adjective clause is non-restrictive, and the comma makes the sentence sexist: it suggests that all women or women in general are disorganized.

Always put the most important thing you want to say in a complex sentence in the independent main clause. Remember that the most emphatic place for important words is at the end (the end of a sentence, paragraph, or piece of writing).

Sentence Types

Sentences are generally described as belonging to one of four basic types:

- Declarative sentences make statements
- Interrogative sentences ask questions
- Imperative sentences give commands or make requests
- Exclamatory sentences express strong feeling.

In terms of grammatical structure, however, the four main categories are simple, compound, complex, and compound-complex:

- A **simple** sentence has a single independent clause:

  o Stephanie scored the winning goal in the women's hockey game.

  But the clause may have more than one verb:

  o Stephanie *scored* the winning goal and *assisted* in many others.

- A **compound** sentence has two or more independent clauses joined by a co-ordinating conjunction or separated by a semicolon:

  o Stephanie scored the winning goal in the women's hockey game, and she assisted in many of the others.

  o Stephanie scored the winning goal in the women's hockey game; she assisted in many of the others.

- A **complex** sentence has one independent clause, and one or more subordinate (or dependent) clauses:

  o Paul's house, which he built himself, has five bedrooms.

  Paul's house has five bedrooms is the independent clause; *which he built himself* is the subordinate or dependent clause. Notice that a subordinate clause may come in the middle of a sentence, separating the parts of the independent clause.

- A **compound-complex** sentence contains two or more independent clauses and one or more subordinate clauses.

  o The doctors diagnosed Mrs. Martinez with cancer and they predicted that she would die within months, but after Mrs. Martinez had lived for six more years, the experts conceded they had been mistaken.

For nearly instant gains in stylistic strength, remember to vary sentence type, length, and rhythm.

Sentence Patterns

Looking at how sentences are put together, we may notice six basic patterns: two for linking verbs and four for action verbs.

Sentences with linking verbs follow either of these patterns:

1. Subject with a linking verb followed by a noun or pronoun:

    ○ My nephew, Auren, became a journalist.
    ○ The winner is he.

2. Subject with a linking verb followed by an adjective:

    ○ The students are intelligent.
    ○ They are also curious, aggressive, and hard-working.

Sentences with action verbs will conform to the following patterns:

1. When the verb is intransitive (i.e. without a direct object), the subject may be followed by the verb alone or by the verb with a modifier or modifiers.

    ○ She sang.
    ○ Birds of a feather flock together.
    ○ The groceries arrived very quickly.

2. When the verb is transitive (i.e. having a direct object), it is followed by a direct object:

    ○ She sang the song.
    ○ The dean addressed the faculty.
    ○ The pitcher threw the ball.

3. A transitive verb may also be followed by both an indirect and a direct object:

    ○ She sang them the song.
    ○ She gave me a gift.
    ○ He wrote her a letter.

If the indirect object comes after the direct object, it takes a preposition to introduce it. (She gave a gift *to* me. He wrote a letter *to* her.) In these cases, the noun or pronoun is the object of the preposition that introduces it.

4. Finally, a transitive verb may be followed by a direct object and an object (or objective) complement:

   ○ She called the song "Amazing Grace."
   ○ They named the baby Arianne.
   ○ She called him dishonest.

An object (or objective) complement is a word (a noun, a pronoun, or an adjective) that follows the direct object of a verb and completes its meaning.

   ○ They called the kitten Azure.

The word *kitten* is the direct object of the verb *called*, and the noun *Azure* is an objective complement. Notice that this structure differs from that for ordinary objects. In the examples given above, the word order could not be changed without changing the meaning, and in fact making the sentence unintelligible (*They named Arianne the baby[?]. She called dishonest him[?].*)

Review Exercises

Exercise 2.A

Identify the simple subjects and predicates, including any compound ones.

1. They discovered that restaurant through friends. _____
2. We decided to build a sandcastle on the beach. _____
3. Mariana collected the papers and handed them to Hassan. _____
4. We could see a couple of people approaching._____
5. Glendon went to the hospital for stitches._____
6. Irene and Scott have been together for years. _____
7. They enjoy watching dramatic films and comedies. _____

Exercise 2.A – *continued*

8. Arianne spent her summer vacation with relatives in Paris. _____

9. Her mother and father attended the ceremony. _____

10. Donations for the rummage sale have been collected. _____

11. Salad and rolls were served first. _____

12. An apple tree grew outside the house._____

13. April returned to the community centre and locked the door._____

14. The train derailed and caused a lot of damage. _____

15. He ran up the stairs and called out her name. _____

16. Carol swept the floor and emptied and the dustpan. _____

17. Her manner indicated a shy, retiring person._____

18. Patrice and Julie stayed for dinner. _____

19. I found some old papers and photographs in the attic _____

20. She got up and closed the window._____

21. Times have certainly changed in recent decades. _____

22. I met Morrie and Alicia at the train station._____

23. Without your help, I would have failed. _____

24. Friends of his invited him to visit them in LA. _____

25. We parked the car and went for a walk along the beach. _____

26. Melissa and Vladimir decided not to get married. _____

27. A couple of friends were planning to drop by for drinks. _____

28. Claire stopped by the gift shop and bought flowers for Jill._____

29. Apparently, about half of marriages end in divorce. _____

30. I like blues and classical music. _____

31. She folded the sheet and put it in the linen closet._____

32. Neither Penny nor Zachary attended the concert last night. _____

33. Hiroshi distributed the assignments to those in his group._____

34. Roses and lilacs adorned the path leading to the house._____

35. Jacqueline and Amir have two lovely and talented daughters. _____

Exercise 2.A – *continued*

36. Roxanne Hall is a great Canadian singer and songwriter. _____

37. The bus and the train ran late that day. _____

38. The boys ran up the stairs with the dogs right behind them. _____

39. Galatea makes a living looking after people's pet dogs. _____

40. I urged him to bury his false pride and speak to his father._____

41. They invited Margie and Bella to dinner and a movie. _____

42. She went out to the garden and picked some lettuce. _____

43. Years ago, writers actually cut and pasted their drafts _____

44. To stay fit, he ran and lifted weights. _____

45. The harder I work, the luckier I get._____

Exercise 2.B

Identify the italicized words as phrases or clauses; identify the phrases as prepositional, participial, gerund, infinitive or absolute, and the clauses as independent (main) or subordinate (dependent).

1. *On the following morning*, we left for Vancouver._____

2. I slept *in the back seat* during most of the trip. _____

3. *When my daughter saw us drive up*, she ran out to greet us._____

4. We spent the evening amiably, *discussing local politics.*_____

5. We toured the area and saw a boat *piled high with fish.*_____

6. *We decided* that we'd try our luck fishing the next day. _____

7. *After a brief discussion*, we agreed to go out for dinner._____

8. *The wind was howling* as we entered the house. _____

9. *Exhausted by the trip*, we fell asleep early. _____

10. I dreamt that night about *what we would do the next day.* _____

Exercise 2.C

Identify the following sentences as simple, compound, complex, or compound-complex.

1. The book that I was reading dropped into the bath water._____

2. Every evening at about dinnertime, my neighbour's dogs start barking. _____

3. I'd love to play, but I'm not allowed. _____

4. When she's good, she's very, very good. _____

5. It was a freezing cold day, so I wore my down-filled parka._____

6. In the corner under my bed, I discovered the missing earring._____

7. You are going to write this exam, even though you feel unprepared. _____

8. She had no money and few resources, but she was determined to persevere. _____

9. Once upon a time, a young man and a young woman fell in love at first sight; they moved to Montreal, where they lived happily ever after._____

10. My possessions, before I grew ill, were most important to me._____

11. Chaim and Frieda walked to the campus activity centre and bought coffee._____

12. We sent gifts to our grandchildren, who live in California. _____

13. Ariel opened the bottle of wine and put it on the table. _____

14. Few people these days remain in the cities where they were raised. _____

15. He and Julie decided to delay their trip and spend the holidays at home. _____

16. The new Harry Potter books were delivered and were sold right away._____

17. I love dramatic films, but he prefers comedies. _____

18. Azar, Emile, and Yossi decided to take their vacations in July. _____

19. Please wait here; I shouldn't be too long. _____

20. I ordered the fish, which looked good, but I soon lost my appetite. _____

Chapter 3

Verbs Revisited

Because verbs are inflected—changing their forms or spellings according to the subject (i.e. whether it is first, second, or third person, singular or plural) and the three basic tenses (present, past, and future)—they are fairly easy to identify. The infinitive is the basic form of the verb; it's usually preceded by the word *to*, called the "sign" of the infinitive: *to walk*, *to eat*, *to run*. The word following the *to* is called the "stem" of the infinitive. In most verbs, the form or spelling of the stem of the infinitive is also the form of the verb in first person, present tense.

To conjugate a verb means to list its various forms or inflections according to the possible subjects or "persons":

to walk	singular	plural
First person	I walk	we walk
Second person	you walk	you walk
Third person	he/she/it walks	they walk

The cardinal rule is that the verb must agree with the subject in person and number; this is why we say *I walk* but *he walks* (not *he walk*), and *it is* but *they are* (not *they is*).

Person

In grammatical terms, there are just three "persons": the one speaking, the one being spoken to, and the one being spoken about. But each "person" can be either singular (one person) or plural (more than one person), so when dealing with the issue of persons, we actually need to consider six possibilities, as the following table shows:

	Singular	*Plural*
First person (speaking)	I	we
Second person (spoken to)	you	you
Third person (spoken about)	he, she, it	they

Tense

Tense is that feature of the verb that locates it in time, showing whether an action or state of affairs belongs to the past, present or future. English has six basic tenses, three of which are "simple" (or "primary"), while the others are called "perfect" (also "compound" or "secondary") and use auxiliary verbs. The six basic tenses are:

- the simple present: *I walk*
- the simple past: *I walked*
- the simple future: *I will walk* or *I shall walk*
- the (compound) present perfect: *I have walked*
- the (compound) past perfect: *I had walked*
- the (compound) future perfect: *I will have walked* or *I shall have walked*

Traditionally, the future tense requires the auxiliary verb *shall* for first person and *will* for second and third persons. In modern usage, however, the distinction is not observed, and the auxiliary will to form the future tense is used for all persons.

Add the progressive tenses (which use the present participle, the *–ing* form of the verb, with the verb *be* as the auxiliary: *I am walking, I was walking, I will be walking*) and then the three perfect-progressive tenses (which use both *have* and *be* as auxiliaries: *I have been walking, I had been walking, I will have been walking*), and you get a total of twelve possible tense variations. The following charts show the conjugation in first person singular of the regular verb *to walk* in all the twelve tenses, and then of the irregular verb *to run*.

to walk	present	past	future
simple	I walk	I walked	I will walk
perfect	I have walked	I had walked	I will have walked
progressive	I am walking	I was walking	I will be walking
perfect-progressive	I have been walking	I had been walking	I will have been walking

to run	present	past	future
simple	I run	I ran	I will run
perfect	I have run	I had run	I will have run
progressive	I am running	I was running	I will be running
perfect-progressive	I have been running	I had been running	I will have been running

Notice that in regular verbs such as *to walk*, the past tense is formed by adding *–ed* to the infinitive form (*walked*) and is the same as the form for the perfect tenses (*have walked*). In irregular verbs such as *to run*, the past tense form (*ran*) doesn't end in *–ed*, and it differs from the form for the perfect tenses (*have run*).

Be sure to use the correct form of the verb for the perfect tenses. It is not "I have *ran*" but instead "I have *run*;" not "I should have *took*" but "I should have *taken*;" not "he had *sang*" but rather "he had *sung*," etc.

Here is the complete conjugation (stating all possible persons—first, second, and third, singular and plural—as subjects) of the verbs *to walk* and *to run*:

to walk

simple present	simple past	simple future
I walk	I walked	I will walk
you walk	you walked	you will walk
he/she/it walks	he/she/it walked	he/she/it will walk
we walk	we walked	we will walk
you walk	you walked	you will walk
they walk	they walked	they will walk

present perfect	past perfect	future perfect
I have walked	I had walked	I will have walked
you have walked	you had walked	you will have walked
he/she/it has walked	he/she/it had walked	he/she/it will have walked

we have walked	we had walked	we will walk have walked
you have walked	you had walked	you will have walked
they have walked	they had walked	they will have walked

present progressive	*past progressive*	*future progressive*
I am walking	I was walking	I will be walking
you are walking	you were walking	you will be walking
he/she/it is walking	he/she/it was walking	he/she/it will be walking
we are walking	we were walking	we will be walking
you are walking	you were walking	you will be walking
they are walking	they were walking	they will be walking

present perfect-progressive	*past perfect-progressive*	*future perfect-progressive*
I have been walking	I had been walking	I will have been walking
you have been walking	you had been walking	you will have been walking
he/she/it has been walking	he/she/it had been walking	he/she/it will have been walking
we have been walking	we had been walking	we will have been walking
you have been walking	you had been walking	you will have been walking
they have been walking	they had been walking	they will have been walking

to run

simple present	*simple past*	*simple future*
I run	I ran	I will run
you run	you ran	you will run
he/she/it runs	he/she/it ran	he/she/it will run
we run	we ran	we will run
you run	you ran	you will run
they run	they ran	they will run

present perfect	*past perfect*	*future perfect*
I have run	I had run	I will have run
you have run	you had run	you will have run
he/she/it has run	he/she/it had run	he/she/it will have run
we have run	we had run	we will have run
you have run	you had run	you will have run
they have run	they had run	they will have run

present progressive	*past progressive*	*future progressive*
I am running	I was running	I will be running
you are running	you were running	you will be running
he/she/it is running	he/she/it was running	he/she/it will be running
we are running	we were running	we will be running
you are running	you were running	you will be running
they are running	they were running	they will be running

present progressive-perfect	past progressive-perfect	future progressive-perfect
I have been running	I had been running	I will have been running
you have been running	you had been running	you will have been running
he/she/it has been running	he/she/it had been running	he/she/it will have been running
we have been running	we had been running	we will have been running
you have been running	you had been running	you will have been running
they have been running	they had been running	they will have been running

Principal Parts of the Verb

Verbs are said to have three principal parts: the infinitive (*to eat*); the past tense (*ate*); and the past participle (the one used with *have* to form the perfect tenses: *eaten*). All other forms and uses of the verb are derived from these. Here are the three principal parts of the verb *walk*:

- I *walk* today—*infinitive form, same as first person, present tense*
- I *walked* yesterday—*past tense*
- I have *walked* a lot in the past two days—*past participle*

Notice that for a regular verb such as *walk*, the form for the past tense (*I walked*) is the same as that for the past participle, used to form the perfect tenses (*I have walked*). As noted above, however, the irregular verb *eat* is another matter:

- I *eat* spaghetti today—*infinitive form*
- I *ate* spaghetti yesterday—*past tense*
- I have *eaten* too much spaghetti recently—*past participle*

Participles

A participle is a word derived from a verb; it can function as a verb or as an adjective. As part of a verb phrase, the participle is the last word and carries the basic meaning. In the following verb phrases, the participles are in italic type:

- am *walk*ing
- have *walked*
- am *eating*
- have *eaten*

English verbs have three participles:

1. The present participle, which is the *–ing* form of the verb, is used with the auxiliary verb *be* to form the progressive tenses (*I am walking*).

2. The past participle, which ends in *–ed* for regular verbs, is used with the auxiliary verb *have* to form the perfect tenses (*I have walked*).
3. The perfect participle, made up of the present participle *having* and any past participle (*having walked*), is not used as a verb at all. It acts as an adjective.

Present and past participles may also be used as adjectives, as in "the *walking* tour" or "the half-*eaten* donut." In the clause "I am singing," the present participle *singing* is the main verb, used with the auxiliary *am* to form the present progressive tense of the verb *sing*. But in the phrase "the singing telegram," *singing* works as an adjective to modify the noun *telegram*. In the clause, "I have grown," the past participle *grown* is the main verb, used with the auxiliary *have* to form the present perfect tense. But in the phrase "a *grown* man," *grown* is working as an adjective to modify the noun *man*.

The perfect participle cannot function as a verb because no conjugation uses "having" followed by a participle. Examine the following construction:

○ *Having eaten* my dinner, I returned to work.

Notice that *having eaten* has no subject; it does not function as a verb (as do, for example, "have eaten" or "has eaten"). Instead, as you may recognize from the discussion in the previous chapter, *having eaten* is a participial phrase, which always works as an adjective. In this case, it modifies the pronoun *I*.

Don't confuse the three participles (present, *eating*; past, *eaten*; perfect, *having eaten*) with the three principal parts of a verb (present infinitive, to *eat*; past tense, *ate*; and past participle, *eaten*). The confusion seems to arise because the past participle appears in both lists.

Note on Verb Auxiliaries

In verb forms composed of two or more words (i.e. verb phrases), such as *will have been going* and *was being held*, the last word is the principal or main verb; all the others are auxiliaries, commonly forms of *to be* and *to have*. When a verb phrase has one or more auxiliaries, the first indicates the basic tense. For example, in *had been sleeping*, the first auxiliary, *had*, is past tense, and the tense of the whole verb phrase is past-perfect-progressive. In *have been sleeping*, the first auxiliary is *have*, present tense, and the verb phrase is present-perfect-progressive. The charts below show the two most basic auxiliary verbs, *to have* and *to be*, in first person singular, in the six basic tenses.

to have	*present*	*past*	*future*
simple	I have	I had	I will have
perfect	I have had	I had had	I will have had

to be	*present*	*past*	*future*
simple	I am	I was	I will be
perfect	I have been	I had been	I will have been

Mood

Verbs are said to be in one of three moods:

- indicative, to make a statement: *it's a beautiful day*
- imperative, to give a command or request: *open the window*
- subjunctive, to express a wish or condition contrary to fact: *if only I were there*

Note that the subject of the imperative is 'you,' often implied rather than stated: *Please take a seat.*

Note also that the subjunctive form is required for the verb in certain "that" and "if" clauses expressing commands, wishes, and other conditions not or not yet existing in reality. Except for the verb *to be*, the subjunctive form of the verb differs from the indicative form only in dropping the *s* from the third-person singular in the present tense (*the doctor ordered that he eat*, not *eats*). In the case of the verb *to be*, the subjunctive differs in present tense (*if I/you/he/she/it/we/they be untrue*) and past tense (*if only I/you/it/she/he/we/they were there*). This quirk of the subjunctive is becoming less common in informal speech, but is sometimes required, and generally preferred in formal writing.

To make this topic more complex, there is a special group of auxiliary verbs, known as "modal" auxiliaries, which also do not change their form for third-person singular subjects in the present tense. The modal auxiliaries include *must* (which has the form *he must*, rather than *he musts*), *ought to*, *used to*, *shall* and *should*, *will* and *would*, *can* and *could*, and *may* and *might*. Certain other words, such as *need*, can act as either modal auxiliaries (as in *she need not go*) or as ordinary indicative verbs (*he needs sugar*).

Verb Types

As we saw in Chapter One, there are two basic kinds of verbs: action verbs, which express actions, telling what the subject *does* or *has* (we *walk*, they *wonder*, she *has* time), and linking verbs, which are used to link information to the subject, rather than to have the subject "do" or "have" anything (I *am* glad, he *is* tall, the room *was* blue). The quintessential linking verb is the verb *to be*. Other linking verbs, such as *to feel*, can function as either linking or action verbs, but *to be* is always a linking verb.

There are other useful ways to categorize verbs, including making the common distinction between "finite" verb forms, which actually function as verbs, and "non-finite" verb forms, which perform quite different duties.

Finite and non-finite verb forms

Verb forms that can be used as predicates or sentence verbs (i.e. ones that have subjects and can act as the main verb in a sentence), such as *ate, was eating, have eaten* or *went, am going, have gone* are called "finite." Non-finite verb forms (also called verbals) cannot serve as sentence verbs because they have no person or number. They look like verbs but function as other parts of speech: as nouns, adjectives, and adverbs.

The phrase *having eaten*, for instance, looks like a verb phrase but instead forms the perfect participle and acts as an adjective. *Having eaten* can also be called a non-finite verb form. One way to check whether a form is finite is to try conjugating it:

- finite: *have eaten* (*I have eaten, you have eaten, he/she/it has eaten, we have eaten, you have eaten, they have eaten*)
- non-finite: *having eaten* (*I having eaten? you having eaten? he/she/it having eaten? We don't thinking so!*)

There are three kinds of non-finite verb forms:

1. participles, which function as adjectives
2. gerunds, which function as nouns
3. infinitives, which can function as nouns, adjectives, or adverbs

Participles: We have already seen how the three participles (present, past, and perfect) can act as adjectives:

○ The girl *finishing* her lunch left a piece of half-*eaten* pie.
○ *Having missed* both breakfast and lunch, I thought it looked not half bad.

The participial phrase *finishing her lunch* modifies *girl*; then *half-eaten* modifies *pie*. In the second sentence, *Having missed* introduces a participial phrase modifying the pronoun *I*.

Gerunds: A gerund is the present participle used as a noun.

sub *obj.*

○ *Singing* is fun. She loves *swimming*. In fact, she loves *singing* and *swimming*.

Infinitives: Most often used as nouns (*to sing is fun*), infinitives can also be used as adjectives (*he had few books to read*), or as adverbs (*she ran fast to make the green light*). Sometimes the *to* is omitted: *Steve helped move the dog house*. The *to* is understood before *move*, which is used not as a finite verb but as a noun—the object of the sentence verb *helped*.

Subjects, Objects, and Complements

Verbs used in sentences and clauses (in other words, finite or sentence verbs) have subjects—someone or something performing the action indicated by the verb (for action verbs), or representing the state or quality indicated by the verb (for linking verbs).

Verbs may also have complements, words that complete their meaning and that answer the question *what* or *who* after the verb. For action verbs, these include direct objects (*she bought a gift*), indirect objects (*she bought him a gift*), and object complements (*he dyed his hair orange*). Linking verbs do not take objects; instead, they take predicate complements: predicate nouns (*she is the doctor*); predicate pronouns (*this is she*); or predicate adjectives (*she is tall*). Some verbs can function as either action or linking verbs (*he feels the material / he feels confident*).

Action verbs

To find the direct object of an action verb, first find the verb, and then ask the question *what* or *who* after the verb. (*She sings a song*. The verb is *sings*. Sings what? A song. The direct object is *song*.)

The indirect object answers the questions *to what* or *to whom*, or *for what* or *for whom* after the verb. Example: *She sings (for) him a song*. She sings for whom? For him. The indirect object is therefore *him*.

When the indirect object comes before the direct object, no preposition is required; the meaning is clear without it (*she gave him a book*). But if the indirect object comes after the direct object, a preposition is necessary (*she gave a book to him*). When this happens, the word *him* is really the object of the preposition *to*, not an indirect object of *gave*.

Transitive/intransitive action verbs

Action verbs that have direct objects are called transitive verbs; action verbs without direct objects are called intransitive verbs.

- transitive: *Julia saved money* — the word *money* is the direct object of the verb *saved*.
- intransitive: *The guests arrived* — the verb *arrived* has no object; it expresses an action but not to, for, or against anyone or anything.

Most action verbs can be used either transitively or intransitively:

○ Lightning struck the tree.

The verb *struck* is used transitively in the above sentence; it has a direct object: *the tree*.

○ Lightning struck.

Here, *struck* is still an action verb, but an intransitive one because it has no direct object.

Particularly in creative or journalistic writing, avoid the tendency to overuse the verb *to be*; find stronger verbs, ones that will show instead of simply tell what you mean. For example, the sentence *He was angry* does not describe the character as well as the following:

○ He fumed. He paced. He shook his fist at heaven.

Also, avoid beginning too many sentences with *there is, there are,* or *it was*, etc. The sentences *There is a tree on the hill* and *It was silent in the woods* would be more powerfully written as follows: *A tree sits on the hill. Silence enveloped the woods.*

Linking verbs

A linking verb expresses a state of being instead of an action, and as mentioned earlier, it takes predicate complements rather than objects. The predicate complement is either a noun or pronoun (identifying the subject), or an adjective (modifying or describing the subject). Notice that unlike an intransitive verb, which can make a complete thought even though it has no direct object, the linking verb cannot make a complete statement without its complement.

○ Fritzraven Sky is a Canadian *dancer*. (*Dancer* is a predicate noun.)

○ The woman I saw at the market was *she*. (*She* is a predicate pronoun.)

○ Your eyes look *bloodshot*. (*Bloodshot* is a predicate adjective.)

Although the quintessential linking verb is *be*—it is always a linking verb and establishes the definition—other common linking verbs are *act, appear, become, continue, feel, get, grow, keep, look, prove, remain, seem, smell, sound, stand, stay, taste*, and *turn*. The sentences below illustrate the use of linking verbs. In the first two examples, the linking verbs (*became* and *remained*) have predicate nouns (*prime minister* and *provost*) that identify the subjects; in the next two, the linking verbs (*looks* and *feels*) have predicate adjectives (*well-rested* and *sad*) that describe the subject.

○ Paul Martin *became* prime minister of Canada.
○ Dr. Evered *remained* the provost of the university.
○ Professor Thobani *looks* well-rested.
○ Mr. Frowning *feels* sad.

Most verbs that can be used as linking verbs can also function as action verbs (either transitive or intransitive). The following examples show the verb *grow* used three different ways:

○ That farmer *grows* vegetables.

A transitive action verb, with *vegetables* as the direct object.

○ The lilac tree *grows* in the back yard.

Again, an action verb, but this time it's intransitive because it has no object.

○ With repeated interruptions, the teacher *grows* tired.

A linking verb, meaning that the teacher *becomes* tired; the word *tired* is a predicate adjective, describing the subject *teacher*.

You can usually tell whether a verb is a linking verb by replacing it with the verb *be* and seeing if the meaning of the sentence stays much the same. Compare the sentences below.

○ Jared *felt* the sofa.

Jared *was* the sofa? The meaning changes; the verb *felt* is not a linking verb here, but a transitive action verb with a direct object, *sofa*.

○ Jared *felt* happy.

Jared *was* happy. The meaning doesn't change; here the verb *felt* is a linking verb, and *happy* is a predicate adjective.

Some verbs that are usually action verbs can act in special cases as linking verbs. This happens in the sentence, *The well ran dry*, in which the word *dry* is not an object but a predicate adjective linked to the subject of the sentence, *well*, by the verb *ran*. Of course, *ran* is normally an action verb—either intransitive (*Sasha <u>ran</u> down the street*) or transitive (*Muhammad <u>ran</u> the company*). Here are two more examples of verbs that are normally transitive used as linking verbs:

○ The words she spoke *rang* true.
○ The door *slammed* shut.

Do not confuse the predicate complement with the object or objective complement. The latter is a noun, pronoun, or adjective that follows the direct object of a verb and completes the meaning. It says something about the object of the verb, not about the subject of the verb. Here is an example:

○ They named the baby *Elana*.

The verb is *named*; its direct object is *baby*; the proper noun *Elana* is an object complement.

Active and Passive Voice

Voice—active or passive—is an important quality of action verbs. A verb is in active voice when the subject of the sentence performs the action of the verb (i.e. when the subject acts). A verb is in passive voice when the subject of the sentence receives the action of the verb (i.e. when the subject is acted upon). Examples:

○ I hold the pen. *(active voice)*
○ The pen is held by me. *(passive voice)*

In the first sentence, the verb, *hold*, is in active voice because the subject, *I*, performs the action. In the second sentence, the verb, *is held*, is in passive voice because the subject, *pen*, is acted upon. The passive voice is always formed with some variant of the auxiliary verb *be* and a past participle.

To illustrate, here's the verb *call* conjugated in third person in the six basic tenses, first in active voice, then in passive voice.

Primary tenses

Active	Passive
she calls	she is called
she called	she was called
she will call	she will be called

Perfect tenses

Active	Passive
she has called	she has been called
she had called	she had been called
she will have called	she will have been called

Review Exercises

Exercise 3.A

Identify the action verbs and the linking verbs. Then identify any direct or indirect objects for the action verbs, and any predicate complements—nouns, pronouns, or adjectives—for the linking verbs.

1. He held the end of the long string and watched the kite rise._____

2. The warm bath water felt good on my aching muscles. _____

3. My sister-in-law broke my sewing machine. _____

4. I spent several hundred dollars on the repair job. _____

5. Rebecca seems content to continue studying. _____

6. My uncle remained a great, if informal, adviser. _____

7. I wrote the novel to recapture the emotions of my childhood. _____

8. Adrian was once a newspaper reporter. _____

9. I felt the grass tickling my feet. _____

10. I felt sad about the lack of gender equity on campus. _____

Exercise 3.B

Identify the verbs in the sentences below as action or linking verbs.

1. They found two kittens in the alley. _____

2. It seems colder today than yesterday. _____

3. That coat looks very warm. _____

4. Saskia became a freelance journalist. _____

5. Always look both ways before crossing the street. _____

6. We cooked the turkey in its own juices. _____

7. The speeding car slowed down. _____

8. Suddenly, the children grew unusually quiet. _____

9. Please pass the salt. _____

10. The trains avoided a collision. _____

11. Edith grew beautiful roses in her garden. _____

12. Francis kept horses on his farm. _____

13. That birthday cake looks wonderful. _____

14. Teenagers are often rebellious. _____

15. The dogs chased the cat down the hall. _____

16. Teachers are an important social resource. _____

17. The new student sat at the front of the class. _____

18. Yves sold his electric guitar to a friend. _____

19. We kept the articles on a shelf in the attic. _____

20. Teddy remained pessimistic about his prospects. _____

Exercise 3.C

Identify the underlined words as one of the following: subject noun or pronoun, verb or verb phrase, direct object, indirect object, predicate noun, predicate pronoun, or predicate adjective.

1. Idell and Tony married and moved to Freeport. _____

2. Please pass me the sugar bowl. _____

3. The owners of the resort were friendly. _____

4. Frannie studied dance from an early age. _____

5. Renée became a well-known and respected artist. _____

6. They have put the packages in the mail. _____

7. She usually calls me on Sunday. _____

8. Rishma showed me the article you mentioned. _____

9. It proved very interesting. _____

10. The vet examined the dog's eyes and ears. _____

11. Nerine became a good friend and colleague. _____

12. Professor Gagnon won a top award for her work. _____

13. We gave Zachary a puppy for his birthday. _____

14. They always arrive a little early. _____

15. She appeared rather distracted and irritable. _____

16. She helped Danielle with her moving. _____

17. Dinner that night was a large all-dressed pizza. _____

18. Emanuel and Alain have been friends for several years. _____

19. Hafiz returned the book to the library. _____

20. Three of the students won scholarships. _____

Exercise 3.D

Identify the complements (the words that come after the verb and complete its meaning) as direct or indirect objects, or as predicate nouns, predicate pronouns, or predicate adjectives.

1. First-rate work habits are rare among students. _____

2. Brent announced the results of the competition. _____

3. They bought her a book about ancient cultures. _____

4. The musicians were seasoned professionals. _____

5. Megan baked a chocolate cheesecake. _____

6. Tara opened the presents under the tree. _____

7. The month's supplies seemed adequate. _____

8. Penny mailed a letter to Rebecca. _____

9. The clerk delivered the groceries. _____

10. Check the car's tires and the oil. _____

11. This is she. _____

12. Patrick threw Jamie the ball. _____

13. Jeffrey has been exercising his biceps. _____

14. The deer ate the flowers in the yard. _____

15. Chris sent Marybeth a birthday present. _____

16. This situation seems quite unusual. _____

17. We prepared several dishes for the party. _____

18. After the storm, everyone grew quiet. _____

19. If I were she, I would resign. _____

20. Put the cups and saucers on the table. _____

Exercise 3.E

Identify the verbs as action or linking verbs; identify their objects as direct or indirect, and their complements as predicate nouns, pronouns, or adjectives.

1. Sandy looks terrific in that outfit._____

2. Meet me in the main lobby after the show. _____

3. Jean bought tickets to Cirque du Soleil._____

4. Her sister is a famous dancer._____

5. The tea roses smell wonderful. _____

6. Those coats are theirs. _____

7. Mohamed plays pool with his friends on Fridays. _____

8. Most of the students proved intelligent and creative. _____

9. It was they. _____

10. The winner could well be she. _____

11. Samantha became a doctor._____

12. The little girl was pale and weak. _____

13. The culprits could be they. _____

14. He investigated the rumour. _____

15. She redecorated the apartment. _____

16. The forest looks colourful in the fall. _____

17. We asked them to deliver champagne._____

18. All the children seemed excited. _____

19. Kara wore a light cardigan over her shirt. _____

20. My favourite performer was she. _____

Part II

Elementary Errors

Chapter 4

Subject–Verb Agreement

One more time: a verb must agree with its simple subject (i.e. the noun or pronoun without the modifiers) in person (first, second, or third) and number (singular or plural). The person and number of the subject determine the person and number of the verb:

	Singular	Plural
First person (the person speaking)	I	we
Second person (the person spoken to)	you	you
Third person (the person spoken about)	he, she, it	they

People rarely make errors in subject–verb agreement when the verb directly follows the subject, as it does in normal sentence order: subject, verb, object (*I go home, he hits the ball, they argue the case*, etc.). You don't often hear people say, "I *goes* home," "they *hits* the ball," or "we *argues* the case." Problems arise with reversed sentence order, or when words come between the subject and its verb.

Reversed Sentence Order

It's easy to make mistakes when the verb comes before the subject, such as in questions and sentences that begin with expletives like *there* and *it*. (Expletives are words with no grammatical or part-of-speech function; they are used only as fillers to allow for more natural-sounding sentences. Don't confuse the grammatical term with the everyday meaning of "expletives" as swear words.)

○ There is no way to mitigate the consequences of this disaster.

There in this sentence is an expletive, with no grammatical function.

We use it so we don't have to say or write this:

- No way to mitigate the consequences of this disaster is (or exists).

The use of *there* to begin a sentence is often unimaginative but not ungrammatical.

- It is true that love conquers all.

It in this sentence is an expletive, used to stress the main idea, *that love conquers all*, by putting it last. Otherwise, we would have to write this:

- That love conquers all is true.

To work out the agreement for sentences with reversed order, you have to find the real subject—the noun or pronoun that performs the action of the verb:

- There (is, are) many reasons why I decided to move.

We want to know the subject of *is/are* so that we can choose the proper form of the verb *to be*. One way to do this is to convert the sentence into normal order:

- Many reasons are (or exist) why I decided to move.

The subject is *reasons* (plural) so the verb must be plural:

- There *are* many reasons why I decided to move.

Here is a more difficult one:

- Where (is, are) Devesh and his buddies going?

Normal sentence order:

- Devesh and his buddies are going where.

The subject is compound—Devesh and buddies—and so the verb must be plural:

- Where *are* Devesh and his buddies *going*?

Words Between the Subject and Verb

It's also easy to err in subject-verb agreement when the verb is separated from the subject by intervening words. No native English speaker would have trouble with the following subject-verb agreement:

> ○ She *is* (not *are*) speaking.

But if we put an intervening phrase between the subject, *she*, and the verb, *is*, errors like the following can occur:

> *Incorrect:* She, along with some other candidates, *are* speaking.
> *Correct:* She, along with some other candidates, *is* speaking.

Examine the examples below.

> ○ My sister, together with her new boyfriend, *is* coming to the concert.

The grammatical subject, *sister*, is still singular. The words *together with her new boyfriend* form a prepositional phrase; *boyfriend* is the object of the preposition *together with*, not another subject. Move the phrase to the end of the sentence and you'll see it:

> ○ My sister is coming to the concert with her new boyfriend.

> ○ My sister and her new boyfriend *are* coming to the concert.

Here the subject actually is plural, made up of *sister* and *boyfriend*. The subject is compound, with the two subjects joined by the conjunction *and*, so the verb is plural.

> ○ Where is Alice, along with her kittens, going?

The singular subject, *Alice*, takes a singular verb, *is going*. The intervening words—*along with her kittens*—are not part of the grammatical subject.

> ○ The result of the social funding cuts *was* obvious to us all.

The grammatical subject is *result*, singular, not *cuts*, plural. *Of the social funding cuts* is just a prepositional phrase, not a subject. It's the result of the cuts—and not the cuts themselves—that is obvious. It would be plural only if the "result" were plural (*the results of the social funding cuts were obvious to us all*).

Relative Pronouns

When the subject of a clause is a relative pronoun (*who, which, that*), it takes its person and number from its antecedent (the word it refers back to or replaces); the verb must agree with the antecedent.

> ∘ I was happy to be one of the women *who were delegated* to represent the union.

Who refers to women, which is plural, so the verb is plural: *were delegated*. The common error in a sentence pattern like this is to assume that the antecedent of the relative pronoun *who* is *one*, rather than *women*, and make the verb singular.

> ∘ I will be happy to be the one *who is delegated* to represent the union.

In this sentence, the antecedent of *who* is *one*, a singular pronoun. Compare it to the next variation:

> ∘ I will be happy to be one of the ones *who are delegated* to represent the union.

Here the antecedent of *who* is *ones*, which is plural and requires a plural verb.

Linking Verbs

What do you do when one noun (or pronoun) comes before a form of the verb *to be* and another noun (or pronoun) comes after the verb, but the two nouns differ in number? Answer: Consider the first noun the subject, and make the verb agree with it, even if the noun that comes after the linking verb differs from it in number.

> ∘ The only *flower* available now *is* tulips.
> ∘ *Tulips are* the only flower available now.

Correlated Subjects

Some compound subjects have two parts (joined by correlative conjunctions such as *either/or*, and *neither/nor*). If both parts of the compound subject are singular (*neither Muhammad nor Michelle*) or plural (*neither the girls nor the boys*), there is no problem. But if one part of the subject is singular and the other part is plural, it seems confusing. The trick is to make the verb agree in person and number with the subject that is nearer to it:

- Neither my mother nor my sisters *are* here.
- Neither my sisters nor my mother *is* here.
- Either my brothers or I *am* going to attend.
- Either I or my brothers *are* going to attend.

Collective Nouns as Subjects

Collective nouns (such as *crowd*, *majority*, *team*, *family*, *army*, and *committee*) are singular in form, yet refer to groups of people rather than to a single person. Collective nouns take singular or plural verbs depending on whether the group is thought of as a single unit or as individual entities.

- The faculty *is* striking for better working conditions.
- The faculty *are* divided on the question of a strike.

Compound Subjects

Usually, compound subjects joined by the conjunction "and" take plural verbs. In some cases, however, two nouns joined by "and" are considered a single unit (for example, *bread and butter*) and the subject, though technically plural in form, is singular in meaning and takes a singular verb. This rule can sometimes pose a difficult judgement call, since you must decide whether to consider the subject as one whole or as separate elements:

- Bread and butter *was* (not *were*) all she served.
- The long and the short of it *is* (not *are*) I quit.
- My friend and colleague *has* (not *have*) just returned from London, England.

If this last example referred to two different people, you would repeat the pronoun and write this:

- My friend and my colleague *have* just returned from London, England.

Plural Nouns

Some nouns—even though they end in *s*—are considered singular and take singular verbs; examples include *athletics*, *news*, and *mathematics*.

- *Athletics* is an interesting topic of conversation among them.
- The CBC *news comes* on at ten o'clock.
- *Mathematics is* a difficult subject for me.

Other nouns that end in *s* are plural and take plural verbs; examples include *scissors*, *pants*, and *shears*.

- These *scissors* are sharp.
- His *pants were* baggy.
- The *shears are* dull; they need sharpening.

Nouns that name a title, price, size, number, or quantity are usually seen as a single unit and take singular verbs.

- *The Ambassadors is* an interesting book.
- Five *dollars is* the price of admission.
- *Six feet is* the minimum height of team members.
- *Twelve makes* a dozen.
- *Two litres is* all I will need.

Phrases involving basic mathematical calculations usually take singular verbs.

- Two plus two *makes* four.
- Ten divided by two *is* five.

Latin and Greek noun plurals

Some of the nouns that came into the English language directly from the ancient languages of Latin and Greek have kept their old plural forms. Be careful not to get the singular and plural forms of these unusual words confused. For instance, most people would consider it wrong to talk about "a single criteria"; the proper singular form is *criterion*. The word *alumni* refers to many people, not a particular *alumnus*. Some words, like *data* and *media*, are troublesome because they are technically plural (the singulars are *datum* and *medium*) but they have singular meanings too. For instance:

- The various *media are competing* for customers.

Here, *media* is a plural referring to the separate media outlets that compete among themselves for the same audience. In this next sentence, however, the noun is treated as singular, referring to one industry:

- The *media is* an important part of democratic society.

Again, the trick is to work out whether the subject should be considered as a single unit or as separate elements.

Indefinite Pronouns

Indefinite pronouns that mean *one* (such as *each, either, everyone, anyone, nobody,* and *none*) are singular and take singular verbs.

- Each of the campers *is* responsible for providing equipment.
- Everyone *was* invited to the party.
- Every plate, bowl, and cup *was* dirty.

The old rule that the indefinite pronoun *none* means *not one,* and thus takes a singular verb, seems to be losing ground rather rapidly, as grammatical change goes. Although there is logic and precision in this traditional view, some grammarians argue that the indefinite pronoun *none* can also mean *not any* and should therefore on occasion take a plural verb. This reasoning obfuscates the issue, however, since *not any* still means *none* (not a single *one*). Eventually the well-wrought rule that *none* takes a singular verb may give way entirely to popular usage, and the distinction cease to be observed even in formal written English. Until then, however, it is best generally to follow the rule for *none* that applies to other singular indefinite pronouns, and use a singular verb.

There are of course exceptions, cases in which other reasons make a plural verb preferable. The following example, cited in the classic *Elements of Style,* constitutes such an exception:

- None *are* as fallible as those who are sure they're right.

It's the plural *those* referring to the subject of the subordinate clause that makes the plural verb sound preferable—or so challengers of the rule would argue. At the same time, with a singular subject in the subordinate clause, there would be no reason to eschew the rule:

- None *is* as fallible as *he* who's sure he's right.

Singular indefinite pronouns as subjects can be especially tricky because they are often followed by prepositional phrases (*none of the students, each of the oak trees,* and *nobody through all the looking-glasses*). Still, the rule holds and the verb must agree with the grammatical subject, which is the indefinite pronoun, not the object in the prepositional phrase. (*None of the students has* arrived; *each* of the oak trees *is* one hundred years old, and *nobody* through all the looking-glasses *looks* back).

Incorrect: One of the cars *were* damaged.
Correct: One of the cars *was* damaged.

Cars is not the simple subject; *one* is. *Cars* is the object of the preposition in the prepositional phrase *of the cars.* Singular *one* needs a singular verb.

Indefinite pronouns that mean more than one (such as *several, few,* and *many*) generally take plural verbs. But some indefinite pronouns, including *some, any* and *all,* take singular or plural verbs depending on their meaning within given sentences. When these indefinite pronouns refer to a single mass or quantity regarded as one unit, they take singular verbs. When they refer to a number of individual items, such as could be counted, they take plural verbs.

- *Some* of the ice cream *is* left.
- *Some* of the people *are* going by plane.

- *Is* there *any* room left in the car?
- *Are any* of the crayons on the floor?

- *All* of the flour *has* been sold.
- *All* of the loaves *have* gone stale.

In phrases such as *all of the meal* and *some of the meal,* the number of the simple subjects *all* and *some* is determined (contrary to the general rule) by the noun in the prepositional phrase. If that noun is a single entity, quantity or mass, or anything else regarded as a whole or single unit, the indefinite pronoun takes a singular verb. If the noun in the prepositional phrase is a number of individuals or things that can be counted, the indefinite pronoun takes a plural verb.

- Some of us *are* dissatisfied with the results.

Some in the above sentence means more than one person.

- Some of the meal *was* left.

Some here means part of a single portion.

Two more examples:

- Some of the cake *is* missing.
- Some of the cakes *are* missing.

Turning to *all,* here is an instance of it meaning more than one person:

- All of us *are* going to the cottage.

In the next sentence, however, *all* means a specific lump sum, and so is singular:

> ○ All the money was spent.

Two more examples:

> ○ All of the meal *is* missing.
> ○ All of the meals *are* missing.

The words *half* and *part* as simple subjects also take singular or plural verbs depending on the context. Again, if they refer to a mass or single unit, they are singular. If they refer to individual people or things that could be counted, they are plural.

> ○ *Half* of the *rink* was flooded.
> ○ *Half* of the *students* are attending the concert.

> ○ *Part* of the *roof* has collapsed.
> ○ *Part* of the *segments have* been re-worked.

The word *number* takes a singular verb when it is preceded by the definite article *the*, and a plural verb when it is preceded by the indefinite article *a* or *an*.

> ○ *The number* of requests *is* growing by the hour.
> ○ *A number* of reporters *are* asking for interviews.

Review Exercises

Exercise 4.A

From the two verbs in parentheses, choose the form that makes the subject–verb agreement correct. (Find the simple subject and make the verb agree in person and number with it.)

1. Kinga and Auren (discuss, discusses) their favourite issues often.

2. The teacher, along with her students, (hope, hopes) to make the trip.

3. The students, along with the teacher, (is, are) taking notes.

4. The reading club (is, are) unanimously in favour of reading that novel.

Exercise 4.A – *continued*

5. The number of requests (is, are) growing by the hour.

6. His trousers (was, were) clearly second-hand.

7. The radio news (says, say) the storm is approaching.

8. The various media (was, were) present at the event.

9. (Does, do) they know the answers to the exam questions?

10. A number of reporters (is, are) asking for interviews.

11. Fifty dollars (is, are) the cost of admission.

12. (Was, Were) either of the girls elected to the council?

13. They all want cookies but no one (want, wants) to drive to the store.

14. The action of the supervisor (was, were) deemed inappropriate.

15. Part of the roof (has, have) collapsed.

16. Half of the food (was, were) consumed in the first hour.

17. In the yard (is, are) several linden trees.

18. A number of cases of beer (was, were) delivered.

19. Part of the segments (has, have) been re-worked.

20. Half of the rink (was, were) flooded.

Exercise 4.B

Choose the verb that agrees with the subject.

1. Some of the cupcakes (has, have) icing on them.

2. Twenty years (seems, seem) like a long time to hold a grudge.

3. That group (was, were) late getting started.

4. Part of the arena (was, were) being renovated.

5. Some of the people (is, are) going by plane.

6. Everything (has, have) been taken care of in advance.

7. Many a town in this region (has, have) seen better days.

Exercise 4.B – *continued*

8. There (are, is) a hundred people lined up to get in.

9. All of the cookies (is, are) baked.

10. Some of the ice cream (is, are) left.

11. The weather or upcoming exams (is, are) the probable reason for his absence.

12. My cousin and my friend (has, have) already arrived.

13. There (was, were) a great deal of food laid out on the table.

14. His aunt, along with her husband,(is, are) coming for a visit.

15. (Is, Are) any of the crayons on the floor?

16. Every cup and saucer (was, were) dirty.

17. Regular work habits (make, makes) for success.

18. The team (is, are) ready to board the bus for home.

19. The only flower available now (is, are) tulips.

20. Tulips (is, are) the only flower available now.

Exercise 4.C

Choose from the words in parentheses the one that makes the sentence correct.

1. Semantics (is, are) a heady discipline.

2. A poll taken by the agencies (seem, seems) to indicate the election will be close.

3. There (is, are) too many cooks working on the main course.

4. Neither Eloise nor Carl (knows, know) what happened at the scene of the accident.

5. Both of the cars in the garage (need, needs) washing.

6. Everyone from first and second years (is, are) welcome to attend the show.

7. News of world events (travel, travels) fast over the Internet.

Exercise 4.C – *continued*

8. Here (is, are) some books for you to peruse.

9. One of my two dogs (is, are) sick.

10. Nuclear physics (has, have) addressed the mysteries of the universe.

11. Neither of you (is, are) willing to help.

12. Neither of your reasons (is, are) acceptable.

13. Only one of these class projects (is, are) first-rate.

14. Either Jared or Jessie (is, are) eligible for the scholarship competition.

15. Neither Robert nor his colleagues (is, are) ready to leave.

16. Neither my parents nor my aunt (is, are) at home now.

17. There (is, are,) several students waiting to speak with you.

18. Bill, Lailani, and Neco (was, were) present at the ceremony.

19. I didn't think you (was, were) going to be able to make it.

20. Where (is, are) your friend and your cousin?

21. There (is, are) fifty ways, the song says, to leave your lover.

22. Greed, as well as incompetence, (is, are) to blame.

23. The consequences of the new bylaw (was, were) obvious to all concerned.

24. I will be happy to be one of the women who (is, are) chosen to represent the group.

25. The problem of high tuition fees (command, commands) our compassion.

26. All of us (was, were) partly responsible for the accident.

27. All of the cake (was, were) gone.

28. Some of the members (has, have) already left town.

29. Every man and woman in the club (was, were) required to help pay for the trip.

30. Where (is, are) the scissors?

31. Mathematics (is, are) my worst subject.

Exercise 4.C – *continued*

32. Neither my sister nor my brothers (is, are) eager for me to leave the country.

33. The leader, as well as the entire team, (is, are) unable to make the game.

34. The main part of the intestines (was, were) removed.

35. Neither you nor she (is, are) one-hundred-per-cent correct.

36. The entire class (is, are) present for the important lesson on parts of speech.

37. Six per cent (is, are) a fairly usual rate of interest for mortgages.

38. The supporters of the new bylaw (is, are) in the minority.

39. All of the food (was, were) consumed by the hungry children.

40. He volunteered to be one of the persons who (was, were) building the new gym.

41. All of us (was, were) right there when you made that promise to the kids.

42. The young woman's dreams (was, were) in the process of coming true.

43. Who (is, are) the bride and groom at this wedding?

44. Either you or I (am, are) eligible for this scholarship.

45. None of us knew that the results of the election (was, were) on our side.

46. Frederica will attend, and her mother and father (is, are) coming too.

47. Not a single one of the movies (was, were) cited for an award.

48. The question of ground rules (was, were) discussed by the debating team.

49. The young woman soon learned that there (was, were) many obstacles facing her.

50. Some of my closest female friends (is, are) quite a bit older than I.

Exercise 4.C – *continued*

51. His appearance, as well as his personality, (is, are) charming.

52. The nature of ambition—its joys and its perils—quickly (become, becomes) apparent.

53. She's one of the ablest musicians who (has, have) attempted this piece.

54. My girlfriend is one of those people who (is, are) always late.

55. None of us (is, are) without limitation.

56. Everybody thinks (they have, he has) the ability to write well.

57. Although both juicers work, neither (work, works) very well.

58. The rose and the tulip (share, shares) a garden bed.

59. Every plate, glass and ashtray (was, were) smashed.

60. Some of the cupcakes (is, are) missing; all of the cherry pie (is, are) gone too.

Chapter 5

Pronouns–Antecedent Agreement and Pronoun Case

A pronoun, because it substitutes for a noun, has an antecedent, the noun or pronoun to which it refers. The pronoun must agree with its antecedent in person (*I* have *my* view; *you* have *yours*; *he* has *his*; every *effort* has *its* rewards) and number (*he* opens *his* book, *they* open *theirs*; *I* open *my* book, *we* open *ours*), as well as in gender. There are four grammatical genders: masculine (*father, he*); feminine (*mother, she*); common (*child, friend*); and neutral (*chair, television, it*).

- The *boy* took off *his* hat.
- The *woman* put on *her* coat.
- *She* wanted to leave, but *he* didn't.
- *They* disagreed.
- The *room* looked large without *its* furniture.

Clear Pronoun Reference

Confusion can arise when a pronoun has two possible antecedents in the same clause or sentence. The simplest way to fix this unclear "pronoun reference" is to repeat one of the noun antecedents. Less awkward results often can be had, however, by recasting the sentence entirely. The examples below show unclear reference, and some possible ways to correct the problem.

> *Unclear:* Twyla loves playing duets with Chantelle because she is so talented.

(Is it Twyla or Chantelle who is so talented?)

> *Clear:* Twyla loves playing duets with Chantelle because Chantelle is so talented.

Or: Because Twyla is so talented, she loves playing duets with Chantelle.

Unclear: I finished the cabinet, which pleased my client.

(Was the client pleased with the cabinet itself, or pleased that I finished it?)

Clear: My client was pleased with the cabinet.
Or: My client was pleased that I finished the cabinet.

(N.B. Now would be a good time to do Exercise 5.A at the back of this chapter, before proceeding to the next section.)

Agreement of Pronoun and Antecedent

Indefinite pronouns: singular or plural?

To recap: Indefinite pronouns can be either singular (*everyone, no one, someone*) or plural (*several, few, both*); some indefinite pronouns are singular or plural (*all, any, some*) depending on their meaning in a given context. Examine these examples:

Singular: Everyone in the men's team has his own equipment.
Plural: Several men in the team have their own equipment.
Singular or Plural: All of the cake is gone. / All of the cakes
are gone.

The following indefinite pronouns are always singular: *anybody, anyone, another, each, either, everybody, everyone, no one, nobody, one, other, somebody,* and *someone.*

- *Each* of the *boys* has *his* own agenda.
- *Each* of the *girls* has *her* own agenda.
- *Each* of the *men* has *his* (not *their*) own agenda.

The following indefinite pronouns are always plural: *few, both, many, several,* and *others.*

- *Both* want *their* children to succeed.
- *Few* would give up *their* vacation time.
- *Many* treasure *their* time with friends.
- *Several* found *their* exams difficult.
- *Others* sailed through *their* finals.

Indefinite pronouns and gender

Indefinite pronouns (*each, one, anybody*) can refer to individuals of either masculine or feminine gender. Until fairly recently, convention authorized the use of the masculine pronoun (*he, his, him*) as generic—that is, to be understood to include females.

> ◦ *Each* student must help if *he* can.
> ◦ *One* should always keep *his* affairs in order
> ◦ If *anybody* calls, tell *him* to wait.
> ◦ *Everyone* must lead *his* own life.
> ◦ *He* who hesitates is lost.

Some writers, teachers, and grammarians still consider it acceptable to use the pronouns *he, him,* and *his,* and nouns like *man* and *mankind* to refer to people in general, but this usage, while still widely considered grammatically correct, is much less acceptable today, perhaps because of the greater presence of women in the academy and the rise of feminist scholarship.

When the group referred to is mixed, made up of females and males, the use of the masculine possessive pronoun *his* to refer to singular but indefinite pronouns such as *each* is incorrect. But the plural possessive form *their,* which is how most people would speak such a sentence (*Each student should bring their raincoat*), is also incorrect because *each* is singular.

This creates a major difficulty. In these next examples, if the "team" in question is composed of boys and girls, all of the sentences are, strictly speaking, incorrect:

> ◦ Each of the team players should bring *their* own towel.
> ◦ Each of the team players should bring *her* own towel.
> ◦ Each of the team players should bring *his* own towel.

There are three ways around this problem:

- Use both the male and female pronouns joined by the conjunction *or: his or her.* This makes the sentence grammatically correct, but awkward:

> ◦ Each of the team players should bring his or her own towel.

- Replace the pronoun with the indefinite article—*a* or *an:*

> ◦ *Each* of the team players should bring *a* towel.

- Use a plural form for both pronouns:

> ◦ *All* of the team players must bring *their* own towels.

Collective nouns as antecedents

Collective nouns, those that are singular in form but refer to groups, can be considered singular or plural; correct usage depends on the context. If the collective noun represents an entity regarded as a single group, it is singular; if the group is acting as individual members, it is plural.

- The *group* chose Marian as *its* leader.
- The *group* chose *their* various positions.
- The *team is* ready to play *its* last game.
- The *team are* arguing amongst *themselves*.

Compound antecedents

When a pronoun refers to compound antecedents—two antecedents joined by *and*—the pronoun is plural if the antecedents refer to two different people or things, and singular if they refer to the same person or thing. In the first two examples below, two separate people are being referred to, and the pronoun that follows is accordingly the plural *their*. The second two examples indicate one person performing two roles, and the pronoun that follows is accordingly singular (*her, his*). Note the repetition of *my* and *the* in the first two examples; this is what indicates that two separate people are being referred to.

- *My* friend and *my* cousin take their vacations together.
  (two separate people)
- *The* president and *the* treasurer are making *their* plans.
  (two separate people)
- *My* best friend and confidante is leaving *her* job.
  (one person playing two roles)
- The president and treasurer of the club is resigning his posts.
  (one person playing two roles)

Pronoun/adjective agreement

We've seen that personal pronouns can act as adjectives, and that when they do, they are called "possessive adjectives." These must agree with the nouns they modify:

- *Every* child likes *his or her* playmates; *some* children like *their* playmates.

Indefinite pronouns may also be used as adjectives and must agree with the nouns they modify:

- *Any* person has *his or her* preferences; *all* people have *their* preferences.

So may demonstrative pronouns: *this and that* are singular and should be used with singular nouns; *these* and *those* are plural and should be used with plural nouns:

- *This* hat, *these* hats
- *That* house, *those* houses

(N.B. Now try exercises 5.B, C, D, and E, checking your answers before proceeding to the next section.)

Pronoun Case

Case is that quality of pronouns that shows their relationship to the other words in a phrase, clause, or sentence. A pronoun can be used in one of three cases: subjective, objective, or possessive. When you wonder whether it's correct to write, "To *who* it may concern" or "To *whom* it may concern," you're wondering about case. (*Whom* is correct; it's the object of the preposition *to* and needs to be in objective case.)

Subjective case is for pronouns functioning as subjects; objective case is for pronouns acting as objects (of verbs or prepositions); possessive case is for showing ownership.

Pronouns change form (spelling) according to their case. For example, for the first person singular pronoun:

- the subjective case is *I*
- the objective case is *me*
- the possessive case is *my*

Like pronouns, nouns can also be said to be in one of the three cases, but they change form only for the possessive case; the spelling is the same for the subjective and objective cases. Examine the examples below:

- Gertrude phoned someone.
(*Gertrude* is in subjective case, subject of the verb *phoned*.)

- Someone phoned Gertrude.
(*Gertrude* is in objective case, the direct object of the verb *phoned*.)

- Give Gertrude the phone.
(*Gertrude* is in objective case, indirect object of the verb *give*.)

- Give the phone to Gertrude.
(*Gertrude* is in objective case, object of the preposition *to*.)

○ That phone number is Gertrude's.
(Gertrude's is a possessive noun, acting as the predicate pronoun of the linking verb *is*.)

Notice that the spelling of *Gertrude* doesn't change to show subjective or objective case, only possessive. Neither would the spelling change for a common noun instead of a proper one:

○ The *girl* phoned the *boy* and the *boy* phoned the *girl* back.

But if you substitute pronouns for either the proper noun *Gertrude*, or the common nouns *girl* and *boy*, you see the different forms:

○ She phoned someone.
(She is in subjective case, subject of the verb *phoned*.)

○ Someone phoned her.
(Her is in objective case, the direct object of the verb *phoned*.)

○ Give her the phone.
(Her is in objective case, indirect object of the verb *give*.)

○ Give the phone to her.
(Her is in objective case, object of the preposition *to*.)

○ That phone number is hers.
(Hers is in possessive case, acting as the predicate pronoun of the linking verb *is*.)

In the sentence, *They gave me a vest just like theirs*, the word *they* is in subjective case (*they* is the subject, performing the action of the verb); *me* is in objective case (*me* receives the action, being the indirect object of the verb); *theirs* is in possessive case (it shows whose vests these are, to whom they belong). The chart below lists the personal pronouns and the relative pronoun *who* in subjective, objective, and possessive case.

Subjective pronouns	Objective pronouns	Possessive pronouns
I	me	mine (my)
you	you	yours (your)
he	him	his
she	her	hers (her)
it	it	its
we	us	ours (our)
they	them	theirs (their)
who	whom	whose

N.B. Most grammar texts include *my*, *your*, *her*, *our*, and *their* (the words listed above in parentheses) as possessive pronouns. This text follows that convention. Strictly speaking, however, these are possessive adjectives because they always modify a noun (*my house*, *their dinner*, etc.) rather than substituting for it.

Subjective case

When a pronoun is the subject of a verb, it's in subjective case.

- *I* like apples. *You* like oranges. *He* and *she* like blueberries.
- *It* goes well with mangos. *We* like melons.
- *They* like kiwis. *Who* likes strawberries?

When a pronoun is a predicate complement (*this is she*), it is in subjective case. (Recall that linking verbs take predicate complements instead of the objects that action verbs take.) Look at this example, which uses a linking verb (*was*) and a predicate pronoun (*she*):

- Was she the girl you spoke of?

When unsure of whether to use *she* or *her*, try testing the case by putting the sentence in normal sentence order (subject, verb, object):

- She was the girl you spoke of.

This simple order tends to answer the question for us because our ears object to *Her was the girl you spoke of*. At any rate, the rule is always to use subjective case for predicate pronouns:

- It was *I* who did the work.
- It was *they* who called.
- This is *he*.

Objective case

When a pronoun is the object of a verb (either direct or indirect) or the object of a preposition, it's in objective case:

- Give those to *me* or *him* or *her* or *us* or *them*.
- You gave those to *whom*?

Direct object of a verb

Here the pronoun *me* is the direct object of *kissed*:

- He kissed *me*.

Here, both pronouns are the direct objects of the verb *see*:

> ○ Did you see *him* and *me*?

Like Maude and Dileep, the pronoun *him* in the next sentence is in objective case, being the direct object of *invite*:

> ○ I'll invite Maude, Dileep, and *him*.

Indirect object of a verb

> ○ He gave [to] *me* a kiss.
> ○ We bought [for] *them* a gift for their anniversary.
> ○ You bought [for] *whom* a gift?

Object of a preposition

> ○ Give that book to *us*.
> ○ Ask not for *whom* the bell tolls.
> ○ Let's keep this information just between *you* and *me*.

(The word *between* is a preposition, and both pronouns—*you* and *me*—are its objects.)

A pronoun is also in objective case when it's used as the subject or object of an infinitive.

> ***Subject of the infinitive:*** I wanted *her* to run for chair of the department.
>
> ***Object of the infinitive:*** We lost the chance to recruit *him* for the post.

Sometimes, the sign of the infinitive—the *to* before the verb—is not stated but only implied or understood. The subject of the implied infinitive is still in objective case:

> ○ They let *us* [to] enter the concert hall at the break.

Even when the infinitive is the quintessential linking verb *to be*, the rule holds. Both the subject and object are in objective case:

> ***Subject and object of the infinitive:*** Did you take *her* to be *me*?

The only time to use subjective case after the infinitive *to be* is when the infinitive has no subject:

- The culprit was assumed to be he.
- The author was thought to be she.

This construction is easy to spot because it's "reversible." You can reverse the two terms on either side of the infinitive and see clearly that the case is subjective:

- *He* was assumed to be the culprit.
- *She* was thought to be the author.

You would never think to write or say, "*him* was assumed to be the culprit" or "*her* was thought to be the author."

Possessive case

When a pronoun indicates possession, it's in the possessive case.

- That book is *hers*.
- Except for the five that are *his* and *yours*, the others are *mine* and *theirs*.
- *Whose* are those?

Note well the general rule that possessive pronouns such as the ones just cited do not take apostrophes.

Commit this one to memory; it's one of the most common mistakes in the English language, so you can easily distinguish yourself by not making it.

The word *it's* is a contraction of *it is*. The apostrophe stands for the missing "i" in *is*. Do not confuse this contraction with *its*—the possessive form of the pronoun *it*. Notice in the chart on pronoun case that none of the possessive pronouns takes an apostrophe. (This rule applies as well to the relative pronoun *who*. The possessive is *whose*; the word that takes an apostrophe—*who's*—is a contraction of *who is*.)

Remember that nouns in possessive case take apostrophes (the *company's* annual report), but pronouns in possessive case do not (*its* annual report).

Parting Tips on Pronoun Case

Appositives

An appositive is a noun or noun substitute (also called a **substantive**—see the glossary) that follows another noun or noun substitute, and that identifies, describes, explains, or expands upon the first (with which it agrees in case and number). Nouns, pronouns, two of the three kinds of verbals—gerunds and infinitives—and some phrases and clauses can be used as appositives (or "in apposition"). Examine the examples below:

○ I've sent something she loves, roses.

Roses is a noun, in apposition with *something she loves*, a subordinate noun clause.

○ David, my best friend, is coming to visit.

My best friend, a noun phrase, is in apposition with the proper noun, *David*.

Problems of correct case can arise when pronouns are used with appositives. Make the case of the noun and pronoun the same:

○ *We girls* (not us girls) just want to have fun.

The noun *girls* is in apposition with the pronoun *we*, which is the subject of the verb *want*; hence, it's in subjective case.

○ Give that prize to *us girls* (not we girls).

Girls is in apposition with *us*, the object of the preposition *to*; hence, it's in objective case.

When using pronouns with appositives, keep the pronoun in the same case as the appositive. If you get confused about which case is correct, try reading the sentence without the noun, with the pronoun alone:

Incorrect: Us cat lovers love to discuss our feline friends.
(Us love to discuss our feline friends?)
Correct: We cat lovers love to discuss our feline friends.

Incorrect: The teacher gave we students a prize.
(She gave we a prize?)
Correct: The teacher gave us students a prize.

Pronouns and nouns joined by *and*, *or*, *nor*, and *neither/nor* or *either/or*

When the subject or object pronouns are compound, the rules of case still apply. If the pronouns are in subjective case, both pronouns are subjective; if the pronouns are in objective case, both pronouns are objective. The classic error here is the phrase "between you and I." Since the word *between* is a preposition, and both pronouns are its objects, both pronouns must be in objective case: between *you* and *me*. If in doubt as to the correct case, read the sentence with the pronoun alone.

> *Incorrect case:* Neither Yossi nor *me* had ever seen a lion that close up before.

Read the sentence without the "Neither Yossi nor" part: *Me had never seen a lion that close up before?* Subjective case is required; use *I*.

> *Correct:* Neither Yossi nor *I* had ever seen a lion that close up before.

> *Incorrect:* Ms. Parker sang nursery rhymes to her small daughter and *I*.

Ms. Parker sang nursery rhymes to *I*? Objective case is needed.

> *Correct:* Ms. Parker sang nursery rhymes to her small daughter and *me*.

When the compound antecedent nouns or pronouns differ in number, make the pronoun agree with the antecedent that's closer to it.

> ○ The teacher or the students will begin by reciting their poems.
> ○ The students or the teacher will begin by reciting his poems.

> ○ Neither Yitzak nor his cousins lost their books.
> ○ Neither his cousins nor Yitzak lost his books.

Elliptical clauses: *than* and *as*

An elliptical clause is one in which some words are left out because their meaning can be inferred from the rest of the sentence. Example:

> ○ He chose the steak; I, the smoked fish.

The verb, *chose*, is missing from the second clause; it's understood. In certain constructions using the conjunctions *than* and *as*, you need to understand what's missing from the elliptical clause to get the pronoun case right.

◦ She is taller than *I*.

This is an elliptical clause; with the missing words inserted, it would read as follows:

◦ She is taller than I am tall.

◦ He wants to compete as much as *I*. (The sentence means that he wants to compete as much as I want to compete.)

To understand why it matters, consider the difference in meaning in the following two sentences:

◦ Gidon loves the children more than me.
◦ Gidon loves the children more than I.

The first sentence means that Gidon loves the children more than he loves me. The second means that Gidon loves the children more than I love the children.

Who, whom, and whose

One of the most common areas of confusion arises for some reason with the cases of the relative pronoun *who*. (This is a grammatical distinction quickly losing ground. No one asks *whom*—instead of *who*—do you love, even though *whom* is correct. Nevertheless, in order to make judicious decisions of this nature in your own writing, you still need to understand case.)

Who is the subjective form; *whom* is the objective form; *whose* is the possessive form. To verify the correct case, try reading the sentence with a more familiar pronoun (*I/me, he/him or she/her, we/us, they/them*).

◦ The boy *who* gave the speech won an award.

Who is the subject of the verb *gave*. You would say *he gave the speech*, not *him gave the speech*.

◦ The boy *whom* I just met won an award.

Whom is the object of the verb *met*. Would you say I just met *he* or I just met *him*?

The *who-whom-whose* conundrum also seems to kick in whenever the word *whom* (or variants such as *whomever*) is or could be involved in subordinate clauses. (The American journalist and humorist Calvin Trillin claimed that *whom* is a word invented to make us all sound like butlers.) Remember that *whom* is objective and *who* is subjective.

○ They decided to give the tickets to (*whoever,* subjective, or *whomever,* objective) came first.

The correct form is *whoever,* because it is the subject of the verb *came* in the subordinate noun clause. But what about the preposition *to* that introduces the clause? Shouldn't that be *whomever* because it's the object of a preposition? No, because in such cases it's the whole noun clause (*whoever came first*) that's the object of the preposition, not the relative pronoun itself.

Interrogative sentences: who or whom

To determine the right case for a pronoun in an interrogative sentence (one that asks a question), first put the sentence in normal sentence order (subject-verb-object). It should then be easy to tell whether the right case is subjective, objective, or possessive.

○ Whom are you calling? (*You are calling whom*—direct object of the verb)
○ Whom is he talking to? (*He is talking to whom*—object of the preposition *to*)
○ Who do you think is the hero of the play? (*You do think who is the hero of the play*—*who* is the subject of the verb *is.*)
○ Whose books are those on the table? (Those books are *whose*—possessive case)

Pronouns with gerunds

Pronouns before gerunds usually take possessive case:

○ She minded *my* speaking.

In that sentence, the simple object of the verb *minded* is the gerund *speaking*; the possessive pronoun *my* simply modifies the object. Examine this next sentence:

○ She minded *me* speaking.

Here, the pronoun *me* is the object of the verb *minded*; the word *speaking* is a participle modifying the object *me*. The first sentence—*she minded my speaking*—implies that she would mind the act of speaking by anyone at all. The second—*she minded me speaking*—means that she minded *me* in the act of speaking.

(N.B. Exercises 5.F and 5.G deal with pronoun case.)

Review Exercises

Exercise 5.A

This exercise tests your understanding of clear pronoun reference. Each sentence contains an ambiguous pronoun, one that could refer to either of two possible antecedents. First, rewrite the sentence two different ways, referencing each of the possible antecedents in turn. Finally, try recasting the sentence, adding or changing words if necessary, to get the best possible arrangement.

1. Although she gave me a gift on my birthday, it wasn't that nice. _____

2. Carol visited Marg whenever she was in town. _____

3. The dog in the shed which is quite large always barks at me. _____

4. My sisters met your sisters when they visited Montreal. _____

5. Hafiz and Narayan went to his brother's place for Christmas. _____

6. That artisan has a sketch of an antique samovar, which I'd like to buy. _____

7. Idell picked up Theresa at her office. _____

8. When the truck hit the van, it was nearly totalled. _____.

9. When Frannie plays duets with Joi, she always plays too fast. _____

10. Parents with young children should ensure they get proper nutrition. _____

Exercise 5.B

This exercise tests your understanding of pronoun/antecedent agreement. Choose the right word from the parentheses; then rewrite the sentence to eliminate the problem.

1. In Israel, everyone must do (his or her, their) army duty at a young age. _____

2. Each one who passes the final exam can consider (himself or herself, themselves) off to a good start. _____

3. None was considered skilled enough to adapt (his or her, their) script to the existing audience. _____

4. If anybody objects, let (him or her, them) think up a better scheme. _____

5. Each citizen in a free country must regard it (his or her, their) duty to vote. _____

6. Everybody was asked to do (his or her, their) best to sell tickets. _____

7. Joan was worried that someone had not received (his or her, their) invitation._____

8. Let everyone try to make (himself or herself, themselves) a market niche. _____

9. Any woman who hates children should re-examine (her, their) values. _____

10. Each one of us had to present (his or her, their) piece of ID at the door._____

Exercise 5.C

Choose the correct form of pronoun from the two in parentheses.

1. Each of the articles sat on (its, their) own shelf.

2. The city had memorials designed to honour (its, their) heroes.

3. Every one of the women has done (her, their) part.

4. Either one or the other must pay for (his, their) ticket.

5. If Kara or Anne calls, tell (her, them) I'll call back.

6. Neither man wants to commit (himself, themselves).

Exercise 5.C – *continued*

7. Each of the candidates had to provide the committee with (her, their) portfolio.

8. All the students paid (his or her, their) fees.

9. Neither man presented (his, their) case with any conviction.

10. Both boys ordered textbooks through (his, their) local bookstore.

11. Everything was in (its, their) own place.

12. Each girl who competes will receive a questionnaire that (she, they) must answer.

13. Neither of the tomcats will touch that new food in (his, their) bowl.

14. The company holds the annual general meeting in (its, their) boardroom.

15. All the new students know how to get to (her, their) classes.

Exercise 5.D

Correct any errors in pronoun usage.

1. If either student finishes the work, they may leave.

2. One may pay online if you prefer.

3. Her girlfriend and colleague contributed their time.

4. Barbara's mother got re-married when she was six years old.

5. Anyone can apply by sending their resumé.

6. One does well to meet their obligations.

7. Each of the items had their special place on the shelf.

8. Either Jim or Ira will give their presentation.

9. The teacher and the student gave her opinions.

10. The company usually hires their new employees in January.

11. Each of the contestants wrote down their phone number.

12. If anyone wants a ticket, they should call Janine.

13. Before you leap, one should look.

14. Some law firms do its recruiting in May.

15. A volunteer is usually motivated to do their part.

Exercise 5.E

Correct any pronoun errors.

1. The family received its passports yesterday.

2. The firm sent a memo to their staff about the new health plan.

3. If anyone else objects, let them speak up now.

4. If a student works hard, they will probably ace the exam.

5. The team is continuing on to their third competition.

6. Everybody has to deal with their own problems.

7. The band took out its instruments.

8. Each girl expected their essay to receive an A.

9. When you are in error, one should be ready to admit it.

10. Some of the teams had its various colours displayed.

11. I love these kind of apple but not those kind of orange.

12. Harry's father became a doctor when he was born.

13. Some of the material has lost their shape.

14. The company has already moved to their new offices.

15. The school has planned their first semester.

16. Who wants to take their own car?

17. Each of the programs will have their own writers.

18. My friends Allie and Sandy have her own way of doing things.

19. Every single chair in the place had a reserve sign on their seat.

20. The faculty has been informed of its vacation dates.

21. One shouldn't leave home without your wallet.

22. Every girlfriend she knew had invited her to their wedding.

23. None signed their name to the petition.

24. This kinds of poems leave me cold.

25. The singers turned to the audience and took its bows.

26. Many a man owes their success to the right education.

Exercise 5.E – *continued*

27. Both the winner and the guy who placed second had his good points.

28. A performer in top form can do their best with ease.

29. The members of the orchestra rose from its seats.

30. When one is in a glass house, you shouldn't throw stones.

Exercise 5.F

Choose the correct case of pronoun from the choices in parentheses.

1. Come swimming with (we, us) this afternoon.

2. I am sure that the winner will be (she, her).

3. (Us, We) writers find ingenious reasons to avoid the blank page.

4. (Him, He) and (I, me) have been colleagues for years now.

5. Did you think the young musician was (he, him)?

6. I'm certain of it; I have no doubt it was (she, her) who complained.

7. It was (they, them) who told me the story about the rabbit.

8. Let (us, we) take care of the children.

9. Did you phone (he, him) and (me, I)?

10. Please wait for Alex and (I, me).

11. Between you and (me, I), I wouldn't believe that story.

12. Everyone has gone but (she, her).

13. You and (I, me) can be relied upon to do a good job.

14. I intend to invite Cynthia, Gail, and (him, he) to the performance.

15. (Who, whom) are you going to see?

Exercise 5.G

Choose from the words in parentheses the correct form in the sentences below.

1. The women (who/whom) fought for the right to vote were called suffragettes.

2. I'll introduce you to my sister, (who/whom) you have yet to meet.

3. I've never known a man (who/whom) is as kind as Ehud.

4. (Who/Whom) will I say is calling?

5. (Who/Whom) do you wish you were?

6. The architect, (who/whom) we hired to renovate our house, did a good job.

7. You can invite (whoever/whomever) you like to the party.

8. I wonder (who/whom) you saw walking down the street.

9. To (who/whom) would you like to speak?

10. There was a bully in my neighbourhood (who/whom) made my life difficult.

11. Will Jack or (she, her) be hired, do you think?

12. After the games were over, the most valuable player turned out to be (he, him).

13. Following a heavy meal, (us, we) health nuts would rather walk than ride.

14. (Who, Whom) is knocking on the door?

15. Give these free clothes to (whoever, whomever) asks for them.

16. Professor Gagnon is the one (who, whom) we think will win.

17. Doctor Cantley is the one (who, whom) we hope to elect.

18. Sunanda bakes better bread than (I, me).

19. The novelist offered Sara and (I, me) some kindly advice.

20. They came to meet the teachers and (we, us).

21. I would rather talk it over privately, just between you and (I, me).

22. (Who, Whom) should I ask for directions?

Exercise 5.G – *continued*

23. A group of (we, us) students protested the new regime.

24. I thought Carla and (he, him) brought the refreshments.

25. My parents disapproved of (us, our) driving on the dangerously icy Coquihalla.

26. (We, Us) instructors have just as much fun as you students do.

27. Frannie and (I, me) planted an apple tree in the front yard.

28. It wasn't (I, me) who called the police.

29. It was (she, her) who said that (we, us) boys were being too rough.

30. (She, Her) and the three boys went swimming in the lake.

Chapter 6

Diction and Danglers

The importance of precision to good writing can hardly be over-estimated. This chapter addresses the correct use of individual words (diction) and the proper placement of modifying words and phrases (misplaced and dangling modifiers).

Diction

Diction is word selection, and precision at this level is essential. In the often cited words of Mark Twain, "The difference between the almost right word and the right word is really a large matter—it's the difference between the lightning bug and the lightning."

Errors in diction include blunders such as using the word *affect* when you mean the word *effect*, or writing *aggravate* when you mean *irritate*, or choosing *like* when you should use *as*, or *contagious* when the right term is *infectious*.

A thorough review of diction is beyond the scope of this book. This section focuses on just one of this topic's major aspects: words commonly misused or confused with other words that sound the same or similar. Study the meanings of the words sets below, then turn to Exercise 6.A. (It's probably best to check your answers before you continue with the rest of the chapter).

ability, capacity: *Ability* is the power to do something (*he has the ability to win*). *Capacity* is the power of containing or experiencing (*the room was filled to capacity; her capacity for work impressed her teacher*).

accept, except: To *accept* means to receive or agree to (*they accepted the gift*). To *except* means to omit or exclude (*Yitzak was excepted from the list of invited speakers*); as a preposition, *except* means *but for* or *with the exclusion of* (*all arrived early except Abdul*).

adverse, averse: *Adverse* is an adjective meaning unfavourable (*he cancelled his trip because of adverse weather*). *Averse* is a predicate adjective, usually followed by *to*, meaning opposed or disinclined (*I am averse to aiding racists*).

advice, advise, inform: *Advice* is a noun meaning an opinion or recommendation offered with the intention of helping the person receiving it (*let me offer you some friendly advice*). *Advise* is a verb meaning to give advice (*let me advise you*). *Inform* means to tell, to provide information (*he informed them of their rights*).

affect, effect: *Affect* is most often used as a verb meaning to produce an effect on (*the recession affected her business*); when *affect* is used as a noun it means 'emotion' (*one sign of depression is lack of affect*). *Effect* is most often used as a noun meaning a result or consequence (*the effects of the storm were severe*); when *effect* is used as a verb, it means to accomplish or bring about (*some activists manage to effect change*).

aggravate, irritate: To *aggravate* means to worsen a condition or situation (*his drinking aggravated his medical condition*). To *irritate* means to bother, anger, or annoy (*the screaming children irritated her*).

all ready, already: *All ready* means that everyone or everything is ready (*we are all ready to go*). *Already* is an adverb meaning "previously" or "as early or soon as" (*they've already left; already at age five, she was writing stories*).

all right, alright: *Alright* is still disputed in formal English as an alternative spelling for all right. (*Is that all right with you?*) Use *all right*.

all together, altogether: *Altogether* is an adverb meaning "completely" or "overall" (*he is altogether confused; altogether, it was a pleasant trip*). *All together* means that "all" are in the same place or occur simultaneously (*the family were all together again; all together now, "Happy Birthday to You"*).

allusion, illusion; allude, elude: An *allusion* is a passing or indirect reference (*the teacher's allusion to Balzac interested him*). An *illusion* is a delusion or deception (*a mirage is an optical illusion*). To *allude* to something is to refer to it indirectly (*the speaker alluded to a well-known novel*). To *elude* is to skilfully escape from something or someone (*she managed to elude her pursuers*).

almost, most: *Almost* is an adverb meaning "nearly or all but" (*the larder is almost empty*). *Most* refers to a majority, or means "the greatest number" or "to the greatest degree"; it can function as a pronoun (*most agreed to the plan*), an adjective (*most people would disagree*), or an adverb (*he was most pleased with his A+*).

among, between: *Among* is for relationships of more than two items or entities (*the goods were divided among the seven siblings*). *Between* is for two only (*the two sisters split the profits between them*).

amount, number: *Amount* is used to refer to a total quantity, a mass (*the storm dumped a large amount of snow*). *Number* is used for countable quantities, for things that could be counted (*the band sold a large number of CDs*).

beside, besides: *Beside* is a preposition meaning "at the side of" (*the boy sat beside his mother*). *Besides* as a preposition means "apart from" or "except for" (*besides Hafiz, nobody entered the contest*); *besides* as an adverb means "in addition" (*Hafiz won the contest, and a free lunch besides*).

breach, breech, broach: To *breach* is to break or break through (you can breach a contract or a wall). A *breech birth* or *breech delivery* is one in which the baby is born buttocks first instead of head first. To *broach* is to raise or open (you can broach a subject or a barrel).

bring, take: To *bring* is to carry or transport to where one is (*she will bring her guitar with her when she comes home*). To *take* is to carry or transport away from where one is (*when she goes to Montreal, she will take her guitar with her*).

burst, bust: *Burst* is a verb meaning "to break suddenly or violently," and all its principal parts are spelled the same (*don't make the balloon burst; the balloon burst; the balloon had burst*). A *bust* is a statue. Used as a verb to mean "burst or break," it is considered slang.

can, could, may, might: *Can* denotes ability (*she can succeed if she wants to*), and *could* is a kind of past tense of *can* (*she could succeed if she wanted to*) and has a weaker meaning than *can*. *May* denotes possibility or permission (*he may attend; yes, you may be excused*), and *might* is a kind of past tense of *may* (*he might have attended; I asked if I might be excused*) with a weaker meaning than *may*.

censor, censure: *Censor* is either a noun meaning someone authorized to vet material intended for public dissemination or a verb meaning to act as a censor and make deletions or changes to such material. *Censure* as a noun is harsh criticism or condemnation (*the new play attracted widespread censure*); as a verb, to *censure* means to criticize harshly.

complement, compliment; complimentary: A *complement* is something that completes (*this red sash will complement your new outfit*). A *compliment* is a flattering or praising remark (*he paid her the usual compliment, mumbling that she looked terrific*). *Complimentary* can mean "praising" or "free" (*complimentary remarks; complimentary tickets*).

compose, comprise, and constitute: To *compose* means to create, constitute, make up or arrange in a certain way (*Bach composed contrapuntal music; the tribes that composed the nation*, or *the tribes that the nation was composed of*). To *comprise* means to contain or include (*her repertoire comprised works by Bach and Beethoven*); don't use "of" with *comprise* (*comprised of* is incorrect). To constitute means to make up or be equivalent to (*the several pieces constituted the whole of her repertoire*).

comprehensible, comprehensive: *Comprehensible* means "understandable, intelligible" (*his lectures were barely comprehensible*). *Comprehensive* means "complete, thorough" (*the textbook is comprehensive*).

contagious, infectious: *Contagious* refers to a disease passed on through physical contact with the sick person (*I've read that a cold is no longer contagious once symptoms appear*). If something is *infectious*, it may be passed on either through contact or by some other means, such as air or water (*the infectious disease was spread largely by people's sneezes*).

continual, continuous: *Continual* means "frequently repeated" (*these continual arguments are stressful*). Something that is *continuous* is uninterrupted (*continuous rainfall for six hours dampened our spirits*).

convince, persuade: To *convince* means to overcome doubt. It may be followed by *of* or *that*, but not *to* (*I convinced him of my suitability for the job, I convinced him that I was suitable for the job*). *Persuade* means to win over, and may be followed by *of*, *that*, or *to* (*I persuaded her of the soundness of my theory; I persuaded him that I was in the right; I persuaded them to go back to school*).

council, counsel: *Council* is a noun meaning an assembly (*the council voted to elect a new leader*). *Counsel* can be a noun or a verb; as a noun, it means "advice" or "a legal adviser"; as a verb, it means "advise." (*His counsel advised caution; his lawyer counselled caution; he received wise counsel*).

credible, creditable, credulous: *Credible* means "believable, reliable" (*the evidence presented was credible enough to convince the judge*). *Creditable* means "deserving praise or credit" (*they gave a creditable performance*). A *credulous* person is gullible, too ready to believe on the basis of slim evidence (*the quack doctor made a living selling his useless remedies to credulous people*).

defuse, diffuse: *Defuse* is a verb meaning to render something harmless (*the bomb squad defused the bomb; the counsellor tried to defuse the tense situation*). *Diffuse* is an adjective meaning "spread out" or "scattered" (*diffuse light filled the room; his efforts were sincere but diffuse*).

deny or repudiate, rebut or refute: All of these are transitive verbs (they take direct objects). To *deny* or *repudiate* is to declare false, or refuse to acknowledge or obey (*he denied he was at the club that night; he denied his angry feelings; the sixties generation repudiated their parents' values*). To *rebut* or *refute* is to prove false or wrong (*she rebutted the evidence with new evidence; she refuted the charge with a solid alibi*).

dependants, dependents: A *dependant* is a noun meaning "one who depends on someone or something else" (*the couple had two dependants, aged two and five*). *Dependent* is an adjective that means "depending on" (*the human child is dependent on others for survival.*)

different from, different than: The word *different* should be followed by *from*, not *than*. The use of *than* after *different*, when *than* introduces a clause, is considered acceptable by some. Since *from* is always considered correct, use *from* (*this coat is different from that one; I want to buy a coat different from the one I bought last winter*).

due to: *Due to* is a preposition meaning "caused by or ascribed to" (not synonymous with *because of*). Use it after a noun or a linking verb (*the plane's late arrival, due to adverse weather, meant a day's wait in Calgary; the delay was due to adverse weather*). Never write the wordy "due to the fact that"; it's more efficient to write "because of" or "since."

elicit, illicit: *Elicit* is a verb meaning to evoke or draw out (*the lecture elicited questions from the audience*). *Illicit* is an adjective meaning "not legal" or "not allowed" (*he got into trouble with illicit drugs*).

farther, further: *Farther* is for physical distances (*he rowed farther out on the lake*). *Further* is for other than physical distances (*let's discuss this matter further*).

fewer, less: *Fewer* is for numbers, for nouns that can be counted (*fewer people, fewer seats*). *Less* is for amounts or degree (*less water, less crowding*).

flair, flare: A *flair* is an aptitude (*a flair for public speaking*). A *flare* is a sudden outburst of flame (*the flare that lit up the night sky*).

flaunt, flout: To *flaunt* means to show off (*if you've got it, flaunt it*). To *flout* means to spurn or scoff at (*this unruly youth loves to flout the rules*).

flounder, founder: To *flounder* means to move clumsily or become confused (*the first-time skier floundered in the deep snow*). To *founder* means to fail or (of ships) to fill with water and sink (*the ship foundered in the Atlantic*).

forbid, prohibit: *Forbid* is followed by *to* (*the dean forbade students to leave campus that day*). *Prohibit* is followed by *from* (*the students were prohibited from leaving campus that day*).

forego, forgo: To *forego* is to precede, to go before (*the horse foregoes the cart*). To *forgo* is to go without, to abstain (*already late, she had to forgo her morning coffee*).

formally, formerly: *Formally* means "in a formal way or manner" (*you are formally invited to attend*). *Formerly* means "at a former or earlier time" (*Jean Chrétien, formerly the prime minister of Canada*).

former, latter: *Former* refers to the first named of two things, as opposed to *latter*, the second named of two things. For more than two things, don't use *former* and *latter*; use *first, last, second, third, fourth,* etc.

fortuitous, fortunate: *Fortuitous* means "by chance, unplanned" (*they met fortuitously at a ball game*). *Fortunate* means lucky (*she felt fortunate to have a decent job*).

fuller, fulsome: *Fuller* means more extensive or complete (*a fuller discussion*). *Fulsome* means disgustingly excessive, loathsome (*fulsome flattery*).

gender, sex: *Gender* is the grammatical term for classification of nouns and pronouns according to biological *sex*. Grammatical genders number four: feminine (*she, mother, queen*); masculine (*he, father, king*); common (*child, teacher, friend*); and neuter (*chair, table, book*). (Examples: *The gender of the noun* actress *is feminine. Writers of both sexes competed in the essay contest*).

grisly, grizzly: *Grisly* means "horrible, gruesome" (*grisly murder scene, grisly details*). *Grizzly* means "grey-haired" (*a grizzly beard, a grizzly bear cub*).

hang, hung: The past tense and past participle for the verb *hang* is hanged when it means "killed by hanging" (*the deserter was hanged at sunrise*). *Hung* is the correct past tense and past participle for all other uses (*they hung the picture in the hall*).

imply, infer: To *imply* is to suggest or hint at; to *infer* is to conclude or deduce (*what the speaker implies is not necessarily what the listeners infer*).

in to, into: *Into* is a preposition meaning "to or toward the inside," used with an object of the preposition (*she walked into the room*). Use two words when *in* is an adverb modifying the main verb, while *to* works alone as the preposition, single-handedly addressing the object (*she handed her exam in to the teacher*).

ingenious, ingenuous: *Ingenious* means "clever, inventive" (*an ingenious plan*). *Ingenuous* means "innocent, unsophisticated" (*an ingenuous person*).

intelligent, intelligible: *Intelligent* means "smart, possessing mental ability" (*an intelligent student*). *Intelligible* means "decipherable, able to be understood" (*an intelligible essay*).

judicial, judicious: *Judicial* means "of the justice system or the administration of justice" (*a judicial process such as a trial*). Something is *judicious* if it is wisely judged, or shows discernment (*a judicious choice, such as telling the truth*).

lay, lie: *Lie* is an intransitive verb meaning "to recline"; its past tense is *lay* (*I am lying on the couch today; I lay on the couch yesterday; I have lain on the couch before*). *Lay*, however, is also a transitive verb meaning "to place or put something down" (*I lay the burden down today; I laid the burden down yesterday; I have laid the burden down before*).

lend, loan: *Lend* is a verb meaning "to give someone the use of something temporarily" (*please lend me ten dollars*). *Loan* is the noun that refers to the thing lent, especially money (*please repay the loan of ten dollars*).

like, as, such as: *Like* is a preposition meaning "similar to"; it should be followed by an object (*she bought flowers like the ones her sister had*). *As* is a conjunction and should be followed by a clause (*she did as she pleased*). *Such as* is a preposition meaning "for example" (*he loved tart fruit such as lemons and limes*).

literally, virtually: *Literally* means "exactly, in fact" (*he literally left without saying a word to anyone*). *Virtually* means "in effect, but not in fact" (*he virtually vanished*).

loath, loathe: *Loath* means "reluctant" (*I was loath to give up my place*). To *loathe* is a verb meaning "to detest" (*they loathed each other*).

nausea, nauseate, nauseous, noxious: *Nausea*, a noun, is a feeling of sickness or disgust (*he was overcome by nausea*). *Nauseate*, a verb, means "to affect with nausea" (*he was nauseated by the fumes*). *Nauseous*, an adjective, means "causing or feeling nausea" (*he felt nauseous*). *Noxious*, an adjective, means "harmful" (*the fumes were not only nauseating but also noxious*).

noisome, noisy: *Noisome* means "harmful and foul-smelling" (*noisome fumes wafted from the barrel*). *Noisy* means "making noise" (*the excited children were noisy*).

oral, verbal, aural: *Oral* means "spoken" (*oral examinations*). *Verbal* means "of or referring to words," often spoken words as distinct from written ones (*a verbal agreement versus a written agreement*). *Aural* means "of or pertaining to the ear or to hearing" (*the aural acuity of the blind*).

pedal, peddle: To *pedal* is to power one's bicycle (*he pedalled his bike*). To *peddle* is to sell (*he peddled his wares*). Hence *pedaller* (one who pushes pedals) and *pedlar* (one who sells something).

precede, proceed: To *precede* is to go before (*the horse precedes the cart*). To *proceed* is to continue (*please proceed*).

principal, principle: *Principal* as an adjective means "chief or most important" (*the child's welfare was my principal concern*). *Principal* as a noun is either a sum of money (*principal plus interest*) or the head of a school (*the principal of North Bay High*). *Principle* is a noun meaning "a rule or code of conduct" (*live according to one's principles*).

quotation, quote: *Quotation* is a noun referring to text or speech borrowed from another source (*that quotation is from the Old Testament*). *Quote* is a verb meaning "to cite or reference the words of another" (*he quoted George Bernard Shaw*).

reason is that, reason is because: *The reason is* should be followed by *that* or *why*, but not by *because* (*the reason I was late is that the car broke down; tell me the reason why you quit*). *Because* is a subordinating conjunction that introduces an adverbial clause (*I was late because the car broke down; I quit because I saw no future in the job*).

reluctant, reticent: *Reluctant* means "unwilling" (*he was reluctant to accept the deal*). *Reticent* means "reserved, not revealing oneself" (*he was reticent throughout the discussion*).

robbed, stolen: A person or place is robbed (*he was robbed at gunpoint; the store was robbed twice in three months*). A thing is stolen (*the thieves stole his wallet; thousands of dollars were stolen*).

stimulant, stimulus: A *stimulant* is a drug or substance that stimulates (*alcohol is not a stimulant but a depressant*). A *stimulus* is a spur or incentive, something that stimulates one to act (*a small success can be the stimulus for more success*).

tortuous, torturous: Something *tortuous* is winding, full of twists and turns (*the long, tortuous road*). Something *torturous* is painful (*she was glad the torturous procedure was over*).

try and, try to: In written English, *try* should be followed by *to*, not *and* (*try to do a better job next time*).

Misplaced and Dangling Modifiers

Just as single modifying words (for example, adjectives such as *only* and *either*) can be misplaced, so too can modifying phrases and subordinate clauses. All modifiers should be placed as close as possible to the word they modify to make their meaning entirely clear. Concentrate on precision of meaning as you consider the placement of the modifiers in the following examples:

> *Misplaced:* I *only* meant that comment for you, not for everyone else.
> *Well placed:* I meant that comment *only* for you, not for everyone else.

> *Misplaced:* You can *either* come today or tomorrow morning.
> *Well placed:* You can come *either* today or tomorrow morning.

> *Misplaced:* The university president hoped to hire a counsellor for troubled youth with an advanced degree.

Clearly the intended meaning here is that the university president hopes to hire a counsellor with an advanced degree, not one for those troubled young people with advanced degrees.

> *Well placed:* The university president hopes to hire a counsellor with an advanced degree to work with troubled youth.

> *Misplaced:* Cheetie watched the moon rise from her front-porch swing.

It was Cheetie who sat on the swing to watch the moon rise; the moon itself did not rise from the swing.

> *Well placed:* From her front-porch swing, Cheetie watched the moon rise.

> *Misplaced:* Harold put the leftover cheesecake in the refrigerator, which we planned to eat later.

It's the cheesecake—we presume—that we planned to eat later, not the whole refrigerator.

> *Well placed:* Harold put the cheesecake, which we planned to eat later, in the refrigerator.

Misplaced: Burnt and foul-smelling, he sent the meal back to the kitchen.

It's the meal, we suppose, and not *he*, that was burnt and foul-smelling.

Well placed: He sent the meal, burnt and foul-smelling, back to the kitchen.
Or: He sent the burnt and foul-smelling meal back to the kitchen.

Notice here that the correction consists in moving the appositive phrase *burnt and foul-smelling* next to the word it is intended to modify, meal.

Misplaced: A writer of considerable erudition, they gave him first prize.

How can *they* be a single writer of any description?

Well placed: They gave him, a writer of considerable erudition, first prize
Or: They gave first prize to him, a writer of considerable erudition.

The above examples may seem obvious, but the errors illustrated in them are a lot easier to commit than you might expect. That's one of the reasons for the oft-repeated advice to put a bit of distance between successive drafts of a work, especially between the penultimate and the last. Otherwise, you can become so familiar with what you're trying to say that you fail to notice when you've actually said something ludicrous.

Misplaced and dangling modifiers are often lumped together as "danglers." But there is a small difference of meaning between the two terms. In the case of misplaced modifiers, as in the examples above, the modifying words are just wrongly placed and the correction consists in moving them to where they belong, as close as possible to the word they modify.

A dangling modifier is slightly more complicated: the word that the modifier is supposed to be describing is absent from the sentence; it must be supplied to correct the error. Dangling modifiers often occur in phrases at the beginning of a sentence, and although there is more than one way to correct them, the answer often involves turning the dangling phrase into a clause that supplies the missing subject. Examine the examples below:

Dangling: On receiving the bad news, her flight was cancelled.

It's not the flight that received bad news, but the missing subject, *she*.

> *Correction:* When *she* received the bad news, she cancelled her flight.
> *Or:* On receiving the bad news, she cancelled her flight.

Notice that these corrections also involve a change from passive to active voice of the verb *cancelled*.

> *Dangling:* While out jogging, the shoelaces on his runners broke.

The shoelaces weren't out jogging; the missing subject, *he*, was out jogging.

> *Correction:* While *he* was out jogging, the shoelaces on his runners broke.
> *Or:* While out jogging, he broke the shoelaces on his runners.

> *Dangling:* Yawning sleepily, the taxi cab drove me home.

The taxi cab wasn't yawning; I was.

> *Correction:* I yawned sleepily as the taxi cab drove me home.
> *Or:* Yawning sleepily, I was driven home in the taxi cab.

> *Dangling:* Standing on the corner, a sports car sped by.

This sentence is logically impossible. It says that a sports car was both standing on the corner and also speeding by!

> *Correction:* Standing on the corner, I saw a sports car speed by.
> *Or:* While I stood on the corner, a sports car sped by.

> *Dangling:* Strolling down the country lane, she saw two men in straw hats.

Strictly speaking, there's no grammatical error in this sentence, but remember that a participial phrase such as *strolling down the country lane* at the beginning of a sentence must refer to the grammatical subject. In this example, it is *she* who is strolling. It would be wrong to write this if you meant instead that the two men were strolling down the country lane. (In that case, you would write this: *She saw two men in straw hats strolling down the country lane.*)

Phrases don't have to contain present participles (the *–ing* form of the verb used as an adjective) or gerunds (the *–ing* form of the verb used as a noun) to dangle. Examine these danglers:

Dangling: Young and naive, the world seemed his oyster.

It's the boy or man—not the world—that is young and naïve.

Correction: Young and naive, he thought the world his oyster.

Dangling: Without a single production credit, the impulse to lie
was sorely tempting.

It's not the impulse that lacked experience, but the job aspirant.

Correction: Without a single production credit, he found the
impulse to lie sorely tempting.

Dangling: To drive safely, a good set of brakes is required.

The brakes aren't driving the car; the driver is. Fix this dangler by supplying the missing subject, the implied *you*.

Correction: To drive safely, you need a good set of brakes.

It's correct to use verbal phrases (participial, gerund, and infinitive) to
express a general viewpoint or to refer to a whole sentence (*generally
speaking, to write requires intelligence*). Also, not all words that end in *–ing* are
present participles or gerunds; some are prepositions (such as *concerning,
regarding, according to, considering*) used to introduce objects. (*Considering
your heavy workload, it's a minor miracle that you met the deadline.*)

Like phrases at the beginning of sentences, phrases that are tacked on
to the end of a sentence (by means of words like *thus* and *therefore*) can
also dangle.

Dangling: I was called to the editing room by Shawn, thus causing
me to lose my place in the book.

This phrase dangles because it has no noun or pronoun to modify. To
correct sentences like this, turn the participial phrase, *thus causing me to
lose my place in the book*, into another predicate:

Correction: I was called to the editing room by Shawn and thus
lost my place in the book.

Or recast the sentence to make the dangling phrase into an independent
clause, and the existing independent clause into a subordinate one:

Correction: When Shawn called me to the editing room, I lost my
place in the book.

Finally, the possibility for error arises with elliptical clauses, those that omit certain words because the omitted words are "tacit"—they can be understood from the context of the sentence.

Dangling: When 21, her first daughter was born.

Grammatically speaking, this sentence means that *her first daughter* was born at the ripe old age of 21. This is not what the writer means, but it's what the sentence actually says. The problem, once again, is that the grammatical subject is missing.

Correction: When Mary was 21, her first daughter was born.

Fixing Danglers

There are three ways to correct misplaced and dangling modifiers:

- Method 1: Place the modifying word(s) as close as possible to the one they modify
- Method 2: Provide the missing subject
- Method 3: Make a dangling phrase into a subordinate clause.

Method 1

Dangling: Singing happily, the bus took the victorious teenage hockey players home to Montreal.

A singing bus? To correct this, move the *singing happily* closer to the teenagers:

Correction: The bus took the victorious teenage hockey players, singing happily, home to Montreal.

Method 2

Dangling: Waiting at the bus stop, a yellow submarine raced by.

We can solve the issue of the racing-and-waiting submarine by providing the missing subject to the main clause:

Correction: Waiting at the bus stop, I saw a yellow submarine race by.

Method 3

Dangling: While sleeping, the phone rang.

Even if we are prepared to entertain the idea of a sleeping phone, it's hard to accept that it could simultaneously sleep and ring. We can use the third method here, and make the dangling phrase that opens the sentence into a subordinate clause, thereby providing the missing subject:

> *Correction:* While I was sleeping, the phone rang.

Conclusion

To avoid dangling modifiers, remember that adjectival (participial) phrases at the beginning of a sentence must refer to the grammatical subject of the sentence, and that in all related matters, such as elliptical clauses, grammatical integrity must be maintained.

Review Exercises

Exercise 6.A

On diction

Choose the word from parentheses that makes the sentence correct.

1. You will receive (complementary, complimentary) tickets to the show in the mail.

2. She has three (dependants, dependents) under the age of six.

3. I am (averse, adverse) to travelling in these (averse, adverse) conditions.

4. A (breach, breech) birth is one in which the baby is born buttocks first.

5. She hesitated to (breach, broach) the topic.

6. With her blinding migraine headache, she found the (tortuous, torturous) country road a (tortuous, torturous) and harrowing experience.

7. The convicted man was (hung, hanged).

8. Even though she was confident of her speaking abilities, she was glad to hear the professor say that he would not include (aural, oral, verbal) components in the final exams.

9. The crime scene presented a (grisly, grizzly) sight.

10. Lying about the matter can only (irritate, aggravate) an already bad scene.

Exercise 6.A – *continued*

11. I had just (laid, lain) down when the phone rang.

12. Chaim was (beside, besides) himself with joy after winning first place in the violin competition.

13. The profits were obtained by (illicit, elicit) means.

14. I'd prefer to discuss this (farther, further) at another time.

15. The captain forbade the troops (from going ashore, to go ashore) but did not prohibit them (from drinking, to drink).

16. A salesperson or (pedlar, pedaller) (peddles, pedals); a cyclist or (pedlar, pedaller) (peddles, pedals).

17. Sunanda had (all ready, already) left by the time Sarah and the children were (all ready, already) to go.

18. One thing (proceeds, precedes) another when it comes before it.

19. Colds are (contagious, infectious); AIDS is (a contagious, an infectious) disease.

20. The reason I didn't attend the party is (because, that) I wasn't feeling well.

21. She appealed to him to (try and, try to) understand

22. I have already stated my (principal, principle) objections in the letter.

23. She hoped her (ability, capacity) for restraint would not desert her as she watched him try to fill the suitcase beyond its (ability, capacity).

24. He taught in the slums and saw every day the (affects, effects) of poverty.

25. By cutting behind the football field, she hoped to (allude, elude) her tormentors.

26. (Among, Between) the three friends, there were few secrets.

27. With a huge bang, the balloon (burst, bust).

28. The collage was (comprised, composed) of dozens of tiny images that (comprised, constituted) an impressionistic whole.

29. With Beren's (accepted, excepted), all the job hunters' applications were (accepted, excepted) for review.

Exercise 6.A – continued

30. The teacher said that (continual, continuous) interruptions would not be allowed.

31. Anyone who believes the witnesses are (credible, credulous) must be (credible, credulous).

32. The odour of sulphur was more (defuse, diffuse) now.

33. Looking after someone else's children is different (from, than) having your own.

34. As the years passed, (fewer, less) former students came to see the professor.

35. How can I (convince, persuade) you to join us?

36. Margot had a certain (flair, flare) for the arts.

37. If you want to win at a game, you can't (flaunt, flout) the rules.

38. The fate of the ship was sealed; it (floundered, foundered).

39. Patrick hated to (forego, forgo) reading the book reviews.

40. The (formally, formerly) plump child was now thin and pale.

41. Of the three dresses you tried on, the (first, former, latter) suits you best.

42. It was only by a (fortuitous, fortunate) meeting that she learned the truth.

43. The faculty members decided to have a (fuller, fulsome) discussion later.

44. Athletes of both (genders, sexes) will compete in the event.

45. Considering the circumstances, his decision was (judicial, judicious).

46. From the information on this graph, we can (imply, infer) that things are improving.

47. Mark walked right (in to, into) the room and handed his application (in to, into) the boss.

48. She was (reluctant, reticent) to accept the assignment.

49. Bill devised an (ingenuous, ingenious) method for moving tools to the shed.

Exercise 6.A – *continued*

50. The letter rambled on for several pages; its meaning was barely (intelligent, intelligible).

51. They flatly (rebutted, refuted, denied) the allegations.

52. He asked his parents if they would (lend, loan) him the money.

53. When the books arrived, the boy (literally, virtually) devoured them.

54. Cigarettes taste bad, (like, as) you might expect.

55. He tried to (advice, advise) them of their rights, but his (advise, advice) was ignored.

56. Police confirmed that the store had been (robbed, stolen) overnight and that the thieves had (robbed, stolen) thousands of dollars.

57. It was (almost, most) midnight when (almost, most) of the guests went home after (an almost, a most) enjoyable party.

58. She narrowed her eyes as she tried to remember the (quote, quotation).

59. Students began to feel (nausea, nauseous) and were sent home even before the reason—(noxious, nauseated) fumes—was discovered.

60. Most people are (loath, loathe) to admit when they are wrong.

61. It's (all right, alright) with us if you want to (bring, take) your dogs when you come to the cottage.

62. A large (amount, number) of these kinds of errors can be attributed to lack of experience.

63. I (can, may) drive there but I (can, may) not drive there this weekend because my father needs the car.

64. (Due to, because of) car trouble, we postponed our trip.

65. Given what they'd had to overcome, they did an (all together, altogether) fine job.

66. The decision to (censor, censure) the film followed the (censor, censure) of critics.

67. Intelligent discussion can act as a (stimulant, stimulus) to positive change.

Exercise 6.A – *continued*

68. She didn't mind the (comprehensible, comprehensive) nature of the 20-page exam, but she found some of the essay questions barely (comprehensible, comprehensive).

69. The (noisome, noisy) machinery gave Sonja a headache and the (noisome, noisy) fumes made it worse.

70. The elected municipal (counsellors, councillors) decided to (council, counsel) caution.

Exercise 6.B

On misplaced and dangling modifiers

Rewrite the following sentences to eliminate the misplaced and dangling modifiers, using whatever method works best to produce the clearest, strongest sentence with the meaning you believe was intended by the original. For misplaced modifiers, you'll need only to place the modifier where it belongs; for dangling modifiers, you'll need to do a bit more. Concentrate on meaning and making sense rather than on labels.

1. This summer Roxanne almost went swimming every day. _____

2. I jumped out of bed as the radio alarm went off in my bare feet. _____

3. Unable to walk because of a stroke, the portable laptop computer helped my grandfather recover his will to live. _____

4. Speaking slowly, the class could hear every word the guest lecturer said. _____

5. Last week I found a box containing an old healthcare card, which was made of beautifully carved mahogany._____

6. Alone, the abandoned lot at night felt scarier than earlier that day with friends. _____

7. Each of the budgie birds has a name in the pet store that is really weird, like Kissing Cousin, Captain Courageous, and Blue Blogger. _____

Exercise 6.B – *continued*

8. Barely daring to breathe for fear of waking her, the baby slept peacefully as we passed her room._____

9. Flying south for the winter, the sky is full of exotic birds from more northern climes. _____

10. While waiting for the fibreglass shower unit to arrive from Vancouver, the bath tub was often used by the whole family. _____

11. Nostrils flaring, I watched the wild black stallion speed away._____

12. Kate and Beth were laughing wildly as they walked across campus at the top of their lungs. _____

13. We only bought a few gifts to take home for the children._____

14. She first fell for the man who would become her lover in a busy airport. _____

15. They dumped the bags in the recycle bin that Anne-Marie had prepared the day before._____

16. A woman who only tries to be as good as a man is said to lack ambition. _____

17. Gail took care of the wonderful artwork she had bought from the artist on the walls in the den. _____

18. Please either sit down on the sofa or in the armchair. _____

19. He begged her to meet him later at the border crossing when night fell behind the weighing station. _____

20. At birth we all know that the human child is utterly vulnerable, and would in fact die without parental care. _____

21. While out jogging, the dog followed her into the woods and chased a bear. _____

22. Alan put the roast in the freezer, which they planned to eat later._____

23. Vivian says she only remembers part of the novel's plot. _____

24. I hardly ever think that we go out dancing anymore. _____

Exercise 6.B – *continued*

25. Surveying the scene with interest, a beautiful house stood on a distant hill._____

26. We decided completely to believe what the actor said. _____

27. Never give food to a baby that hasn't been cut into small pieces._____

28. The housekeeper bent down and picked up the umpteenth pair of socks groaning loudly._____

29. An author of two books, with a third coming out soon, his office was always full of printed material. _____

30. Swearing profusely, the dog was put out after he bit a visitor. _____

31. While giving a lecture outside on a beautiful spring day, a giant panda bear rounded the corner from the direction of the Clocktower. _____

32. To understand Canadian literature, seminal figures such as Timothy Findley and Margaret Atwood should be studied carefully. _____

33. Being the youngest child in the family, Father and Mother relaxed the rules for me._____

34. At the age of five, Sandy's father decided to marry again. _____

35. If studied correctly, one can learn a lot from the literature of fiction. _____

36. Looking over her shoulder at her pursuer, home seemed distant._____

37. Entering the foyer, a large park can be seen from the window._____

38. Being a big city, the stores were open day and night, including Sunday._____

39. Just before crashing into a thousand pieces on the floor, Fritz almost caught the flying plate._____

Exercise 6.B – *continued*

40. Having never before lived in Kamloops, the organic food co-op was a delightful surprise. _____

41. When writing articles, several good reference texts should be close at hand. _____

42. Flies are easier to catch when using honey instead of vinegar. _____

43. Falling lightly as if in a dream, we watched the first snowfall of the season. _____

44. Having lost consciousness, the teacher called an ambulance for her ailing student. _____

45. To reward me for getting top grades, I got the family car for the whole of Saturday evening. _____

46. Feeling sick and tired, the work was difficult. _____

47. Rounding the corner, the house could be seen. _____

48. Marsha hoped to find a private teacher for her two-year-old with a PhD. _____

49. While washing dishes, her favourite wineglass broke. _____

50. Returning from his linguistics seminar, his pet parrot finally spoke. _____

Part III

Points of Style

Chapter 7

Parallelism and Faulty Constructions

Parallelism

If you keep the grammatical structure for closely related ideas parallel, your style will improve accordingly, and your readers will understand your meaning instead of having to ferret it out for themselves. To keep the grammatical structure parallel means to combine nouns with nouns, verbs with verbs, infinitives phrases with infinitive phrases, noun clauses with noun clauses, and so on.

> *Unparallel:* I have always liked to sew and cooking.
> *Parallel:* I have always liked to sew and to cook.
> *Or:* I have always liked sewing and cooking.

In the following examples, the parallel elements are in italic type.

- The Canadian Charter of Rights and Freedoms calls for freedom *of expression, of communication* and *of assembly.* (parallel prepositional phrases)
- She wrote that she would *leave in August, travel to Montreal by plane,* and *stay for several weeks.* (parallel subordinate noun clauses, objects of the verb *wrote*)
- Birds *fly;* flowers *bloom;* friends *care.* (parallel independent clauses joined by semi-colons)

When you use co-ordinating conjunctions (such as *and, but, for*) or correlative conjunctions (such as *both/and, neither/nor*), make sure you are using them to join elements of equal rank (phrases to phrases and subordinate clauses to subordinate clauses, for example).

> *Unparallel:* Anne is a woman with leadership qualities and who therefore should be elected chair.

Here, the co-ordinating conjunction *and* is used to join a phrase, *a woman with leadership qualities*, to a subordinate clause, *who therefore should be elected chair*. Several solutions are possible:

- Lose the conjunction *and*, as well as the conjunctive adverb, *therefore*:

  ○ Anne is a woman with leadership qualities who should be elected chair.

- Begin the sentence with a phrase:

  ○ A woman with leadership qualities, Anne should be elected chair.

- Write two independent clauses joined by *and*:

  ○ Anne is a woman who has leadership qualities, and she should therefore be elected chair.

- Use two independent clauses joined by a semicolon:

  ○ Anne is a woman with leadership qualities; therefore, she should be elected chair.

Some constructions are so close to parallel that errors are easy to miss:

> *Unparallel:* Professor Wong is intelligent, creative, and works hard.

Because the sentence is short and simple, and because it's obvious what the writer means, it's easy to miss that the conjunction *and* is being used to join unequal elements: two predicate adjectives (*intelligent* and *creative*) to a verb/modifier (*works hard*). The need for parallelism dictates that the conjunction *and* be used to join elements of equal rank only.

> *Parallel:* Professor Wong is intelligent, creative, and hardworking.

If for some reason you wanted to retain two predicate adjectives followed by a verb, you would have to repeat a pronoun for the subject of the clause:

  ○ Professor Wong is intelligent and creative, and he works hard.

Faulty parallelism can be easy to miss with correlative conjunctions (such as *either/or, neither/nor, both/and,* and *not only/but also*). Remember that the forms following the two parts of the correlative conjunction must be equal.

> *Unparallel:* I hope *either* to spend my vacation in Mexico *or* Cuba.

In this sentence, the first conjunction of the pair, *either,* is followed by an infinitive, *to spend;* the second part of the correlative conjunction, *or,* is followed by a noun, *Cuba.*

> *Parallel:* I hope to spend my vacation *either in* Mexico *or in* Cuba.
> *Or:* I hope to spend my vacation in *either* Mexico *or* Cuba.

To turn a fuzzy, unparallel construction into a clear, parallel one, you sometimes need only to repeat a word—an auxiliary verb, the *to* of the infinitive, a subordinating conjunction, an article, or a preposition.

> *Fuzzy:* The chair of the department must advise students who undertake a degree and also take part in the work of the university's various committees.
> *Clear:* The chair of the department *must* advise students who undertake a degree and *must* also take part in the work of the university's various committees.

> *Fuzzy:* He thought that weather conditions were improving and the wildfires crisis was nearly over.

Ambiguity exists here regarding the words *the wildfires crisis was nearly over.* Do these words indicate another of the man's opinions, or simply an independent fact?

> *Clear:* He thought *that* weather conditions were improving and *that* the wildfires crisis was nearly over.

When you use the words *than* and *as* to link parallel constructions, again make sure that the elements joined by those words are equal or parallel.

> *Incorrect:* A plumber's earnings are often as hefty as a professor.
> *Correct:* A plumber's earnings are often as hefty as a professor's.

(The words *earnings are* are understood after *a professor's.*)

> *Incorrect:* He is as short if not shorter than his brother.
> *Correct:* He is *as* short *as,* if not shorter *than,* his brother.

Error can also result when one verb form is used to serve two predicates:

Incorrect: I never have and never will abide fools gladly.

In this sentence, *never will* is correctly used before abide, but *never have* must be followed by the past participle, *abided*—it is incorrect to say *never have abide.*

Correct: I never have abided and never will abide fools gladly.

Incorrect: I was fairly impressed, but most of my students, wildly unimpressed.

The right verb form after *most of my students* is *were*, not *was*. The verb *was* cannot serve for both subjects because they differ in person and number.

Correct: I was fairly impressed, but most of my students were wildly unimpressed.

The same goes for a single article or preposition.

Incorrect: We gave him an orange and pear.
Correct: We gave him an orange and a pear.

Incorrect: I was distressed and anxious about his near-disaster in Bali.
Correct: I was distressed by and anxious about his near-disaster in Bali.

Parting words on parallel constructions

Parallel structure is for sentence elements that are parallel in meaning. Don't try to make all sentences consist of a series of parallel elements, and never sacrifice good style or usage just for the sake of parallelism.

As well, sometimes strict parallelism is not possible, and when that's true, it's much better to write clearly than to try to force a parallel construction out of some misguidedly rigid attachment to the idea of correctness over meaning. Examine this sentence:

∘ She accepted the award graciously and with quiet pride.

Having just finished reading about the importance of parallelism, you might be tempted to rewrite this sentence with something like *graciously and quietly proudly*. There's nothing wrong, however, in using *and* to join *graciously* (an adverb) to *with quiet pride* (a prepositional phrase). Even though the first is an adverb and the second a phrase, both are used as adverbial modifiers, and no grammatical errors have been introduced in the joining.

Faulty Constructions

Predication is the act (and sometimes, we hope, the art) of saying something about a subject, of putting subjects and predicates together in a way that results in readable prose. Faulty predication is a common failing, one that involves imprecise and illogical thinking. Where predication is faulty, a lapse of logic rules: the subject and predicate do not fit. The following sentences illustrate faulty predication.

> *Confusing:* Success in university appears to be a lottery.

The error is not in the grammar *per se*, but in the imprecision and illogic of the sentence. Success means "the securing of a desired outcome"; a lottery is a game of chance. One might succeed at *winning* a lottery, but success cannot itself *be* a lottery—the two terms are not comparable.

Here's a possible fix:

> ○ Success in university appears to be a matter of luck rather than ability.

Although there's nothing necessarily wrong with the pattern, sentences with linking verbs followed by predicate nouns appear to court confusion:

> *Confusing:* My memories of that day are hot and humid.

How can memories be hot and humid? Possible fix:

> ○ I remember that day was hot and humid.

> *Confusing:* The best kind of revising is the scalpel.

A scalpel does cut but it is not, in itself, a form of revising. Possible fix:

> ○ The best way to revise is to cut.

> *Confusing:* One way to better society is the golden rule.

The rule by itself is inert; people would have to follow the golden rule to have it better society. Possible fix:

> ○ One way to better society is to follow the golden rule.

Confusion can also arise when compound subjects share a sentence verb:

Confusing: For the wedding to proceed as planned, hundreds of
details and dozens of purchases had to be made.

You can "make" purchases, but not details. Fix:

o For the wedding to proceed as planned, we had to finalize
hundreds of details and make dozens of purchases.
Or: For the wedding to proceed as planned, hundreds of details
had to be finalized and dozens of purchases had to be made.

Here are more examples of faulty predication fomenting lapses in logic
(and vice versa!):

Confusing: The reason for earning money eventually offered
Penelope a job at the National Film Board.

A reason, no matter how sound, can't offer anyone a job. Possible fix:

o Her need to earn money eventually led Penelope to a job at the
National Film Board.

Confusing: Your first reporting job at a big-city daily is a feeling
that emboldens.

A job is not a feeling. Possible fix:

o Landing a first reporting job at a big-city daily tends to embolden
the aspiring journalist.

Reducing predication is one way to shorten sentences and increase clarity. As an editorial technique, it involves cutting down the number of
words in a sentence by deleting those that are unnecessary. Other ways
to reduce predication include:

• Combining sentences:
o She was a singer in a rock band. The band she played with
specialized in heavy metal.
Combined: She was a singer in a heavy metal rock band.

• Making clauses into phrases:
o A white chiffon dress that looked like a summer cloud.
This could become: A white chiffon dress like a summer cloud.

- Shortening phrases:
  - a wall the colour of rubies
  This could be: a ruby-red wall

- Reducing the number of words:
  - a man who serves on city council.
  This could be shortened to: a city councillor.

Since faulty predication involves illogical and imprecise thinking, the trouble with it—at least from the reader's point of view—lies in the difficulty of divining the writer's meaning. This difficulty should not discourage us from using metaphors or other higher-level functions of language in our writing; rather, it should impress us with the need to master the fundamentals of logic and grammar in order to retain clarity throughout.

Subordination and faulty construction

Logic is the science of correct reasoning; grammar is, in a sense, the logic of a language, providing the logical underpinnings of correct usage. In English sentences, words that show logical relationships between various elements of the sentence must be used correctly for the meaning to be clear. Subordinating conjunctions are such words; for example, they show that the idea in the subordinate clause is less important than the one in the main independent clause. When errors of subordination occur, they are more complex than simple errors of subject/verb agreement or pronoun case. They occur at the level of the sentence, impairing its logic and making its meaning harder to grasp.

Subordination involves the use of certain words (conjunctions, prepositions, and relative pronouns) to link less important sentence elements—modifying words, phrases, or subordinate clauses—to the main independent clause of a sentence. The examples below show the subordination of secondary information:

- In our front yard, there is a fountain, which is carved from marble.

In this version, the less important idea, that the fountain is carved from marble, is placed in a subordinate clause, *which is carved from marble.*

- In our front yard there is a fountain *carved from marble.*

Here, the subordinate idea is reduced to a three-word participial phrase, *carved from marble.*

- In our front yard there is a *marble* fountain.

Here, the participial phrase is reduced to the single word, the adjective *marble*.

Simple errors of subordination can occur when the subordination is reversed:

> *Incorrect:* Though she won the race, she showed signs of tiredness.
> *Correct:* Though she showed signs of tiredness, she won the race.

> *Incorrect:* Though he had to leave, he loved her.
> *Correct:* Though he loved her, he had to leave.

Errors can also arise when the wrong conjunction is used:

> *Incorrect:* I read in the paper *where* the Strawberry Hill fire is completely contained.
> *Correct:* I read in the paper *that* the Strawberry Hill fire is completely contained.

> *Incorrect:* While they are not perfect, they certainly have merit.
> *Correct:* Although they are not perfect, they certainly have merit.

Closely related to the problem of faulty subordination is that of incomplete or incorrect comparison, a problem we touched on earlier when we examined elliptical clauses. The following sentence, for instance, might confuse a reader:

> ∘ Polly loves crackers more than me.

Grammatically, this sentence means that Polly loves crackers more than Polly loves me, the writer. If the intended meaning is that Polly loves crackers more than I, the writer, love crackers, then the sentence must read either *Polly loves crackers more than I,* or *Polly loves crackers more than I do.*

Here's another example:

> ∘ We helped Margaret more than them.

We can't be sure in this sentence whether the writer means that we helped Margaret more than we helped them (which is what the sentence literally means) or that we helped Margaret more than they helped Margaret, in which case writing "we helped Margaret more than them" would constitute an error of pronoun case. If the latter meaning is intended, the sentence should read:

> ∘ We helped Margaret more than they.
> *Or:* We helped Margaret more than they did.

Unnecessary shifts in clause construction also confuse meaning and sap energy. Possible corrections for the examples are given below. (You may see other, perhaps more elegant, corrections.)

>*Incorrect:* She bought the dark blue chiffon dress, which by taking down the hem a bit she hoped to wear to the ball.
>*Correct:* She bought the dark blue chiffon dress; she planned to take down its hem a bit, and wear the dress to the ball.
>*Or:* She bought the dark blue chiffon dress, planning to wear it to the ball after taking down the hem a bit.

>*Incorrect:* Because she had no ride prevented her from attending the protest.
>*Correct:* The lack of a ride prevented her from attending the protest.
>*Or:* Because she had no ride, she couldn't attend the protest.

>*Incorrect:* He had a bad cold was why he missed the exam on Monday.
>*Correct:* He missed the exam on Monday because he had a bad cold.
>*Or:* Because he had a bad cold, he missed Monday's exam.

Extra conjunctions also confuse meaning and sap strength:

>◦ Barb realized *that* during the show *how* bored she had been.

To correct this badly constructed sentence, go with one conjunction or the other; you don't need both.

>*Either:* Barb realized how bored she'd been during the show.
>*Or:* Barb realized that she'd been bored during the show.

>*Incorrect:* That's the professor about whom Mohamed was talking about.
>*Correct:* That's the professor about whom Mohamed was talking.
>*Or:* That's the professor (whom) Mohamed was talking about.

>*Incorrect:* I think that if he were serious about doing the work, that he would call me.
>*Correct:* I think that if he were serious about doing the work, he would call me.

Review Exercises

Exercise 7.A

Rewrite the following sentences to correct faulty parallelism.

1. Shawnee is a young wolf dog with a thick black coat, beautiful amber eyes and he has a bark much worse than his bite. _____

2. The entire Grade 6 class was worried about but also happy to move to the new location._____

3. In the glove compartment, they found several items: a book of bus tickets, half-eaten orange, and keys to the house. _____

4. It is normal to have greater muscle content in a newborn male than a newborn female. _____

5. Lainey grabbed the megaphone, climbed on top of the car, then the protesters heard her begin to speak._____

6. My mother always has and always will iron towels. _____

7. You must hand in your final exam either before the end of class or I must dock you ten points. _____

8. We decided that we should stay the night in Cache Creek and to leave early the next morning for Kamloops._____

9. Timothy Findley's novel *The Wars* is as good if not better than other novels written by Canadian authors about the First World War. _____

10. The piano movers were built like tanks with massive chests and shoulders and strong arms and hands, and their backs were strong. _____

11. Dana's favourite desserts were chocolate ice cream, chocolate donuts and she loved baklava. _____

12. Eating and drinking are not allowed in the classroom, and you may not smoke. _____

13. Lulu couldn't make up her mind whether she wanted to eat, clean her paws, or to go outside. _____

14. I have neither the time nor do I feel inclined to help you. _____

15. They agreed they would re-convene at 9:00 the next morning and to settle the dispute._____

Exercise 7.A – *continued*

16. Kelly's essay was well written and quite a bit longer than Kara. _____

17. This digital watch is pretty, reliable, and it keeps accurate time. _____

18. The exercises were not only lengthy, but they were also quite hard. _____

19. Planning to exercise does not provide the same benefit as if you actually do the exercises. _____

20. Marcel is a writer and athlete. _____

21. I have always liked to sew and cooking. _____

22. The Canadian Charter of Rights and Freedoms calls for freedom of expression, communication, and to assemble. _____

23. She wrote that she would leave in August, travel to Montreal by plane, and to stay for several weeks. _____

24. Anne is a woman with leadership qualities and who therefore should be elected chair. _____

25. Professor O'Regan is intelligent, creative, and works hard. _____

26. I hope either to spend my vacation in Mexico or Cuba. _____

27. The chair of the department must advise students who undertake a degree and also take part in committee work. _____

28. The drama coach wants to meet with people who enjoy theatre and stage an amateur production at the high school. _____

29. He thought that weather conditions were improving and the wildfires crisis was nearly over. _____

30. A plumber's earnings are often as hefty as a professor. _____

31. He is as short if not shorter than his brother. _____

32. I never have and never will abide fools gladly. _____

33. I was fairly impressed, but most of my students, wildly unimpressed. _____

34. We gave him an orange and pear. _____

35. I was distressed and anxious about his near-disaster in Asia. _____

Exercise 7.B

Repair the faulty constructions in the examples below.

1. In looking for her raincoat was Penny's excuse for keeping us all waiting. _____

2. The grammatical error called a dangling modifier is when a participial phrase has no grammatical subject. _____

3. I always believed that if I did the work, that I would become a professional. _____

4. The reason is because she had a toothache._____

5. She had always thought that with adobe, what a good color white is. _____

6. His body, which after he started exercising and eating right, he no longer thought was his worst enemy._____

7. We are as tall if not taller than they._____

8. George, after he finished the last novel of the trilogy, he finally took a holiday._____

9. The new school lab has flat-screen computers, thus which are harder to hide behind. _____

10. Success in university appears to be a lottery._____

11. My memories of that day are hot and humid. _____

12. One way to better society is the golden rule. _____

13. In order to have the wedding in August, hundreds of details and dozens of purchases had to be made. _____

14. A bias is when you make a judgment about something before you have the facts._____

15. The reason for earning money eventually offered Penelope a job at the National Film Board._____

16. Your first reporting job at a big-city daily is a feeling that emboldens. _____

17. Though she won the race, she showed signs of tiredness._____

18. Though he had to leave, he loved her. _____

19. I read in the paper where the Strawberry Hill fire is completely contained. _____

Exercise 7.B – *continued*

20. While they are not perfect, they certainly have merit. _____

21. She was extremely tired, although she managed to finish her homework. _____

22. He was a great believer in learning by doing and never gave long lectures. _____

23. I wanted to bake a cake and I had no flour or sugar in the house. _____

24. Cristine tried hard and paid attention in class, and she didn't get the A she wanted. _____

25. The event was well-planned although the turnout was low. _____

26. Since no one else showed up, we decided to leave. _____

27. As she was the only one in the office at the time, she took the call. _____

28. She wanted to impress him, which she put on her best clothes for him._____

29. Because they couldn't decide who should drive, they took a cab because it was getting late. _____

30. Sunny says she wants to meet someone although she doesn't go out much. _____

31. He got to know her better, however he no longer judges her harshly._____

32. When they finished the rehearsal they went for coffee after they closed the studio._____

33. As I was busy with the baby, I asked Jeremy to prepare dinner._____

34. An example of their stubbornness is when they refuse to engage in teamwork. _____

35. In the article on video games explains why the games grew popular. _____

Exercise 7.C

For this exercise in subordination, combine the sentences in the paragraphs below to make one complex or compound/complex sentence. Delete and change the forms of the words as necessary.

1. The English word "language" is derived from the Latin word *lingua*. The Latin word *lingua* means "tongue." One way to define language is to say that language is made up of sounds that are produced with the human tongue.

2. Yet some sounds made by humans do not qualify as "language." Speech is the basic form of communication, the way the vast majority of communications take place. Humans have been speaking for much longer than they have been writing.

3. Do animals, or only humans, possess language? Animals do produce sounds that communicate meaning to other animals of the same species. The range of communication may be limited, but some sort of meaning is nevertheless conveyed.

4. Any satisfying definition of language would have to say something about "meaning." It would also have to include the various methods of conveying meaning. It would have to include both spoken words, and visible gestures, and of course, the complex system of symbols that make up written language.

5. It would seem that humans are set apart from other mammals not so much by their capacity for and use of spoken symbols to communicate. They are set apart more by their invention and use of writing. That invention has allowed humans to communicate across time and space. It has also allowed humans to expand their knowledge and understanding of the world.

Chapter 8

Punctuation

The classic writing text *Elements of Style* opens with eleven "elementary rules of usage." Eight of these involve points of punctuation. (Only three address matters other than punctuation: subject-verb agreement, pronoun case, and dangling participial phrases at the beginning of sentences.)

Punctuation matters; it constitutes the "graphics" of grammar and indicates the patterns of the spoken word. Consider that while humans have been speaking for hundreds of thousands of years (approximately 700,000), they have been writing for only about 3,500, and they have been using the modern system of punctuation for barely 300. Punctuation allows us to bring precision to written words, to indicate how the words would sound when spoken. The correct and skilful use of punctuation can do a lot for your writing, and the rules are few and reliable.

There are two basic kinds: terminal punctuation (used at the end of a sentence), which includes the period, the question mark, and the exclamation point; and internal punctuation (used within sentences), which includes the remaining nine marks of punctuation (comma, semi-colon, colon, dash, parentheses, brackets, quotation marks, the apostrophe, and the ellipsis).

Another way to look at the system is in terms of function. Punctuation generally serves four possible functions: to separate or set off, to join or link, to enclose, and to indicate omissions. Just as the same word can function as different parts of speech in a sentence, the same mark of punctuation can serve different purposes depending on the context. The following list illustrates this principle, indicating the various marks under the four possible functions they can serve:

- *Separate or set off:* period, question mark, exclamation point, and comma
- *Link:* semicolon, colon, and dash

- *Enclose:* paired commas and dashes; parentheses, brackets, and quotation marks
- *Indicate omissions:* apostrophe, ellipsis (three evenly spaced periods), and the single dash

Remember that many minor variations occur at the discretion of individual writers, and that certain professions or organizations have their own preferences in matters of style. For example, journalists tend to favour minimal punctuation, while the legal profession makes copious use of it. Some style guides prescribe an apostrophe before the *s* when writing the plurals of letters and numbers, while others eschew the apostrophe and use only the *s*. As well, British punctuation differs slightly from that used in North America, particularly with regard to the placement of quotation marks.

Terminal Punctuation

Of terminal punctuation, there are three kinds: the period, the question mark, and the exclamation point. All are used to end sentences, separating them from other sentences.

Period
Use the period:

- To end sentences and separate them from those that follow. Use the period to end declarative sentences and imperative sentences (ones that give commands or make requests).

  Declarative: The weather forecaster predicts rain.
  Imperative: Stop playing that video game and answer the door.

- For abbreviations or initials within sentences. If the abbreviated form appears at the end of the sentence, one period suffices to end both the abbreviation and the sentence.

  Abbreviation: He lives at 45 Sherbrooke St. West and has lived there for a long time.
  Abbreviation at the end: He lives at 45 West Sherbrooke St.
  Initials: J. R. Ewing was one of the main characters in a TV series.

Question mark
Use the question mark to end interrogative sentences, those that ask direct questions.

- Where will I put these books?
- Is Lienne at home?

If there are questions within a sentence that already asks a question, use one mark for each actual question:

> ○ Can we be sure of her ability? Her experience? Her honesty?
> *Or:* Her ability, her experience, her honesty—can we be sure
>   of them?

Exclamation point

The exclamation point at the end of a sentence shows emphasis, urgency, surprise, or other strong emotion. Overuse of the exclamation point is like an admission of defeat. It implies that you are unable to make your words adequately express your meaning. (F. Scott Fitzgerald advised the excision of all exclamation marks; he said they were like laughing at your own joke.) Assuming the mark is not used too often, it is correct in sentences such as the following:

> ○ I do not want to have to tell you again!
> ○ Hey, watch out for that truck!
> ○ She surely was a sight for sore eyes!

Exclamation points are also correctly used with interjections, commands, and rhetorical questions.

> ○ Wow! That was unusual.
> ○ Come out with your hands raised above your heads!
> ○ Are you serious!

Internal Punctuation

Of internal punctuation, there are nine kinds: comma, semicolon, colon, dash, parentheses, brackets, apostrophe, ellipsis, and quotation marks.

Comma

The comma sets off or separates words or phrases in a sentence. It may be used alone and in a pair.

The single comma

This humble and much-misused mark is used correctly:

- Between words, phrases, and clauses in a series of three or more. Authorities disagree on whether writers should insert a comma before the conjunction joining the last two members of the series. Do so unless you are directed otherwise by your teacher or employer.

∘ She asked for a ruler, a pen, and a piece of paper.
∘ Alice planned to have fish, potatoes, salad, and apple pie
for dinner.
∘ He walked out of the room, turned around, came back in, and
glowered at me.
∘ At the meeting, we decided to: 1) institute core courses,
2) raise the entrance requirements, and 3) vote in a new
department chair.
∘ We ate sandwiches, potato chips, Caesar salad, and pickles.

N.B. No comma is required before a co-ordinating conjunction
that joins two words considered as a single unit (e.g. *bacon and eggs*):

∘ Hiking and camping, jogging and running, and dancing and
singing are some of their favourite activities.
∘ He ordered a breakfast of orange juice, toast, coffee, and bacon
and eggs.

• Before a co-ordinating conjunction (such as *and, or, but, yet, for, nor,*
and *so*) that joins two independent clauses. Don't confuse a sentence containing two independent clauses (such as *You can come to
the fair with me, or you can go to the game with your father*) with a sentence containing two predicates (*You can come to the fair with me or
go to the game with your father*). The following sentences have two
independent clauses, separated by a comma:

∘ Montreal is a large and vibrant city, and it has many cultural
attractions.
∘ He decided he would not go to Mexico, for he wanted to spend
the time at home.
∘ I dictated the letter without omissions, but she did not
transcribe it correctly.
∘ She was glad to be leaving, yet she felt a bit nostalgic for
the place.
∘ We did not stop for breakfast that day, nor did we take a full
hour for lunch.

Many writers and editors believe it's appropriate to omit the comma
between independent clauses when the clauses are short, so long as
no error or ambiguity results.

∘ He looked right at her but he didn't see her.
∘ I walked the dog and then I took a shower.

If there is no co-ordinate conjunction between two independent clauses, use a semi-colon to join them, not a comma. To use a comma between two independent clauses without any co-ordinate conjunction is to commit the error known as the "comma fault" (or "comma splice"). The sentence below illustrates this error:

Incorrect: The people in the department are not following
instructions, they continue to proceed without
regard to the plan.

To correct the comma fault, do one of the following:
(a) Insert a co-ordinate conjunction after the comma:

○ The people in the department are not following instructions,
and they continue to proceed without regard to the plan.

(b) Replace the comma with a semicolon:

○ The people in the department are not following instructions;
they continue to proceed without regard to the plan.

(c) Rewrite the sentence as two shorter sentences:

○ The people in the department are not following instructions.
They continue to proceed without regard to the plan.

• To set off or separate introductory expressions (ones that begin a sentence) from the rest of the sentence, whether these introductory expressions are single words, participial phrases, or subordinate clauses. Notice in the final two examples that when a subordinate clause follows a main clause (i.e. when it does not introduce the sentence), no comma is required.

○ Yes, I will come to the party.
○ As always, she chose the seat at the very back of the café.
○ Without the children, the house seemed empty.
○ According to Jim, the ice road is not safe.
○ Seeing the rental sign, he wrote down the address in his notebook.

○ After he wrote the letter, he made an important phone call.
But: He made an important phone call after he wrote the letter.

○ Before you can graduate, you must complete this assignment.
But: You must complete this assignment before you can graduate.

Note also that when an infinitive phrase functions as the subject of a sentence, it should not be separated by a comma from its verb:

○ To be a good editor was her goal.

• To set off elements in apposition, whether words, phrases, or clauses. When the words in apposition come in the middle of the sentence rather than at the end or beginning, two commas are required to "enclose" the words.

○ They sent the manuscript to Clara, the editor-in-chief.
○ Clara, the editor-in-chief, is my best friend.
○ The university gave an award to Dr. Asher, our English teacher.
○ Dr. Asher, our English teacher, won an award from the university.
○ He believes the smell is caused by pollution, severe as the day is long.
○ The bad smell, severe as the day is long, was blamed on pollution.

• To set off names or nouns used in direct address or in the salutation of a letter. If these words fall within the sentence rather than at the beginning or end, two commas are required to enclose them:

○ Fritz, please pass the salt. (Please, Fritz, pass the salt.)
○ I'm glad that we waited for you, Bill. (I'm glad, Bill, that we waited for you.)
○ Have you seen my keys, Finnegan?

The salutation and comma in a letter is followed by a capital letter:

○ Dear Felicity, How have you been?

• To separate any words that might be ambiguous or confusing without the separation.

Not this: From outside the cabin appeared deserted.
But this: From outside, the cabin appeared deserted.

• To separate co-ordinate adjectives (ones that equally modify the same noun and could be joined by the conjunction *and*, or be reversed in order).

○ The efficient, orderly secretary got a raise.

Both of the adjectives modify secretary; they are co-ordinate adjectives. The conjunction *and* could be used instead of a comma:

○ The efficient and orderly secretary.

The adjectives could be in reverse order:

○ The orderly, efficient secretary.

Each adjective is modifying *secretary* equally, distinguishing this secretary from all those *disorderly* and *inefficient* ones. Compare to this next example:

○ This big old house needs repairs.

In the noun phrase *this big old house*, the adjectives are not co-ordinate. They modify the same noun, but not equally, and they should not have a comma separating them.

• To set off words or phrases that fall at the end of a sentence and express contrast or ask questions:

○ I asked you to file the papers, not to hide them.
○ You may be excused, but just this once.
○ The train should be on time, shouldn't it?
○ They were supposed to move to Toronto, weren't they?

• To separate the parts of an address or a date:

○ The beautiful young woman had been born on April 15, 1970, at 225 Riverview Avenue in Montreal, Quebec.
○ They decided to convene at nine o'clock, on Friday, Feb. 4.

• With direct quotations, to separate the quoted material from the rest of the sentence:

○ Dr. Lambert said, "If you don't feel better by tomorrow, call me."
○ "If you don't feel better by tomorrow, call me," said Dr. Lambert
○ "If you don't feel better by tomorrow," Dr. Lambert said, "call me."

○ "In the first place," Pablo said, "you should have told me you went to the meeting."
○ "In the first place, you should have told me you went to the meeting," Pablo said.

○ Pablo said, "In the first place, you should have told me you went to the meeting."

○ "Many are in favour of this change in policy," said the dean.
○ The dean said, "Many are in favour of this change in policy."
○ "Many are in favour," said the dean, "of this change in policy."

• To indicate the omission of certain implied words.

○ He ordered the steak; Marnie, the shrimp; I, the veggie burger.
○ I voted for the motion; he, against.

The paired comma
Use paired commas as follows:

• To enclose non-restrictive clauses (ones that convey additional or parenthetical information not essential to the meaning of the sentence). A restrictive clause, by contrast, is never enclosed in commas because it is necessary to the sentence; it is not parenthetical or "optional" in any way. Consider these sentences:

○ All the students who failed the music proficiency test must attend a special summer course.
○ All the students, who failed the music proficiency test, must attend a special summer course.   *poor example*

The words are the same in both sentences, but the first sentence contains no commas, while the second sentence has a pair of commas. Yet the sentences mean radically different things. In the first sentence, the clause *who failed the music proficiency test* is restrictive, and the sentence means that some of the students failed the test. In the second sentence, the clause is non-restrictive, and the sentence means that all the students failed the test.

In the examples below, the first sentence of each pair contains a restrictive clause (no commas), and the second contains a non-restrictive clause (commas). Try to understand the difference in meaning between the two sentences in each pair, and you will see why the distinction matters.

○ The man who lives next door came to work at our office.
○ The man, who lives next door, came to work at our office.

○ The lawnmower that is in the garage is broken.
○ The lawnmower, which is in the garage, is broken.

- The bridge that connects the South Shore communities to the Island of Montreal was built in the sixties.
- The bridge, which connects the South Shore communities to the Island of Montreal, was built in the sixties.

The words *that* and *which* are often used interchangeably with restrictive and non-restrictive clauses, but there is a difference in meaning between the two words. When you need to choose between *that* and *which*, use *that* and no commas for restrictive clauses; for non-restrictive clauses, use *which* and paired commas.

- To enclose transitional words (*however, therefore, moreover, yes, besides*), phrases (*after all, by the way, without doubt, so to speak, of course*), and clauses (*I think, we suppose, he says, they all agree*) that occur within a sentence.

  - You will, I believe, receive credit for that course.
  - We have decided, therefore, to accept your offer.
  - Mr. Berzan, as you know, is an expert in his field.
  - They tried, of course, to do their very best.

Since the purpose here is to enclose the parenthetical expression between two commas, don't forget the second comma. In the next example, assuming the speaker has a sister named Penny who lives in Nelson, the last comma is essential to the meaning:

Not this: Penny, my sister lives in Nelson.
But this: Penny, my sister, lives in Nelson.

- To enclose any intervening or explanatory expressions (such as *and I agree with him, as far as he is concerned*) that fall within sentences, rather than at the beginning or the end.

  - That's the end, as far as I'm concerned, of the whole affair.

Semicolon

The semicolon shows that one thought has ended, and another closely related thought is about to begin. It indicates a stronger separation than the comma does. Used effectively (and sparingly), the semicolon can enhance your style. Use a semicolon:

- Instead of a conjunction such as *and, but, or, yet, for, nor,* and *so* in a compound sentence between independent clauses:

  ○ French was one of my best subjects; trigonometry gave me trouble.
  ○ He meets with the editors every other week; he talks to reporters rarely.
  ○ They did not approve the expenses claimed; they called them excessive.
  ○ The weather was wonderful; we decided to spend the day outdoors.

- Between independent clauses that are connected not by co-ordinate conjunctions, but by transitional words that show the logical relationship between the clauses (so be careful to choose the right transitional words):

  ○ Baroque music is restrained; on the other hand, it can also be quite moving.
  ○ She said she was glad to do the work; nevertheless, she thought the task difficult.

- To separate phrases or clauses in a series that already contains internal punctuation.

  ○ Tom, the president, conferred with Star, the vice-president; Jeanette, the chief shop steward; and Bernard, the chair of the human rights committee.
  ○ Our history professor, Anne, really keeps us on our toes with her tough assignments; our English teacher, who taught us in our first two years, tended to be less demanding.
  ○ His father, a kind and decent man, was not easily angered; but his son's disrespect, which everyone noticed, made him see red.

- Before words (such as *for example, for instance, namely*) that introduce a list or an example.

  ○ Many of the school's policies changed; for example, students now had to wear uniforms.
  ○ These shorts are available in only three colours; namely, yellow, green, and blue.

Colon

The colon sets up whatever follows it: a quotation, an example, an appositive, a list. It's true that the semicolon may also be used with transitional words to introduce these elements, but the colon does more to throw the emphasis forward to what follows. (The dash, on the other hand, throws the emphasis backward.) Use the colon:

- To introduce such as a list, an appositive, or an example.

  o In class, we read works by the following authors: John Irving, Alice Walker, and George Szanto.
  o To succeed in the arts you need at least two things: talent and a thick skin.
  o He had a list of chores: get groceries, have the car washed, and go to the bank.
  o The dog looked like his owner: squat and surly.

- To introduce a long quotation.

  o In his inaugural address, former U.S. president John F. Kennedy said: "Let the word go forth from this time and place that the torch has been passed to a new generation of Americans."

- After the salutation in a business letter.

  o To whom it may concern:
  o Dear Mr. Flanz:

- To divide parts of titles, citations, and references to time.

  o Chapter One: Parts of Speech
  o He cited a passage from Part 1: Chapter 5.
  o The time was 9:15 p.m.

Dash

The dash can give your writing a certain liveliness or drama, but don't use it indiscriminately, or where more pedestrian punctuation would serve. It is counter-productive; by overusing the dash, you soon forfeit its literary effects. Use the dash:

- To set off something that sharply interrupts the flow of a sentence.

  o The judges have chosen me—I can hardly believe it—to compete in the essay contest.
  o As I started to explain to you just the other day—hey, what was that noise?

- After a list at the beginning of a sentence.

    ○ Timothy Findley, John Irving, and George Szanto—these were the Canadian novelists that she most admired.

- To announce an appositive or a summary.

    ○ The creature began to howl—a screeching, piercing, heart-stopping howl.
    ○ Contacts, loans, moral support—they gave everything they could to help.

- To set off words for emphasis.

    ○ I could not—I mean could not—believe it.
    ○ That was how I—and everyone else on staff—felt about the new rules.

Parentheses

Use parentheses to enclose independent constructions—words, phrases, clauses, or sentences used to provide material that is explanatory, secondary, additional, or in apposition. These elements are independent of the main clause; they are not essential to complete the meaning of the sentence. The "parenthetical" comments add new information, but you could remove them and the remaining words would still constitute a grammatical sentence.

    ○ Bessie Hall (a post-baccalaureate student from the Maritimes) won the award.
    ○ The French have a saying: *"Plus que ça change, plus que c'est la même chose."* (The more things change, the more they stay the same.)
    ○ We ordered forty-five (45) textbooks for the new course.

When punctuating sentences that have words in parentheses and also other punctuation, punctuate the main clause the same way you would if there were no parentheses. Put a punctuation mark outside (after) the close parenthesis when the mark applies to the entire sentence and not just to the material within the parentheses. Put a punctuation mark inside the close parenthesis when the mark applies only to the material within parentheses.

    ○ Since the new student was shy (she had recently arrived from Italy and spoke little English), we decided to befriend her and make her feel accepted.

- Tanya planned to visit the daughter (she has three) who lives in Paris.
- Janice (an old friend from college) is coming to dinner.
- Having missed the noon bus (he woke late), he decided to stay another day.
- She wrote to him in French: *"Tu me manques."* ("I miss you.")

Comparing commas, parentheses, and dashes

Several paired marks of punctuation may be used to enclose parenthetical matter: paired commas, parentheses, and dashes. All three are used to set off words, phrases, and clauses. When should you use which?

It comes down more to the writer's discretion than to hard and fast rules, but in general, use commas for shorter material closely related to the main clause of the sentence; parentheses for longer material less closely related; and dashes, sparingly and for effect, to indicate abrupt change or emphasis.

Brackets

Brackets are used to enclose words of comment or explanation inserted by the writer into quoted material. The brackets indicate that the words within them are not part of the original quotation. (This convention is not universally observed; for example, Canadian Press style uses parentheses, not brackets, to insert comments by the writer into quoted material. For Standard English in formal venues, including scholarly and technical writing, use brackets for this purpose.) Use brackets as follows:

- To enclose material—editorial comments or additions, for example —added by the writer to a quoted passage.

  - An official at the courthouse said, "The trial will begin soon [next week]."
  - "This writer [Alice Walker] is one of my favourite American novelists," the teacher said.

- To enclose parenthetical matter in a sentence or clause that already uses parentheses.

  - Your book order (including Strunk and White's *Elements of Style* and Dorothea Brande's *On Becoming a Writer* [excluding Brenda Ueland's *If You Want to Write*]) was shipped yesterday.

Apostrophe

The apostrophe has three possible functions: it indicates possession (*Lienne's movie, Dan's sailboat, the professors' association*); it shows missing letters in contractions (e.g. *don't* for *do not*; or *isn't* for *is not*); and it is used to form the plurals of letters, numbers, and short words being referred to as words. Use the apostrophe:

- To indicate possession in nouns. Form the possessive of singular and plural nouns by adding an apostrophe and an "s" to the word (*girl, girl's*); if the plural form ends in *s*, add only the apostrophe (*girls' hats*). Certain expressions of time, distance, and value take apostrophes (*a full week's work; in a year's time, five dollars' worth*).

  For compound nouns (*sister-in-law, sisters-in-law*), add *'s* to the last word in the series (*sister-in-law's, sisters-in-law's*). To show joint ownership when two nouns are involved, make only the second noun possessive; to show individual ownership when two nouns are involved, make each noun possessive (*Mark and Goa's car* indicates joint ownership, a car belonging to both *Mark and Goa. Mark's and Goa's cars* shows individual ownership of two separate cars.)

  To show possession in indefinite pronouns, add *'s*, just as you do for nouns; but remember that possessive pronouns take no apostrophes (*mine, yours, his, hers, its, ours, theirs*). As explained in detail in Chapter 5, *it's* and *its* should not be confused; in *it's*, the apostrophe is used to indicate the omitted letter *i* from *is*; the word *its* is a possessive pronoun, which takes no apostrophe.

  ○ It's a wise woman who keeps her own counsel.
  ○ He consulted the *I Ching*, but its advice eluded him.
  ○ It's an old book, and its cover is worn and tattered.

- To indicate omitted letters in contractions (*isn't, aren't, weren't, hadn't, it's*).

  ○ It isn't a question of time, but of funds.
  ○ We weren't pleased with being rushed through the ceremony.
  ○ They hadn't had a chance to read the report.

- To form the plural of letters, numbers, and short words being referred to as words.

  ○ I will be certain to dot all my i's and cross all my t's.
  ○ The 1960's were a time of turbulent change.
  ○ There are no if's, and's, or but's about it.

Ellipsis

Use the ellipsis to indicate omissions from sentences or quoted passages, and to indicate a reflective pause or drifting off at the end of a sentence or within it. The ellipsis (plural: ellipses) consists of three evenly spaced periods. If the missing words come at the end of the sentence or passage, use four evenly spaced periods (three for the ellipsis to indicate an omission, and one to end the sentence). Consider the following examples:

- "Please close the window and open the door."
- *Words omitted from within the sentence:* "Please close . . . and open the door."
- *Words omitted at the end:* "Please close the window and open. . . ."
- Let me think. . . . Yes, they did discuss local politics.
- And they all lived happily ever after . . .

Quotation marks

Use quotation marks:

- To enclose direct quotations, showing the reader that what is placed inside the quotation marks is a verbatim reproduction, representing the speaker's precise words. Remember that while direct quotations need quotation marks, indirect quotations do not. The examples below illustrate the difference; the first sentence is a direct quotation; the second, an indirect quotation.

  - Mr. Purdon said, "Complete this exercise for homework."
  (This is a direct quotation, reproducing the speaker's precise words.)

  - Mr. Purdon told the class to complete an exercise for homework.
  (This is an indirect quotation, which requires no quotation marks, because it doesn't purport to be a record of the speaker's very words.)

- To refer to or emphasize words or phrases that are slang, or used in some other non-standard way, or that are being referred to as words.

  - The sixties generation used the word "bread" to mean money.
  - What does the French word "châpeau" mean?
  - His "apology" had come a little late and left a lot to be desired.
  - The word "proceed" is often confused with the word "precede."

- To set off the titles of parts of works, such as a chapter in a book, an article in a magazine, or an essay in an anthology. For the titles of full-length works—books, plays, movies—use italics instead.

  - We studied George Orwell's famous essay, "The Politics of the English Language."
  - *The Poisonwood Bible* was written by Barbara Kingsolver.
  - Last night we saw the movie *The War Zone*.
  - The first chapter in Gabrielle Lusser Rico's book, *Writing the Natural Way*, is entitled "Releasing Your Inner Writer."
  - He loves to read "The Talk of the Town" in *The New Yorker*.

Placing quotation marks

Quotation marks separate the direct quotation (the actual words of the quoted speaker) from the attribution or from the rest of the sentence.

  - "Here is your ticket to the game," said Angela.
  - He said the tickets were "compliments of a client" that was unable, for some reason or other, to use them.

Use quotation marks to enclose each part of an interrupted quotation.

  - "Joan," said Nicole, "would you mind eating a bit earlier this evening?"

When a sentence introducing a quotation begins with the attribution, use a comma after the attributive verb to separate it from the quotation.

  - Mark said, "You can't drive all night in this horrid weather."
  - He told the court, "I am innocent."

Use single quotation marks for a quotation within a quotation.

  - The lecturer said, "The words 'when I was a child I spoke as a child' come from the Bible."
  - Our teacher said, "I expected your paper today. You said yesterday, 'I will bring in my paper tomorrow.' "
  - "His exact words were 'be home by ten,' and I think he meant it," Jan said.

For dialogue, start a new paragraph every time the speaker changes.

  - "What time will you be ready?" asked Marvin, scowling.
    "As soon as I put the roast in the oven," replied Janice.

"What's up?" asked Barb, the couple's teenage daughter. She
walked into the kitchen and sat on a stool.
"Nothing," said Janice, rolling her eyes in Marv's direction. "Your
father appears to be worried that we might be late for the game."
"What? Me worry?" Marvin said acidly, once again checking
his watch.

If a direct quotation goes on for more than one paragraph, put quotation
marks at the start of each paragraph but at the end of only the last one.

- "Blah, blah, blah," the politician said. "I say again, blah, blah, blah.
  "I cannot say it too many times: blah, blah, blah.
  "I said it last week as well. But you may not have read the report
  in the local paper, so it bears repeating.
  "Blah, blah, blah."

Periods and commas should always go inside the closing quotation mark:

- "I would love to sail around the world," Martin said.
- But Dahlia replied, "I'd rather stay home."
- "I want you to stop at the grocer's," she said. "I need a quart
  of milk."
- "I have enough time for a quick shower," she said.
- "I need a vacation," Marnie said.
- Some praised the work as "inspired," but others judged it only "fair."
- He called her "unlucky."
- That show was "a real dog," according to my brother.

The question mark and the exclamation point should go inside the close
quotation mark when they refer to the quoted material only, and outside
when they refer to the unquoted material.

- She asked, "When are you going on vacation?"
- Did she say, "I plan to leave for the coast on Monday"?
- What is meant by "a deal he couldn't refuse"?
- "What a sight for sore eyes!" he said.
- I can't believe you said, "I'll drink to that"!

When both the quoted material and the non-quoted material are questions, put a single question mark inside the close quotation mark.

- Did she ask, "When are you going on vacation?"
- Did he say, "Have I understood you correctly?"
- Did Marnie ask, "Who will help me?"

The colon and the semicolon should go outside the close quotation mark unless they are part of the quoted material.

○ She said, "You are to be promoted next month"; consequently, I expected to be promoted.

Review Exercises

Exercise 8.A

Supply the missing punctuation in the following sentences. Where a sentence uses the attributive verb *say*, assume it's a quotation. (Where necessary, make other changes, such as capitalizing the letter that begins a new sentence.)

1. He believes he won the essay contest because he chose an excellent topic and wrote well

2. The girl standing beside Janine is my sister

3. The disorganization was to put it mildly rather disconcerting

4. Before she could enter the swimsuit contest she had to convince her mother it was a good idea

5. All students without exception are welcome to attend the senior prom

6. Please pass the sugar Naomi its right beside you

7. On reading his letter I learned he had finished graduate school married and moved to Los Angeles

8. Many people know Noam Chomsky the brilliant linguist only by his political writings

9. My sister who lives in Big Trout Lake in Northern Ontario is coming to visit me

10. No John you shouldn't send cash through the mail

11. Professor Belshaw won an award for his book and plans to celebrate with his colleagues

12. I give you my word that I will treat your application confidentially please let me know if I can be of further assistance

13. She felt truly grateful for all the information and help that her teachers had provided over the course of her job hunt

Exercise 8.A – *continued*

14. I am most concerned about her progress in English mathematics science and social studies

15. When I sat down she stood up

16. After I sat down she stood up

17. She stood up after I sat down

18. He was writing in response to their letter of February 5 2002 from Montreal Quebec to say he would accept the job in Vancouver BC

19. Some people seek to fix the blame others in my opinion more intelligent seek to fix the problem

20. Despite our desire to see the program flourish we possessed insufficient funds to continue the work

21. Please pass the sugar he said

22. Where did I put the car keys he asked

23. I dont know where you put your keys she said

24. Would you mind holding open the door for me Jack

25. Sandy she said where did you get those shoes

26. Shes planning a trip to Europe with friends however she has yet to inform her mother

27. My older brother lives in Los Angeles California and my younger brother in Montreal Quebec

28. Jessica the brides cousin sang the Simon and Garfunkel song Like a Bridge Over Troubled Water

29. The word accommodate is often misspelled remember to double the c and the m

30. The provost said Id like to announce that all faculty members with more than ten years service at Thompson Rivers University will receive raises of ten per cent or more that is at least ten per cent

Exercise 8.B

Supply the missing punctuation marks.

1. We now have more than 50 tomato plants ready to harvest Fritz dont you think we should begin.

2. Who was it who said ask not what your country can do for you ask what you can do for your country

3. Even the committee chair Vivians strongest supporter had to admit that when Vivian said stuff it to the director her chances of getting funding evaporated

4. Professor Edges latest article The Press We Deserve appeared in an academic journal called Textual Studies in Canada where it provoked much interest

5. Its such a lovely day Harold she said Lets hop in the car and take the kids for a country outing

6. Did you say you would pick me up at the train station at 6:15

7. Hey Bugsy said Kevin show Adam how you wiggle your eyebrows like Groucho Marx

8. Warren please help your sister with the dishes as you promised to do Im too tired Warren said And anyway she didn't help me last week when it was my turn

9. Sorry he said Ive got to split In the sixties the word split meant leave.

10. She seemed to think everything would work out if we all just agreed never to discuss the problem to keep it a secret

11. Would you like a cup of coffee Eloise he asked kindly Thanks no said Eloise Ive already had too much coffee and its barely noon

12. Sit down and be quiet If I want your opinion Ill ask for it

13. Martin turned to Mikelle and made a motion toward the far end of the table Please pass the wine he said coolly avoiding her eyes Why certainly she answered her voice dripping ice

14. Open your mouth and say Ah the nurse said She peered down into Toms mouth and frowned Looks like a bad infection she half whispered Ill prescribe antibiotics Are you sure theyre absolutely necessary Tom asked

15. The word bienvenue means welcome in French Canadas other official language

Exercise 8.B – *continued*

16. Pointing to a large evergreen in the distance Paula said that evergreen marks the northern boundary of our property Then her eyes clouded over as she thought about the fires that still threatened to consume the BC Interior Almost to herself she added Pray for rain.

17. The house was a small stucco bungalow that she fell in love with at first sight Its small she said to her guests but its the perfect size for us We love it

18. To remember the parts of speech and the way they work use mnemonic and organizational aids she said For example take the word grammar itself

19. It will be a long time before I forget the look on his face when you said we should have some guts and show some leadership here I think it took him a full minute to regain his composure before he responded I agree but I can nevertheless do nothing to change managements decision

20. The old Blackfoot elder told his grandson the story about how every human has two wolves battling for control of the human soul the good wolf and the bad wolf Which wolf wins in the end the grandson asked The one you feed the elder answered

Part IV

Writing Essentials

Chapter 9

Writing Well: A Compendium of Tips

The art of writing non-fiction is fundamentally the art of predication, of saying something *about* a subject. Although the essence of good writing is surely debatable, if not ineffable, the qualities that mark it, including of course correctness, are well known. This chapter is intended as the briefest of introductions to a few parameters of style; it cannot substitute for thorough study of the many elements that constitute good writing, including logical thinking, paragraphing, and subordination (insubordination too, according to some), as well as coherent point of view and appropriate techniques for creating variety and emphasis. The chapter uses a broad brush to picture a few of the elements of good prose, and ends with a collection of twelve favourite writing tips.

Good writing says something in particular, with an authentic voice, to a specific audience, and says it lucidly, even unequivocally. That doesn't mean that you can't express ambivalence or uncertainty about a subject or your conclusions on it; it means you should be clear in doing so. After all, the only alternative to saying what you really mean is trying to hide or obfuscate your true thoughts. Beyond being intellectually dishonest, this injures your own writing "muscles" and ultimately your style (since you never get to first base, which is discovering what you have to say).

In fact, of the four essential qualities all good writing shares, the most important is the first: have something to say (which you arrive at by free- and exploratory writing).

Without that "something to say," all the other effort is bound to be mis-guided. In order to know whether your words are expressing your true thoughts and feelings about a given topic, you must first examine those thoughts and feelings. You need to become fully aware of them, and then to subject them to a process of conscious discrimination as you engage in the research and exploration that will familiarize you with the range of existing knowledge and opinion to which your work is intended to contribute.

In other words, the first step is the fashioning of a clear and primary purpose for the piece of writing. (Your purpose in writing doesn't need to be earth-shattering or unprecedented; it simply needs to be clear.) Good writing is heavy on content, not decoration—that is how it satisfies, at some level, a need to know or understand.

Good writing compels the reader's attention by speaking clearly in an authentic voice—the writer's own. Voice is that quality in writing that tells us a real person is behind the words, and that thus compels us to go on reading. The strengthening of voice in your writing goes hand in hand with the evolution of your personal style. Think of style as the articulation of voice.

No one can tell you how to get a voice, but then, no one needs to; it's not so much a question of crafting a voice as of finding and freeing your own. The catch is that real freedom in writing takes a lot of know-how. And acquiring that know-how takes discipline and dedication.

Good writing speaks directly to a particular audience. It doesn't address itself to readers or people in general (because in terms of who will be reading your written words, there is no such entity), but to specific readers for a specific purpose in a tone and manner suitable to the purpose.

Good writing is always preceded, or at least attended, by clear thinking. Lucidity or clarity in writing is probably the characteristic that most immediately distinguishes the professionals from the rest. When writing is consistently clear, readers can follow along without difficulty or interruption; they can ride a wave of momentum created by the careful writer's attention to the details of the craft. The way to create clarity is to concentrate on precision, and choose, for example, the precisely right word, not the nearly right one. Incompetent writers habitually use the word that first springs to mind; they leave the precision work—figuring out what the writer means—to the hapless reader.

If purpose, voice, specificity, and clarity make for good writing, what makes for great writing? One quality that most critics would agree sets apart great writing is its somewhat mysterious power to penetrate superficial awareness, to leave a residue, to resonate long after the initial reading experience. Thus great writing tends to get re-read by individuals as well as by successive generations.

Four Stages of Writing

We can divide the process of writing into four stages:

1) gathering and generating material,
2) drafting or writing successive drafts,
3) revising and re-working the drafts, and
4) editing, to catch any errors and put the finishing touches to the work.

It is helpful to proceed in this way because breaking down the task makes it less overwhelming.

The stages, however, are not in fact discrete. Instead, they blend into each other, and a certain amount of "doubling back" is nearly inevitable. For example, let's imagine you are writing a term paper on the history of access to post-secondary education in Canada. After you've finished gathering and generating material, you would move to the next stage of drafting and begin by making a rough, provisional outline or plan. Suppose that during the writing of the first draft, you decide to do a little more research over what you believe is a minor matter, but that in the process of this "minor" research, a new and important question or angle occurs to you. Clearly you don't want to ignore this idea simply because it failed to occur to you earlier or because, theoretically at least, you have completed the research stage.

Even more overlap occurs between drafting and revising. How could it be otherwise, when you create each successive draft from the ashes of its immediate predecessor? You refine the writing on the basis of the weaknesses detected in the preceding draft, so that the processes of writing and revising are not merely closely linked, but more properly regarded as two ways of looking at a single phenomenon: the attempt to create meaning with words on a page.

The final editing stage continues the process and involves the same kinds of activity. While editing the final draft, you may well decide to return briefly to the revision stage, with its perpetual questioning, in order to clarify and revise. Editing entails asking the same classic questions you have been asking throughout the process:

- Does it make sense?
- Are there any unnecessary words?
- Is it as clear and as strong as it can be?

One last question does constitute an exclusive focus of the editing stage:

- Are there any remaining errors of spelling, grammar, usage, punctuation, or style?

Now let's look at each of the four stages in detail.

Generating and gathering

The classic generating technique is called free-writing; it simply means writing on a topic for a set time (say about ten minutes) without stopping. The only requirement of free-writing—and its only point—is to let yourself write continuously and without restraint, to loosen up the writing "muscles" and warm to the topic.

Even a straightforward research topic should begin with a session of free-writing, if only to distinguish what you already know about the subject from what you need to find out. The advantage to writing on the topic before you do any research is twofold: it allows you to do your own thinking before you are influenced by the views of others; and it helps you focus your research plan (helping you to avoid the number one pitfall in researching anything: trailing off-topic). This kind of early free-writing will often help streamline your research, and may even constitute much of the blueprint or plan for it.

Many other techniques are used to get the words flowing. If you find yourself feeling overwhelmed or intimidated by a writing task, try writing a letter to yourself or to a friend about the topic, or even about why you're having trouble getting started.

You can also try to "talk on a page": Simply imagine yourself speaking about the subject to an interested friend, and write down the words you would say. If it helps, you can make the friend talkative, and play both parts, writing down what "each" of you has to say about the matter.

You can also engage in more structured forms of free-writing, for instance by starting with a main clause ending in a subordinating conjunction, and then finishing the sentence with as many different subordinate clauses as you can think of. Say you are trying to write an essay about your stand on a controversial issue like capital punishment. You could use the subordinating conjunction *because*. Begin with something like this: *Capital punishment should be reintroduced because*—and then complete the sentence as quickly and in as many ways as possible, without excessive deliberating over what to write down. For example:

I think capital punishment should be reintroduced because:
o there would be fewer murders committed
o the ultimate crime needs the ultimate punishment
o someone who takes a life deserves to lose one
o people would take the laws more seriously
o there are too many people in prison
o it is more humane than keeping someone in jail

Finish the clause as many times as you can until you have exhausted the possibilities and are beginning to repeat yourself.

When you're finished writing clauses, go through your list and eliminate any redundancies or anything that is extraneous to your purpose. Then go through the list again and mark anything (with an asterisk or whatever) that strikes you as especially important, even if you are not yet sure why. Now go through this edited list and pick one of the new clauses from it to pursue in the same way, always ending with the culling and revising of the list. The process can be repeated until you have exhausted the possible associations and put them down on paper where they can be analyzed.

No matter what you're writing (an assignment for school, a magazine or journal article, a chapter in a book, even a long-owed letter) the process begins with generating material. Count on generating a lot more material than you expect to appear in the finished piece; you want to be able to throw out liberally, to distill the major elements of the final piece from a wide range of initial options and ideas, to focus it from a wealth of possibilities.

Many texts on writing provide help ranging from friendly advice to "how-to" exercises for the aspiring writer. Five of the best I know are Dorothea Brande's *On Becoming a Writer*, Julia Cameron's *The Right to Write*, Peter Elbow's *Writing with Power*, Gabrielle Lusser Rico's *Writing the Natural Way*, and Brenda Ueland's *If You Want to Write*.

Remember at this initial stage that your purpose is simply to generate thinking on the subject, thinking diverse and substantial enough to lead to a solid perspective, from which you can then fashion the prime requisite: something to say.

Once you've arrived at a provisional thesis, go to the library to do your research. (Library research doesn't cover all the options, of course; journalists, for example, rely more on interviews and first-hand observation.) Start by compiling a list of sources likely to be useful. The Resource List at the back of this book refers you to texts that can help you finesse your note-taking skills, but basically you use one of the following tools: index cards, a laptop, or a notebook.

Some people swear by old-fashioned index cards. It is often best to keep a separate stack of smaller cards on which you record full bibliographic information for each source, and then use larger cards for the main notes. Each larger card should list (at the top left-hand corner) the author's name, a short version of the work's title if necessary, and the page number of the source material. Use one card per note even if you plan to cite a single source more than once. It's best to put the information in your own words (rather than copy out direct quotations) because this forces you to process the material. Thinking takes more time than copying (or worse, photocopying); on the other hand, no amount of copying amounts to thinking.

Other people prefer to record their notes on a laptop computer, which offers the advantage of searchable text files. The pitfalls include a tendency, because of the ease of cutting-and-pasting, to fail to really process the source material, to dump too much raw material into your first draft without pondering it sufficiently.

Another popular tool is lined, three-hole notepaper, which can be arranged and re-arranged in a binder as necessary.

This first stage is complete when, after generating your own responses and doing the research, you have made the material your own, narrowed the focus of your piece, and know basically what you want to say. At this point, you are ready to begin writing.

Drafting or writing stage

The drafting stage is best summed up in the familiar phrase "divide and conquer." After your research is completed, you know what you want to say, but you are still left with a mass of material. To organize this mass, you need two things: a single-sentence expression of what you want to say and a plan of attack for getting it down on paper. You need, in more conventional terms, a working thesis statement and a draft outline. To establish your thesis statement (the main thing you're trying to say), write it out in the form of a complete sentence; this way you force yourself to assert something and not just talk about or around the subject.

If you have used index cards for note-taking, read and shuffle them, trying out various sequences to come up with a basic order; then begin the first draft, turning each card over as you complete the writing based on it. (Don't become frustrated when trying to come up with the right order for the note cards; just go with the best order you can devise given the time constraints involved.) If you have recorded your notes electronically, you can order them in a similar way. As for notes taken in notebooks, instead of shuffling cards, use words or short phrases—called "slugs"—in the margin of the page to indicate what each note deals with. From these "annotated" notes, devise a preliminary outline, lumping together the sources that have related slug words. From this outline, you will construct your first draft.

Dozens of texts offer methods and advice on this stage of the process; they basically come down to various ways of dividing and conquering—of making intellectual chaos into readable prose. Two of my favourite methods are Peter Elbow's "direct writing process," described in his book *Writing With Power,* and Rudolf Flesch's system of "gather, list, sort, and order," as outlined in *A New Guide to Better Writing*.

Elbow's suggestion lowers the frustration level immediately with its initial injunction to divide the available time for writing the piece into halves, one for writing and the other for revising. If, after you've finished researching, your head is swimming with things you've been considering and other points you want to express beyond the thesis topic, apply Rudolf Flesch's method. His "gather" stage refers to generating personal material and doing research; since you have already done that, you can proceed straight to stage two: "list." Simple enough, this means to put that information down in the form of a list. "Sort" means to go through the list and pare it down, getting rid of anything extraneous or repetitive, and consolidating items that are saying the same things in slightly different ways. This process should substantially reduce the number of items on the list. Finally, put the list in "order," deciding where to begin, where to end, and where to put everything else as you navigate the way. The process leaves you with a final ordered list that serves as an outline; it allows you to eliminate from your notes, before you start drafting, whatever is irrelevant or redundant, and to separate merely additional information from the essence or backbone of the piece.

Flesch proposed this technique as a way to get the first draft done, but I've found it can be applied at virtually any stage of the writing process because it constitutes a succinct pattern for any kind of information organizing or ordering. (For example, if a single paragraph is giving you trouble, break it down into its constituent parts, and then re-sort and re-order.)

To draft is to write, and a draft is a complete version, however rough, of what you mean to say in the final version. It is not a partial statement. This stage begins with identifying your purpose and audience because the whole tenor and approach of the writing will differ according to these two elements. Regard your first draft, though it must be complete, as a guide to your second; see the first draft as the one that's meant to expose deficiencies—that tells you what you need to add or fix—and not as any kind of final result. There are many other ways to put your work notes in order and get that first draft done, including:

- *Leave-in-the-blanks:* Leave blank spaces in the draft for material you need to acquire but don't have yet.
- *First-draft-or-bust:* Set and meet a ridiculously early deadline for a first draft. Period. This is best accomplished by writing fairly quickly and without referring to notes.
- *World's-worst-draft:* Set out to write a blatantly bad draft; this way, you get it out of your system and usually discover that the draft is not all bad. Identify the good parts and keep going. This tip comes from the wonderful *Bird by Bird: Some Instructions on Writing and Life*, by Anne Lamott.
- *Letter-to-a-friend:* Write about the issue or subject as if you were explaining it to a friend, existing or imaginary.
- *Sum-it-up:* Write a single paragraph that encapsulates and summarizes what you want to say. Then use the sentences of the paragraph as your basic outline and expand on each sentence, offering illustrations, examples, statistics, and quotations to flesh out the piece.
- *Shuffle-cards:* Even if you haven't used index cards to do your research, you can still write the main ideas on cards and shuffle them to help you structure the piece.

All these methods address the basic reticence to "spit out" what you think more than directly tackling the difficulty of putting things in the right order. But in fact, once you really know what you are trying to say, a possible order tends to become fairly obvious.

Revising stage

By the time you are ready to write the second draft, your thinking will have begun to take serious shape; you arrive at the second draft by questioning and rewriting the first. Delete what needs to be deleted and make notes in the margins regarding what needs more work. Read the draft out loud, noting awkward phrases or parts that do not make sense. It's stunning how effective this technique is for improving your style. (Peter Elbow maintains that free-writing and reading your work out loud are the two best ways to improve your writing.) Whatever process you use for revising, make sure that at this stage you "worry" the draft, allowing objections and questions to arise. In revising successive drafts, continue to ask the critical questions:

- Does this passage say what I mean?
- Does it say this as clearly and forcefully as possible?
- Is it true?
- Does the draft need something more—examples, perhaps—to make its meaning clear, concise, and compelling?

Editing stage

Cutting and polishing best define the final editing stage. Now is the time to hunt down any remaining redundancies, awkward phrasings, wordiness, clichés, and grammatical and other errors. Delete everything that can be deleted.

Read the piece out loud a final time, marking the draft with additional notes whenever you find something that needs fixing or refining. After addressing these notes, print a clean copy of your final draft.

The essence of editing is eliminating unnecessary words, phrases, and clauses, and catching any last-minute inconsistencies or errors. The most common grammatical errors include unnecessary changes in tense, improper reference and case of pronouns, faulty subject-verb agreement, and misplaced and dangling modifiers. On a sentence level, the most common errors are those of faulty construction, including a lack of parallel structure or adequate subordination.

There's a wealth of excellent books to help you improve your writing and achieve your potential as a writer. Ultimately, though, you learn how to write by writing and revising. (Of course, how well you write does correlate with the amount of time you spend writing. In fact, in studies of how people learn to write, that is the only consistently reliable correlation.) Some of the characteristics of good writing are well known and therefore easily passed along. Here are my personal favourites.

Top Twelve Writing Tips

• Vary sentence type, length, and rhythm.

If all the sentences are of the same basic type, length, and rhythm, the writing works only as a soporific. Variety is as enlivening in writing as in life.

• Write with strong nouns and with verbs in active voice.

A conscious preference for strong nouns and for verbs in active voice helps you to avoid the wordiness enforced by over-use of the passive verb *to be*. One of the fastest and surest ways to make your writing sit up and breathe is to take the editor's scalpel to all forms of the verb *to be*. Begin to notice the preponderance of this passive linking verb in your writing, and see, in each instance, if a change to an action verb or the active voice won't automatically tighten the prose.

> *Not this:* The threats against Sally were made by both managers.
> *But this:* Both managers threatened Sally.

> *Not this:* The grey wolf is an exquisite animal that lives mostly in
> northern climates.
> *But this:* The exquisite grey wolf lives mostly in northern climates.

Of course, sometimes the passive voice is useful, necessary, or preferable; for example, when the subject is either unknown or unimportant:

> ○ The chair was re-elected with a majority of the twenty votes.

There would obviously be no point in revising thus:

> ○ A majority of the twenty voters re-elected the chair.

Can the chair be re-elected with a minority of votes, or by anything other than voters?

Excessive use of the passive voice tends to coincide with overuse of nominalizations (abstract nouns made from verbs, such as *intention* from *intend*). Notice how in the examples below, the nominalizations (plan and rectification) force wordier constructions and the use of the passive verb "is." Both suck the energy from your writing, and both can be avoided if you use active verbs instead.

Not this: The plan of the committee is the rectification of problems cited by students.
But this: The committee plans to rectify the problems cited by students.

Not this: The running of the firm was done by the owner's son.
But this: The owner's son ran the firm.

Nominalizations do have their uses (they weaken your prose only when they're used excessively). They can sum up earlier elements, afford appropriate emphasis, and help avoid the awkward phrasing that would follow from a slavish adherence to rules without consideration for the meaning or rhythm of the words.

Nominalizations become a problem when they creep into your writing as an element of your style, when you use them habitually, without recognizing the possibility of a cleaner, clearer, more direct (and hence stronger) route to your meaning.

Much scholarly writing is replete with nominalizations. These ought to be excised just as much as in other kinds of writing, but for whatever reason—perhaps the difficulty of the material—the necessary editing tends not to happen in scholarly texts. This may be how some students and aspiring writers get the idea that nominalizations indicate an advanced or elevated style.

• Ease up on the modifiers.
Too many adjectives and adverbs weaken the writing. Look at the two simple sentences below and ask yourself which of the two versions is stronger.

◦ I was really so very terrified.
◦ I was terrified.

The modifiers, while meant to add emphasis, actually weaken the sentence.

• Learn to play fast and furious with the editor's scalpel.
Your writing should have no unnecessary words, phrases, clauses, or marks of punctuation. Every single element should earn its keep; ditch all "freeloaders"—they are working only to enervate your prose.

• Insist on precision at every level from word usage to overall significance.
In other words, find precisely the right words in precisely the right order. Ask yourself, "What do I want to say? What am I trying to say?" and then "Have I said it?"

• Read your work out loud.

This may be the single most effective way to improve your style. Your ear and your voice working together will not allow you to pass over what your eye blithely overlooks. Students who read their work out loud show marked progress; I've heard hundreds of students automatically correct errors in their writing when they read aloud in small group sessions, even when their command of grammar is clearly less than perfect. Your eye can trick you into believing you have said clearly what you mean, but your ear will prove a more astute and less forgiving critic every time. Never underestimate the inherently musical power of language; use your voice to exploit it.

• Keep the flow, even if you have to push the river.

Good prose is cohesive; you are drawn along by the words because they hang together, with one word, one paragraph, one idea, leading with some force or momentum, and apparently without effort or seams, to the next. Maintaining that coherence throughout a piece of writing requires focus and a careful attention to detail at all levels: consistency, active verb choices, clear subjects, and sensible structuring.

If you want to emphasize something in a sentence, put it last. Conversely, the place for less important words (modifying words, or transitional words such as "however") is near the start of a sentence. Putting lesser elements at the end seems to make the sentence peter out; it saps energy and rhythm from the whole, as if the misplaced words, by usurping the privileged position, have destroyed the opportunity for any emphasis at all.

> *Not this:* I bristled with emotion at the memory of his betrayal, nevertheless.
>
> *But this:* I nevertheless bristled with emotion at the memory of his betrayal.

To ensure that successive sentences form a logical sequence, try reducing them to their simple subjects and predicates. If the sequence doesn't make sense, re-order it until it does, and then write a new draft.

• Search and destroy: Combatting wordiness.

Say exactly what you mean with the fewest words possible. (Shakespeare called brevity the soul of wit; it is also the soul of good writing.)

The motive for wordiness is often a fear of the writing process itself, first of finding out what you mean, and then of coming right out and saying it. On a more prosaic level, wordiness comes from all variety of redundancy and circumlocution, including token phrases ("as you know"—if you already know, why am I telling you again?); redundant or unnecessary modifiers (very lethal, seriously destroying); and over-reliance on the passive verb *to be*. Keep a sharp eye for energy-wasters, and treat them as you would weeds in a garden.

• Control the urge to take refuge in long, rambling sentences.
There's nothing wrong with long sentences, except that they are easy to hide in (the longer the sentence, the more easily you can convince yourself it isn't empty of content). Ask yourself if a long sentence can be revised into separate, shorter sentences to make your meaning more precise, emphatic, or effective.

> *Not this:* Although I was frantically worried about my dentist appointment the next day, during which three titanium implants were to be placed in my lower jaw on the left side, I still remembered a couple of things on my list, like my name.
>
> *But this:* I was frantically worried about my dentist appointment the next day, during which three titanium implants were to be placed in my lower jaw on the left side. But I still remembered a couple of things on my list—like my name.

The *although* at the beginning of the first sentence has been replaced by a *but* at the beginning of the third, and a dash is used to set off and emphasize the last phrase.

When you do write long sentences, be careful to maintain forward rhythm. Don't just keep tacking phrases and clauses together with no regard for the meaning or effect of the whole.

Use repetition and parallel phrasings to help keep up momentum in longer sentences.

> ○ They loved each other completely and with a fierce passion, one destined to last their whole lives.
> ○ A recent survey showed that more than half of Canadians say they approve of same-sex marriage, a stand at odds with that of the Catholic Church.

To combat sprawl, especially in long sentences, use the active voice.

> *Not this:* A decision on the part of each journalism student with regard to the securing of a summer internship has to be made well ahead of time for the student to make a smooth progression toward graduation.
>
> *But this:* To graduate on time, journalism students must secure summer internships early in the program.

• Think chain-link.

Enforce clarity at each step of the way by linking subjects to verbs, and verbs to objects. For example, if a sentence requires a long subordinate clause, lead with it rather than have it separate the subject from its verb.

> *Not this:* Maxine, having moved to B.C. five years ago to teach at a new School of Journalism, found herself homesick for Montreal.
>
> *But this:* Having moved to B.C. five years ago to teach at a new School of Journalism, Maxine found herself homesick for Montreal.

Notice how much tighter and more direct the second sentence is, even though both sentences contain exactly the same words, and all that has changed is their order.

• Embrace revising as an integral part of writing.

Revising should be treated as a creative and integral part of the whole process, not a half-hearted clean-up job. In fact, revising is much more like writing than it is like editing, because it requires you to produce meaning rather than simply correcting errors. In revising, you should be able to "see" the draft again almost as if it had been written by someone else; any major changes of direction should originate at this stage. It's been said so often and it remains true: the art of writing is the art of re-writing.

If possible (and if you plan ahead, it will be possible), leave a bit of time between the completion of your penultimate and final drafts. When you tackle revising and rewriting, read critically (in fact, reading your copy as if someone else wrote it makes it a lot easier to be tough on the writer). This is the right stage in the process to begin to unleash the carping editor (the same one you must sometimes subdue or ignore when you're drafting). This is the time to ask all the tough questions, ditch all the freeloaders or non-sequiturs, to make sure all the parts connect logically and compel the reader's attention forward, and to ensure you've said what you meant to say as lucidly and forcefully as you are able.

• Go get style.

You get style by thinking about it, by reading good stylists, and by reading critically, as a writer. You get it from reading what you write aloud and from refusing to write anything you would be embarrassed to hear coming out of your own mouth; by running a tight page, on which each word earns its place. You get it by being true to what you think, feel, and mean, and by expressing it all with the greatest clarity. Style cannot be forced and does not need to be forced; it emerges naturally over time as a function of doing the work.

Chapter 10

Style and Documentation

The word "style" has more than one meaning in the world of writing. Aside from referring to a writer's manner of expression, it also denotes the set of rules followed by an organization regarding such things as punctuation, typesetting, and the treatment of various nouns, numbers, and technical and legal terms. For all questions of stylistic convention, consult the style guide assigned by your instructor, or the one followed by the organization you're working for or the publication you're writing for. (If you're an aspiring freelancer, never submit work to a magazine without first sussing out its style!)

Except for certain nearly universal conventions, such as capitalizing proper names or spelling out numbers that begin sentences, the mechanics of the English language vary with the style guidelines followed by a given country, discipline, or profession. For example, Canadian spelling differs from American spelling; most Canadian publications follow certain British conventions, such as doubling the consonant in the present participle (*travelling* rather than the American *traveling*, for instance) or putting a *u* in words such as *labour* (Americans would spell this word *labor*).

Each scholarly discipline has certain quirks in its style conventions, and most major professional bodies publish their own style guides. Most newspapers in this country follow the conventions suggested by the Canadian Press (CP) as laid out in the *CP Stylebook*. Yet both national Canadian newspapers—the *Globe and Mail* and the *National Post*—use style guides that differ from all the others.

Canadian Press style differs substantially from Modern Language Association style—the style used by scholars and students in the humanities. For example, while MLA style follows tradition and uses square brackets to distinguish material inserted by the writer into a quoted passage (usually to explain or expand on the quotation), CP style dictates the use of parentheses instead. In fact, the *CP Stylebook* treats "brackets" as synonymous with "parentheses." This procedure is highly idiosyncratic—I'm aware of no style manuals other than those used by newspapers that follow this "convention." The practice is potentially dangerous, since it renders less than clear to the reader the status of the words in parentheses (whether or not they have been inserted by the writer).

The important thing to understand about stylistic conventions is that the rules, are to a great extent, arbitrary; their main purpose is to help you achieve consistency. No one will thank you for spelling a word two different ways, even if one of your "choices" turns out to be "right."

Applying a scrupulously consistent style is particularly important when documenting your sources. Bibliographies and endnotes are notoriously difficult to punctuate and organize, and they require extreme clarity. Readers ought to be able to locate all the sources you cite without undue effort, and it should always be clear when you are using someone else's words or ideas. Attribute everything that is not your own—whether you are quoting, paraphrasing, or only drawing on someone else's thoughts or research. To fail to do so is to commit a transgression that may range from idle carelessness through mild dishonesty to outright plagiarism. None of these will be acceptable.

The business of documenting your sources has two parts: first, either footnotes or in-text notes that appear throughout the body of the article; and second, a corresponding list of references—called by various names including "Works Cited," "Notes," and "References"—usually arranged alphabetically at the end of the piece. A "Bibliography" or "Works Consulted" may follow, listing all the sources consulted (not just cited). Compile your Works Cited section first, so that you can refer to it when referencing sources in the text.

Three of the most widely known and used citation systems are the Modern Language Association style (as detailed in the *MLA Style Manual and Guide to Scholarly Publishing*), generally used for work in the arts and humanities; APA style (*Publication Manual of the American Psychological Association*), used for the social and physical sciences; and Chicago style (*The Chicago Manual of Style*), also used mostly in the humanities.

Both the MLA and the APA style use parenthetical references (notes in parentheses) in the body of the text, and a final alphabetized list called Works Cited (in MLA style) or References (in APA style), to which the in-text parenthetical notes are keyed. Chicago style uses a footnote/endnote system, with superscript numerals in the body of the text keyed to numbered notes—either footnotes at the bottom of each page or endnotes in a separate list at the end, called Notes or Endnotes. Full bibliographic information in Chicago style is found in the Bibliography section that follows the Notes. (Chicago style has another citation method for the social and physical sciences; it uses an author-date system similar to APA style.) The names of the official style manuals and their URLs (updates are available online) are listed below.

- MLA Style Manual and Guide to Scholarly Publishing and the MLA Handbook for Writers of Research Papers. *http://webster. commnet.edu/mla/index.shtml*
- Publication Manual of the American Psychological Association. *http://www.apastyle.org/elecref.html*
- The Chicago Manual of Style: The Essential Guide for Writers, Editors, and Publishers. *http://www.press.uchicago.edu/Misc/Chicago/ cmosfaq/tools.Documentation.html.*

Note in the following examples that the titles of books and other full-length works are in italic type, not underlined. The latter convention is a throwback to the days before computers, when underlining indicated italic type to the printer. Thus what would have appeared at the manuscript stage as Literary Theory: An Introduction, once printed would look like this: *Literary Theory: An Introduction.*

We will compare these three major citation styles for the following ten sorts of sources:

1) a book with a single author;
2) a selection from an anthology or collection;
3) a book with more than one author;
4) a book with a group or corporate author;
5) a book whose author is unknown or not given;
6) a book with an editor or editors;
7) a journal article;
8) a magazine article;
9) a newspaper article; and
10) an online source.

Each system of documentation, then, includes two basic formats: one for the notes within the text and the other for the alphabetical or numbered list to which the in-text notes refer. Examine the following comparison of the three styles of documentation for various sources. The first entry for each example refers to the in-text notes, and the second, to the format for that note in the Works Cited, References, or Notes section. For the Chicago style examples, the Bibliography style is shown in addition to that for the Notes section; they differ slightly.

1) Book with a single author

MLA

> "What Eliot was in fact assaulting was the whole ideology of
> middle-class liberalism, the official ruling ideology of industrial
> capitalist society" (Eagleton 39).

> Eagleton, Terry. *Literary Theory: An Introduction*. Oxford: Basil
> Blackwell, 1983.

Note the lack of punctuation between the author's last name and the page number in the in-text note. If you mention the source's name in the body of the text, you put only the page number in parentheses, like this:

> Eagleton has written: "What Eliot was in fact assaulting was the
> whole ideology of middle-class liberalism, the official ruling ideology
> of industrial capitalist society" (39).

If the reference to the word is general, and you mention both the full title and the name of the author, no parenthetical note is required:

> Terry Eagleton discusses middle-class liberal ideology in *Literary
> Theory: An Introduction*.

MLA style uses a comma in the in-text note only if the author has more than one work cited, in which case a short form of the title of the work follows the author's last name to identify the work that's meant. A comma follows the author's name and separates it from the short form of the title, in italic type, but no comma separates the title from the page number: (Eagleton, *Literary* 39).

APA

> "What Eliot was in fact assaulting was the whole ideology of
> middle-class liberalism, the official ruling ideology of industrial
> capitalist society" (Eagleton, 1983, p. 39).

> Eagleton, T. (1983). *Literary theory: An introduction*. Oxford: Basil
> Blackwell.

Note that in APA style, the year of publication follows the author's name in both the in-text reference and the references section. The elements of the in-text reference—author's name, publication year, and page number— are separated by commas, and the page number is preceded by "p." for a single page and "pp." for multiple pages. In the references section, the citation begins with the author's last name, and gives only initials for first and middle names; in titles and subtitles, only the first words are capitalized.

If you mention the author's name in the text, you don't have to give it again in the parenthetical note:

According to Eagleton: "If reality was constructed by our discourse rather than reflected by it, how could we ever know reality itself, rather than merely knowing our own discourse?" (1983, pp. 143–44).

If you mention the author's name but don't quote him, you put only the publication year in the parenthetical note, generally after the name:

Terry Eagleton (1983) has written about the idea that we construct reality with discourse.

To cite multiple authors in parenthetical references, APA style starts with authors' last names and initials, reversed, and puts an ampersand (&) instead of the word "and" before the last name. As in MLA style, the titles of books and other full-length works are italicized, but APA style does not use quotation marks to indicate parts of a work, such as an article in a magazine or a selection or chapter in a book.

Chicago

"What Eliot was in fact assaulting was the whole ideology of middle-class liberalism, the official ruling ideology of industrial capitalist society."[1]

1. Terry Eagleton, *Literary Theory: An Introduction* (Oxford: Basil Blackwell, 1983), 39.

And, for the Bibliography:

Eagleton, Terry. *Literary Theory: An Introduction*. Oxford: Basil Blackwell, 1983.

Notes in Chicago style traditionally use superscript numbers for the in-text citations, but ordinary numbers in the notes section, and a tab indent instead of a hanging one. (Some traditions like these have been superseded by computer software that may impose its own style guidelines; most academic writers would agree that the time saved by computers in the collating and arranging of notes electronically more than compensates for minor departures from traditional form.) The major difference in the footnotes or endnotes section is that the authors' names are given in normal order, not reversed as they are in the other styles. As well, the elements of the entry are separated by commas, and the publication information is enclosed in parentheses. If specific pages are cited, give the numbers following the publication details in parentheses, preceded by a comma. If a second reference to the same work immediately follows the full citation, use the abbreviation "Ibid.," followed by the page number. If a subsequent reference does not follow directly the full citation, give the author's last name and a short form of the title.

2) Selection from an anthology or collection

MLA

According to one expert, the very idea of parts of speech "depends on a stable relation between form and function" (Myers 100).

If you cite the author's name in the text, you don't need to repeat it in the parenthetical note:

According to L. M. Myers, the idea of parts of speech "depends on a stable relation between form and function" (100).

Myers, L. M. "The Patterns of Grammar." *Introductory Readings on the English Language.* Ed. Richard Braddock. Englewood Cliffs: Prentice-Hall, 1962. 93–105.

One critic maintains that "Anglo-Saxon culture has upheld, as if it were a universal truth, the distinction between fiction and non-fiction" (Ruy-Sanchez 1).

Ruy-Sánchez, Alberto. "Introduction: The Rituals of Writing." *Word Carving: The Craft of Literary Journalism.* Eds. Moira Farr and Ian Pearson. Banff, Alberta: Banff Centre Press, 2003. 1–7.

APA

According to one expert, the very idea of parts of speech "depends on a stable relation between form and function" (Myers, 1962, p. 100).

Myers, L. M. (1962). The patterns of grammar. In R. Braddock (Ed.), *Introductory readings on the English language* (pp. 93–105). Englewood Cliffs: Prentice-Hall.

One critic maintains that "Anglo-Saxon culture has upheld, as if it were a universal truth, the distinction between fiction and non-fiction" (Ruy-Sanchez, 2003, p. 1).

Ruy-Sánchez, A. (2003). Introduction: The rituals of writing. In M. Farr, I. Pearson (Eds.), Word carving: The craft of literary journalism (pp. 1–7). Banff, Alberta: Banff Centre Press.

Chicago

According to one expert, the very idea of parts of speech "depends on a stable relation between form and function."[1]

1. L. M. Myers, "The Patterns of Grammar," in *Introductory Readings on the English Language*, ed. Richard Braddock (Englewood Cliffs: Prentice-Hall, 1962), 100.

Bibliography:

Myers, L. M. "The Patterns of Grammar." In *Introductory Readings on the English Language*, edited by Richard Braddock, 93–105. Englewood Cliffs: Prentice-Hall, 1962.

One critic maintains that "Anglo-Saxon culture has upheld, as if it were a universal truth, the distinction between fiction and non-fiction."[2]

2. Alberto Ruy-Sánchez, "Introduction: The Rituals of Writing," in *Word Carving: The Craft of Literary Journalism*, eds. Moira Farr and Ian Pearson (Banff, Alberta: Banff Centre Press, 2003), 1.

Bibliography:

Ruy-Sánchez, Alberto. "Introduction: The Rituals of Writing." In *Word Carving: The Craft of Literary Journalism*, edited by Moira Farr and Ian Pearson, 1–7. Banff, Alberta: The Banff Centre Press, 2003.

3) Books with more than one author

MLA Style

"Canadian universities and colleges have shown themselves quite willing to live by high standards of accountability" (Bruneau and Savage 59).

Bruneau, William, and Donald C. Savage. *Counting Out the Scholars: The Case Against Performance Indicators in Higher Education.* Toronto: Lorimer, 2002.

Some critics question whether freedom of expression in cyberspace should be treated differently from that in traditional media (Johnston, Johnston, and Handa 161–62).

Johnston, David, Deborah Johnston, and Sunny Handa. *Getting Canada Online: Understanding the Information Highway.* Toronto: Stoddart, 1995.

For a work with four or more authors, use the first author's name and the expression "et al." in both the in-text note (followed by a page number if the reference is a direct quotation) and the Works Cited entry.

> Prosser, William, et al. *Torts: Cases and Materials*. 7th ed. New York: Foundation Press, 1982.

APA Style

> "Canadian universities and colleges have shown themselves quite willing to live by high standards of accountability" (Bruneau & Savage, 2002, p. 59).

> Bruneau, W., & Savage, D.C. (2002). *Counting out the scholars: The case against performance indicators in higher education.* Toronto: Lorimer.

> Some critics question whether freedom of expression in cyberspace should be treated differently from that in traditional media (Johnston, Johnston, & Handa. 1995, pp. 161–62). On subsequent references, use only the first author's last name and the expression "et al." followed by a comma and the publication year: (Johnston et al., 1995).

> Johnston, D., Johnston, D., & Handa, S. (1995). *Getting Canada online: Understanding the information highway.* Toronto: Stoddart.

For a work with six or more authors, use the first author's name and the expression "et al." in both the in-text note (followed by a page number if the reference is a direct quotation) and the entry in the References section.

> Prosser, W., et al. (1982). *Torts: cases and materials* (7th ed.). New York: Foundation Press.

Chicago Style

> "Canadian universities and colleges have shown themselves quite willing to live by high standards of accountability."[1]

> 1. William Bruneau and Donald C. Savage, *Counting Out the Scholars: The Case Against Performance Indicators in Higher Education* (Toronto: Lorimer, 2002), 59.

> Bruneau, William, and Donald C. Savage. *Counting Out the Scholars: The Case Against Performance Indicators in Higher Education.* Toronto: Lorimer, 2002.

Some critics question whether freedom of expression in cyberspace should be treated differently from that in traditional media.²

    2. David Johnston, Deborah Johnston, and Sunny Handa, *Getting Canada Online: Understanding the Information Highway* (Toronto: Stoddart, 1995), 161–62.

Johnston, David, Deborah Johnston, and Sunny Handa. *Getting Canada Online: Understanding the Information Highway*. Toronto: Stoddart, 1995.

For a work with more than three authors, use the first author's name (not inverted) followed by the expression "et al."

William Prosser et al., *Torts: Cases and Materials*, 7th ed. (New York: Foundation Press, 1982).

4) Books with Corporate or Group Author

MLA Style
If the author is a group instead of one or more individuals, begin the in-text reference with the name of the group, followed by the page number(s) if necessary. For a smoother transition, use the name of the corporate or group author in the text itself to avoid a long note in parentheses.

Novels are not "didactic, like tracts or morality plays" (Encyclopaedia Britannica 329).

Encyclopaedia Britannica, Inc. *The Treasury of the Encyclopaedia Britannica*. New York: Viking Penguin, 1992.

APA Style
Novels are not "didactic, like tracts or morality plays" (Encyclopaedia Britannica, 1992, p. 329).

Encyclopaedia Britannica, Inc. (1992). *The treasury of the Encyclopaedia Britannica*. New York: Viking Penguin.

Chicago Style
Novels are not "didactic, like tracts or morality plays."[1]

    1. Encyclopaedia Britannica, Inc., *The Treasury of the Encyclopaedia Britannica* (New York: Viking Penguin, 1992), 329.

Encyclopaedia Britannica, Inc. *The Treasury of the Encyclopaedia Britannica*. New York: Viking Penguin, 1992.

5) Author not known or stated

MLA Style

If the author is not known or stated, begin with the title of the book.

"Egypt had four creation myths, each of them connected with a major city" (*Great Civilizations* 107).

Great Civilizations. Bath, UK: Parragon Publishing, 2002.

APA Style

"Egypt had four creation myths, each of them connected with a major city" (*Great civilizations* 2002, p. 107).

Great civilizations. (2002). Bath, UK: Parragon Publishing.

Chicago Style

"Egypt had four creation myths, each of them connected with a major city."[1]

1. *Great Civilizations* (Bath, UK: Parragon Publishing, 2002), 107.
Great Civilizations. Bath, UK: Parragon Publishing, 2002.

6) Books with an editor or editors

MLA Style

If the work you are citing has no author but does have an editor, translator or compiler, begin with the name of the editor, translator or compiler. (Use the following abbreviations: ed. or eds., trans., comp.)

I referred to a book on memoirs containing short autobiographical pieces by five well-known American writers (Zinsser).

Zinsser, William, ed. *Inventing the Truth: The Art and Craft of Memoir*. Boston: Houghton Mifflin, 1987.

Then I mentioned an anthology of Canadian literary journalism (Farr and Pearson).

Farr, Moira, and Ian Pearson, eds. *Word Carving: The Craft of Literary Journalism*. Banff, Alberta: Banff Centre Press, 2003.

APA Style

I referred to a book on memoirs containing short autobiographical pieces by five well-known American writers (Zinsser, 1987).

Zinsser, W. (Ed.). (1987). *Inventing the truth: The art and craft of memoir*. Boston: Houghton Mifflin.

Then I mentioned an anthology of Canadian literary journalism (Farr & Pearson, 2003).

Farr, M. & Pearson, I. (Eds.). (2003). *Word carving: The craft of literary journalism*. Banff, Alberta: Banff Centre Press, 2003.

Chicago Style

I referred to a book on memoirs containing short autobiographical pieces by five well-known American writers.[1]

1. William Zinsser, ed., *Inventing the Truth: The Art and Craft of Memoir* (Boston: Houghton Mifflin, 1987).

Zinsser, William, ed. *Inventing the Truth: The Art and Craft of Memoir*. Boston: Houghton Mifflin, 1987.

Then I mentioned an anthology of Canadian literary journalism.[2]

2. Moira Farr and Ian Pearson, eds., *Word Carving: The Craft of Literary Journalism* (Banff, Alberta: Banff Centre Press, 2003).

Moira Farr and Ian Pearson, eds. *Word Carving: The Craft of Literary Journalism*. Banff, Alberta: Banff Centre Press, 2003.

7) Journal Article

To document journal articles, give the following information in the order stated: the author's name in inverted order, the title of the article in quotation marks; the name of the journal in italicized type; the volume number; the issue number in parentheses; an immediate colon after the close parenthesis; a space and the page numbers occupied by the article within that issue of the journal.

MLA Style

One feminist scholar has brilliantly explored the differences between liberal and anarchistic versions of individualism, stressing the latter's "uncompromising and relentless celebration of individual self-determination and autonomy" (Brown 23).

Brown, L. Susan. "Anarchism, Feminism, Liberalism, and Individualism." *Our Generation* 24.1 (Spring 1993): 22–61.

APA Style

One feminist scholar has brilliantly explored the differences between liberal and anarchistic versions of individualism, stressing the latter's "uncompromising and relentless celebration of individual self-determination and autonomy" (Brown 23).

Brown, L.S. (1993). Anarchism, feminism, liberalism, and individualism. *Our Generation, 24.1,* (Spring 1993) 22–61.

Notice that in APA style for journal articles, the journal name and volume number are italicized and separated from each other and from the final page numbers by commas. (For journals with continuous pagination, give the issue number in parentheses immediately following the volume number, but do not italicize the issue number.)

Chicago Style

One feminist scholar has brilliantly explored the differences between liberal and anarchistic versions of individualism, stressing the latter's "uncompromising and relentless celebration of individual self-determination and autonomy."[1]

1. L. Susan Brown, "Anarchism, Feminism, Liberalism, and Individualism," *Our Generation* 24.1 (Spring 1993), 23.

The corresponding entry in a bibliography would give the range of page numbers for the article and separate the elements with periods instead of commas.

Brown, L. Susan. "Anarchism, Feminism, Liberalism, and Individualism." *Our Generation* 24.1 (Spring 1993): 22–61.

8) Magazine Article

MLA Style

Some critics say that Canadian journalists have stopped investigating international politics for fear of displeasing their managers (Hughes).

Hughes, Lesley. "What's Wrong with Canadian Journalism." *Canadian Dimension* Jan./Feb. 2003: 48.

Anthony Wilson-Smith believes there's a double standard applied by Canadian journalists to wrong-doing, and writes that interviews are sometimes re-edited to make the interviewer's questions "more eloquent" (16).

One magazine writer believes there's a double standard applied by Canadian journalists to wrong-doing, and writes that interviews are sometimes re-edited to make the interviewer's questions "more eloquent" (Wilson-Smith 16).

Wilson-Smith, Anthony. "Media Hits—and Misses." *Maclean's* 11 June 2000: 16.

APA Style

Some critics say that Canadian journalists have stopped investigating international politics for fear of displeasing their managers (Hughes, 2003).

Hughes, L. (2003, Jan./Feb.). What's wrong with Canadian journalism? *Canadian Dimension*, 48.

Anthony Wilson-Smith believes there's a double standard applied by Canadian journalists to wrong-doing, and writes that interviews are sometimes re-edited to make the interviewer's questions "more eloquent" (16).

One magazine writer believes there's a double standard applied by Canadian journalists to wrong-doing, and writes that interviews are sometimes re-edited to make the interviewer's questions "more eloquent" (Wilson-Smith 16).

Wilson-Smith, A. Media hits—and misses." *Maclean's* 11 June 2000: 16.

Chicago Style

Some critics say that Canadian journalists have stopped investigating international politics for fear of displeasing their managers.[1]

1. Lesley Hughes, "What's Wrong with Canadian Journalism," *Canadian Dimension*, January/February 2003, 48.

Hughes, Lesley. "What's Wrong with Canadian Journalism." *Canadian Dimension*, January/February 2003, 48.

Anthony Wilson-Smith believes there's a double standard applied by Canadian journalists to wrong-doing, and writes that interviews are sometimes re-edited to make the interviewer's questions "more eloquent."[2]

2. Anthony Wilson-Smith, "Media Hits—and Misses," *Maclean's*, 11 June 2000, 16.

Wilson-Smith, Anthony. "Media Hits—and Misses." *Maclean's*, 11 June 2000, 16.

9) Newspaper Article

MLA Style

Zerbisias, Antonia. "Airbus Affair Fallout Blow to Journalism." *Toronto Star* 3 Sept. 2004: C6.

Schachter, Harvey. "Social Intelligence New Gauge of Abilities." *The Globe and Mail* 4 Feb. 2005: C1.

APA Style

Zerbisias, A. (2004, Sept. 3). Airbus affair fallout blow to journalism. *Toronto Star*, p. C6.

Schachter, H. (2005, Feb. 4). Social intelligence new gauge of abilities. *The Globe and Mail*, p. C1.

Chicago Style

1. Antonia Zerbisias, "Airbus Affair Fallout Blow to Journalism," *Toronto Star*, 3 September 2004, C6.

Zerbisias, Antonia. "Airbus Affair Fallout Blow to Journalism." *Toronto Star*, 3 September 2004, C6.

2. Harvey Schachter, "Social Intelligence New Gauge of Abilities," *The Globe and Mail*, 4 February 2005, C1.

Schachter, Harvey. "Social Intelligence New Gauge of Abilities." *The Globe and Mail*, 4 February 2005, C1.

10) Online Source

There are no special rules for citing electronic sources, but such sources often lack publishing information. If you want to cite something from an online source, but no author is given, use a short form of the work's title instead and the appropriate page number(s). If there are no page numbers, give section, chapter, or paragraph numbers if available. In the Works Cited, References or Notes section, give the following information: name of the author or website creator, a title or description of the work, a date of publication or latest update, the date you accessed the material, and the URL (within angle brackets for both MLA and Chicago style). In APA style, if the material carries no date, indicate that with the abbreviation "n.d." after the name of the website, and include the date retrieved.

MLA Style

CAUT. Canadian Association of University Teachers. 10 Jan. 2005
   <http://www.caut.ca/en/about/index.asp>
World Literacy of Canada. 27 Jan. 2005. "Defining Literacy." 5 Feb.
   2005 <http://www.worldlit.ca/defininglit.html>
Mason, Eric. "Remediating the Magic Kingdom: Notes Toward a
   Poetics of Technology." *Currents in Electronic Literacy*. Fall
   (2004): 10 Jan. 2005 <http://www.cwrl.utexas.edu/currents/
   fall04/mason.html>

APA Style

CAUT. Canadian Association of University Teachers. (n.d.) Retrieved
   January 10, 2005, from http://www.caut.ca/en/about/index.asp
World Literacy of Canada. (2005, Jan. 27). Defining Literacy. Retrieved
   February 5, 2005, from http://www.worldlit.ca/defininglit.html
Mason, E. (2004, Fall). Remediating the magic kingdom: Notes
   toward a poetics of technology. *Currents in Electronic Literacy
   Fall* (2004). University of Texas at Austin. Retrieved January 10,
   2005, from http://www.cwrl.utexas.edu/currents/fall04/
   mason.html

Chicago Style

1. *CAUT*, Web site of the Canadian Association of University
   Teachers, <http://www.caut.ca/en/about/index.asp>
   (accessed Jan. 10, 2005).
2. "Defining Literacy," World Literacy of Canada Web site, updated
   Jan. 27, 2005, <http://www.worldlit.ca/defininglit.html>
   (accessed Feb. 5, 2005).
3. Eric Mason, "Remediating the Magic Kingdom: Notes Toward a
   Poetics of Technology," *Currents in Electronic Literacy* Fall (2004),
   University of Texas at Austin <http://www.cwrl.utexas.edu/
   currents/fall04/mason.html> (accessed Jan. 10, 2005).

Answers to Review Questions

Chapter 1

Exercise 1.1

1. saucer: object
2. bushel: object/measure
3. dancing: action
4. camel: animal
5. home: place
6. talent: quality/idea
7. Montreal: place
8. client: person
9. magazine: object
10. year: measure
11. tree: object
12. humour: quality/idea
13. mountain: object
14. pilot: person
15. Canada: place
16. month: measure
17. talking: action
18. steel: substance
19. playing: action
20. performer: person

Exercise 1.2

1. <u>Mordecai</u> bought a used <u>guitar</u> from his <u>friend</u>.
2. <u>Editors</u> are looking for certain <u>kinds</u> of <u>writing</u>.
3. The <u>staff</u> at the <u>plant</u> signed a <u>petition</u>.
4. The <u>book</u> contains <u>examples</u> of feature <u>writing</u>.
5. The <u>teacher</u> had <u>patience</u> and <u>skill</u>.
6. The young <u>musician</u> played his <u>flute</u> in <u>class</u>.
7. A <u>car</u> sped down the quiet <u>street</u> at <u>noon</u>.
8. <u>Oranges</u> and <u>lemons</u> are grown in <u>Israel</u>.
9. Despite <u>predictions</u>, <u>TV</u> has not replaced the <u>book</u>.
10. <u>Pina</u> and her <u>friends</u> went to the <u>festival</u>.

Exercise 1.3

1. Never is an awfully long *time*. – *abstract, common*
2. An old saying has it that *beauty* is in the eye of the beholder. – *abstract, common*
3. My *sister-in-law* is performing at the café tonight. – *concrete, common, compound*
4. I thoroughly enjoyed reading Joy Kogawa's book, *Obasan*. – *concrete, proper*
5. The *Parliament Buildings* are located in the capital city of Ottawa. – *concrete, proper, compound*

6. My best friend and I really treasure our *relationship*. – *abstract, common*
7. The *truth* is I won't come to the event because I disapprove of it. – *abstract, common*
8. I hope the *Blue Birds* won the relay race. – *concrete, proper, compound*
9. A *gaggle* of geese could be seen in the distance. – *concrete, common, collective*
10. I know that middle-aged *couple*; they live on Battle Street. – *concrete, common, collective*

Exercise 1.4

1. The <u>dog</u> dug a <u>hole</u> under the <u>fence</u>.
2. Our <u>mother</u> graduated this <u>year</u>.
3. <u>Maps</u> were distributed among the <u>students</u> in the <u>class</u>.
4. The <u>captain</u> congratulated the <u>winners</u>.
5. The <u>leader</u> had <u>vision</u> and <u>talent</u>.
6. <u>Singing</u> and <u>dancing</u> are her favourite <u>activities</u>.
7. <u>Bernard</u> bought a new <u>home</u> in <u>Westmount</u>.
8. Our <u>class</u> was interrupted by the <u>student</u>.
9. <u>Sky-diving</u> is a dangerous <u>sport</u>.
10. <u>Books</u> and <u>magazines</u> lay scattered around the <u>room</u>.
11. <u>Jeremy</u> hoped to take <u>lessons</u> in <u>swimming</u>.
12. <u>Flour</u> and <u>sugar</u> are useful <u>ingredients</u>.
13. The <u>school</u> made many <u>changes</u>.
14. The <u>doctor</u> prescribed <u>rest</u> for her exhausted <u>patient</u>.
15. The <u>train</u> leaves the <u>station</u> in an <u>hour</u>.
16. That <u>student</u> has <u>initiative</u>.
17. Two <u>friends</u> just returned from a <u>trip</u> to <u>Boston</u>.
18. Her <u>bracelet</u> fell into the <u>water</u>.
19. <u>Heat</u> from the <u>fireplace</u> warmed the <u>room</u>.
20. <u>Caviar</u> and <u>champagne</u> were served at the <u>event</u>.

Exercise 1.5

1. Valarie has been busy; <u>she</u> won't be at the party tonight.
2. The books are on the desk. Please take <u>them</u>.
3. George and Kit are coming to visit; <u>they</u> will stay a week.
4. <u>I</u> looked for the car but couldn't find <u>it</u>.
5. A society owes <u>much</u> to <u>its</u> (possessive adjective) writers.
6. The couple entered the contest and won <u>it</u>.
7. Yingqing invited people to dinner but <u>they</u> didn't show.
8. <u>All</u> the students attended and <u>some</u> stayed on to ask questions.
9. <u>Each</u> of the contestants paid a fee, <u>which</u> was refundable.
10. I overheard <u>them</u> discussing <u>your</u> (possessive adjective) plans.
11. I ate <u>all</u> the cookies <u>that</u> <u>you</u> made; <u>they</u> were delicious.
12. He gave the money to a charity; <u>he</u> kept <u>none</u>.

13. <u>We</u> have pets <u>whom</u> <u>we</u> consider part of the family.
14. <u>It</u> is the thing <u>that</u> matters most to <u>me</u>.
15. <u>Those</u> are <u>my</u> (possessive adjective) daffodils; hand <u>them</u> over.
16. <u>Anybody</u> may join the club, but <u>he</u> must obey <u>its</u> (possessive adjective) rules.
17. <u>Many</u> attended the concert and <u>few</u> forgot <u>it</u>.
18. <u>They</u> say <u>you</u> catch more flies with honey.
19. <u>Why</u> would <u>you</u> want to catch <u>them</u>?
20. Among the reviewers, <u>several</u> mentioned <u>it</u>.
21. The child <u>who</u> was missing returned.
22. <u>These</u> are <u>my</u> (possessive adjective) papers.
23. <u>They</u> asked <u>her</u> to show <u>them</u> to <u>me</u>.
24. <u>We</u> went to Montreal with <u>them</u>.
25. Eileen will not tell <u>her</u> why <u>I</u> quit.
26. <u>He</u> objected to the procedure, and the committee amended <u>it</u>.
27. <u>Anyone</u> can apply for the job.
28. <u>That</u> is the meal <u>they</u> served.
29. The dress <u>that</u> <u>you</u> wore was admired by <u>others</u>.
30. Although <u>I</u> questioned <u>her</u>, <u>she</u> did provide much information.
31. <u>These</u> are on reserve, but <u>those</u> are not.
32. <u>She</u> held the baby in <u>her</u> arms.
33. The meal was excellent and <u>it</u> was consumed heartily.
34. <u>That</u> is the movie <u>I</u> told <u>you</u> about.
35. <u>He</u> didn't wait for <u>them</u> as <u>they</u> had instructed <u>him</u> to do.
36. <u>That</u> was the story <u>that</u> <u>I</u> heard from <u>them</u>.
37. Years passed and <u>many</u> forgot the tale, but <u>some</u> remembered.
38. The horses seemed uneasy when <u>we</u> entered the barn.
39. <u>Each</u> brought <u>his</u> (possessive adjective) or <u>her</u> (possessive adjective) resumé and work samples.
40. <u>She</u> can tell <u>you</u> where the <u>others</u> have gone with <u>their</u> (possessive adjective) friends.

Exercise 1.6

1. He found it behind the sofa. — *He, P; it, P; sofa, N*
2. The crowd cheered the home team. — *crowd, N; team, N*
3. Some got overtime pay but others got nothing. — *Some, P; pay, N; others, P; nothing, N*
4. All the teenage girls bought jeans at the same store. — *All, P; girls, N; jeans, N; store, N*
5. She looked for the textbook but couldn't find it. — *She, P; textbook, N; it, P*
6. He wore an expensive suit that was made in London. — *He, P; suit, N; that, P; London, N*
7. Only the federal government can make criminal law. — *government, N; law, N*

8. He found a seat at the back of the bus and sat down. — *He, P; seat, N; back, N; bus, N*

9. Those were the literary works that she most enjoyed. — *Those, P; works, N; that, P; she, P*

10. All of us decided to help her. — *All, P; us, P; her, P*

Exercise 1.7

1. The bicycle <u>swerved</u> off the road. — *action*
2. Parents usually <u>know</u> their children well. — *action*
3. Snowflakes <u>fell</u> for hours. — *action*
4. You <u>put</u> your coat on the couch. — *action*
5. The kittens <u>meowed</u> at her. — *action*
6. The weather <u>was</u> cold. — *linking*
7. He <u>leapt</u> over the barriers. — *action*
8. The companies <u>merged</u>. — *action*
9. Kinga <u>went</u> to graduate school in London. — *action*
10. Allie <u>won</u> an essay contest at school. — *action*
11. They <u>travelled</u> to Maine for a vacation. — *action*
12. We <u>stopped</u> the car. — *action*
13. The temperature <u>is</u> just right. — *linking*
14. They <u>complained</u> about poor writing skills. — *action*
15. She <u>read</u> the novel three times. — *action*
16. The incident <u>provoked</u> controversy. — *action*
17. The sun <u>shone</u> brightly that day. — *action*
18. Jenny <u>met</u> her future husband in college. — *action*
19. Slowly, the conductor <u>turned</u> to the audience. — *action*
20. My associate <u>is</u> a true scholar. — *linking*

Exercise 1.8

1. The accident <u>affected</u> his vision, but he still <u>drives</u>. — *V,V*
2. The rain <u>had been falling</u> for hours. — *VP*
3. Movies <u>are</u> a popular form of entertainment. — *V*
4. You <u>broke</u> it; you <u>should fix</u> it. —*V,VP*
5. The new journalism school <u>is attracting</u> students. — *VP*
6. After we <u>arrived</u>, we <u>began</u> unpacking. — *V,V*
7. Felicity <u>was studying</u> for her final exam. — *VP*
8. Nanette <u>will drive</u> to Vancouver on Saturday. — *VP*
9. The children <u>were growing</u> fast. — *VP*
10. You <u>must have left</u> the keys in the car. — *VP*

Exercise 1.9

<u>Auxiliary verbs</u> are underlined; *principal verbs* are in italics.

1. He <u>would</u> *live* to regret that decision.
2. All the details <u>had been</u> *finalized* by friends.

3. I was *walking* the dog down Main Street.
4. We did *object* to the plan.
5. They will *decide* later whether to attend.
6. The first storm clouds had been *seen*.
7. The policy does *allow* returns.
8. Billy had *grown* a lot in the last year.
9. Hiroshi was *named* a bureau chief of the Canadian Press.
10. She is *creating* the sets for the play.
11. The twins were *saving* their allowance.
12. The signs of a struggle were *noted* in his police report.
13. The curtains were *blowing* lazily beside the open window.
14. She had been *sleeping* when the phone rang.
15. It had never been *done* before.

Exercise 1.10

Adjectives are underlined; the *nouns* they modify are in italics.
1. A dozen *roses* were delivered.
2. The spare *room* was converted into a study.
3. The accountant gave a short *speech*.
4. They swam in the deep *end* of the pool.
5. A new *scholarship* was offered to the candidate.
6. Many famous *actors* live in Hollywood.
7. The pouring *rain* soaked my *clothes*.
8. Ten *students* attended the free *concert*.
9. The dress has bright *sequins*.
10. He found the wet *towels* in the kitchen.
11. They gave her a gold *watch*.
12. Teenagers like the company of other *teenagers*.
13. I tried to revise the second *draft*.
14. The teacher assigned a critical *reading*.
15. She tried to butter the fresh *bread*.
16. Bright *panels* were added to the display.
17. He gave a provocative *lecture* on journalism.
18. The excited *puppies* raced around the yard.
19. Cold *drinks* were served to the clients.
20. The house was hidden by large *trees*.
21. The clean *glasses* gleamed.
22. Sufficient *food* was provided for the event.
23. What a lovely *sight*!
24. I interviewed a former *boxer*.
25. Aline lives in a small *city*.
26. The school has an innovative *approach*.
27. A colourful *poster* was made for the march.
28. A trio of senior *officials* introduced the show.

29. Anne is a <u>respected</u> *historian.*
30. She sang <u>sweet</u> *lullabies* to the baby.
31. He overcame so <u>many</u> *obstacles.*
32. We climbed to the <u>highest</u> *peak.*
33. <u>Tiny</u> *raindrops* began to fall.
34. <u>Nutritious</u> *food* helps build health.
35. The storyteller related a <u>sad</u> *tale.*

Exercise 1.11

1. <u>Her</u> dress was the colour of lilacs. — *adjective*
2. Auren gave Fred <u>his</u> notes. — *adjective*
3. He made a call on <u>his</u> cell phone. — *adjective*
4. Audrey gave <u>Fred's</u> notes to Scott. — *adjective*
5. <u>Your</u> keys are on the shelf; <u>mine</u> are in <u>my</u> purse. — *adjective, pronoun, adjective*
6. <u>Tanya's</u> are the wrong size; try <u>mine</u>. — *noun, pronoun*
7. <u>His</u> father will call <u>Steve's</u> friend tomorrow. — *adjective, adjective*
8. We helped get <u>her</u> keys out of the lock. — *adjective*
9. They stopped at <u>his</u> place for the gifts. — *adjective*
10. I carried the baby in <u>my</u> arms and rocked her. — *adjective*
11. <u>Our</u> boots are here; <u>theirs</u> are in the closet. — *adjective, pronoun*
12. She gave <u>hers</u> to Fritz and kept <u>Joannie's</u>. — *pronoun, noun*
13. Brenda drove Shawn to <u>his</u> office. — *adjective*
14. <u>His</u> essays are good; <u>hers</u> are brilliant. — *adjective, pronoun*
15. We read <u>their</u> names from <u>Henry's</u> list. — *adjective, adjective*
16. Cristina wrote <u>her</u> essay on censorship and <u>its</u> ills. — *adjective, adjective*
17. <u>Dani's</u> internship at the newspaper went well. — *adjective*
18. <u>Their</u> houses blended; <u>his</u> stood out. — *adjective, pronoun*
19. I loved <u>her</u> sense of fairness and <u>her</u> honesty. — *adjective, adjective*
20. The box fell and <u>its</u> contents tumbled to the floor. — *adjective*

Exercise 1.12

1. The paper was delivered <u>daily</u>. — *time*
2. I <u>seldom</u> have a chance to read novels. — *time*
3. Ross can throw the ball <u>farther</u>. — *degree*
4. Five years have passed since she moved <u>here</u>. — *place*
5. They went <u>everywhere</u> to collect donations. — *place*
6. The wounded bird <u>soon</u> grew stronger. — *time*
7. <u>Quietly</u>, he left the room. — *manner*
8. She plays that piece <u>beautifully</u>. — *manner*
9. She said she had to leave <u>now</u>. — *time*
10. The weeds grew <u>fast</u>. — *manner* or *time*
11. The lost earring could be <u>anywhere</u>. — *place*
12. Spending was <u>sharply</u> reduced. — *manner* or *degree*

13. I see him <u>occasionally</u>. — *time*
14. She wants to speak to you <u>privately</u>. — *manner*
15. <u>Sometimes</u> we go to the farmers' market. — *time*
16. I've been staying at home <u>lately</u>. — *time*
17. Kimberly is <u>slowly</u> but <u>surely</u> recuperating. — *manner* or *degree*
18. The little girl <u>cautiously</u> opened the jar. — *manner*
19. They <u>often</u> take that route to work. — *time*
20. I waited <u>impatiently</u> in line. — *manner*

Exercise 1.13

1. We were *tired* and *hungry* after our journey. — *adjective, adjective*
2. I am *appalled* at your behaviour! — *adjective*
3. I had a *really good* time at your party. — *(really) adverb, (good) adjective*
4. I found a *gold* ring in my living room. — *adjective*
5. I was *never good* at public speaking. — *(never) adverb, (good) adjective*
6. I *very nearly* lost control of the car just then. — *(very) adverb, (nearly) adverb*
7. *Yesterday*, I dreamed I saw a *giant* lobster. — *adverb, adjective*
8. I had *two* cream puffs for lunch. — *adjective*
9. You look *ill*. — *adjective*
10. We painted the *small* bedroom *midnight* blue. — *adjective, adjective*

Exercise 1.14

Prepositions are in italics; <u>phrases</u> are underlined.

1. They will vote *on* <u>the motion</u> *at* <u>this meeting</u>.
2. We found his wallet *on* <u>the back seat</u>.
3. We found your pocketbook *in* <u>the house</u>.
4. Flowers were planted *along* <u>the path</u>.
5. His birthmark looked *like* <u>a large plum</u>.
6. The author read *from* <u>his new novel</u>.
7. We copied those pages *from* <u>the book</u>.
8. The doctor walked *into* <u>the room</u>.
9. A large box sat *beside* <u>the main door</u>.
10. The lovers walked *along* <u>the beach</u>.
11. The lilacs *in* <u>the yard</u> smell wonderful.
12. Rumours began to spread *throughout* <u>the town</u>.
13. My cousin moved *to* <u>Boston</u> *with* <u>her husband</u>.
14. She was tutored *by* <u>a college student</u>.
15. He wrote a play *about* <u>Canadian politicians</u>.

Exercise 1.15

1. They wore long coats <u>and</u> fur hats. — *coats, hats*
2. The girls baked cakes <u>and</u> cookies for the sale. — *cakes, cookies*
3. I can bring the drinks <u>or</u> the salad to the party. — *drinks, salad*
4. Anne <u>and</u> I prefer the same kinds of books. — *Anne, I*

5. She left the room <u>and</u> closed the door behind her. — *left, closed*
6. The erosion occurred slowly <u>but</u> surely. — *slowly, surely*
7. He <u>and</u> I are planning the convocation events. — *He, I*
8. Lienne writes movie scripts <u>and</u> TV shows. — *movie scripts, TV shows*
9. The boutique sold no tams <u>or</u> berets. — *tams, berets*
10. The bed was covered with papers <u>and</u> clothes. — *papers, clothes*
11. Every Saturday, I visit my friends Lu <u>and</u> Morris. — *Lu, Morris*
12. The doctor ordered her to eat well <u>and</u> get some rest. — *eat well, get some rest*
13. Singing <u>and</u> dancing are both fun. — *singing, dancing*
14. I like pasta, <u>but</u> I don't like pesto. — *I like pasta, I don't like pesto*
15. The tired <u>but</u> happy couple returned home. — *tired, happy*

Exercise 1.16

1. The boy loved hiking <u>and</u> swimming. — *conjunction*
2. <u>Wow</u>! That was invigorating. — *interjection*
3. Call back this evening <u>or</u> tomorrow morning. — *conjunction*
4. Cristine <u>and</u> Danielle worked together. — *conjunction*
5. I felt happy <u>but</u> tired. — *conjunction*
6. The dinner was elaborate <u>and</u> delicious. — *conjunction*
7. <u>Oh no</u>! I left the keys in my other bag. — *interjection*
8. They discussed profits <u>and</u> losses. — *conjunction*
9. <u>Oh boy</u>! That was the day from hell. — *interjection*
10. She must decide on one <u>or</u> the other — *conjunction*
11. The hotel was lovely <u>but</u> expensive. — *conjunction*
12. Sweat bathed his arms <u>and</u> chest. — *conjunction*
13. They liked the resort <u>yet</u> decided to leave early. — *conjunction*
14. They wanted to vacation in Paris <u>or</u> London. — *conjunction*
15. He ordered soup <u>and</u> salad. — *conjunction*

Chapter 1 Review Exercises

Exercise 1.A

1. *sand*, adjective; *on*, preposition
2. *Joi*, noun; *well*, adverb
3. *removed*, verb; *jacket*, noun
4. *told*, verb; *all*, pronoun
5. *They*, pronoun; *cherries*, noun
6. *Everyone*, pronoun; *old*, adjective
7. *She*, pronoun; *Montreal*, noun
8. *Oh*, interjection; *beautiful*, adjective
9. *were*, verb; *greedy*, adjective
10. *was waiting*, verb; *school*, noun
11. *down*, preposition; *road*, noun

12. *recently*, adverb; *jobs*, noun
13. *can call*, verb; *or*, conjunction
14. *scholarly*, adjective; *wolves*, noun
15. *Music*, noun; *engaging*, adjective
16. *has*, verb; *beautiful*, adjective
17. *Nobody*, pronoun; *new*, adjective
18. *He*, pronoun; *with*, preposition
19. *has been repairing*, verb; *pipe*, noun
20. *takes*, verb; *day*, noun
21. *Carolyn*, noun; *and*, conjunction
22. *Gee*, interjection; *that*, pronoun
23. *quickly*, adverb; *go*, verb
24. *to*, preposition; *threads*, noun
25. *scraped*, verb; *badly*, adverb
26. *layer*, noun; *now*, adverb
27. *better*, adjective; *so*, conjunction
28. *excited*, adjective; *yard*, noun
29. *love*, verb; *niece*, noun
30. *two*, adjective; *on*, preposition
31. *Health*, adjective; *has become*, verb
32. *massive*, adjective; *suddenly*, adverb
33. *has reached*, verb; *low*, noun
34. *her*, adjective; *under*, preposition
35. *home*, noun; *heartbreaking*, adjective
36. *Many*, adjective; *complain*, verb
37. *but*, conjunction; *home*, noun
38. *Experts*, noun; *very*, adverb
39. *Wow*, interjection; *really*, adverb
40. *Ray*, noun; *who*, pronoun
41. *If*, conjunction; *down*, adverb
42. *team*, noun; *down*, noun
43. *by*, preposition; *marched*, verb
44. *conductor*, noun; *down*, adjective
45. *opposition*, noun; *round*, noun
46. *little*, adjective; *shiny*, adjective
47. *When*, conjunction; *round*, verb
48. *young*, adjective; *fast*, noun
49. *was travelling*, verb; *fast*, adverb
50. *like*, verb; *fast*, adjective
51. *part*, noun; *system*, noun
52. *Those*, pronoun; *her*, pronoun
53. *I*, pronoun; *many*, adjective
54. *Most*, pronoun; *us*, pronoun
55. *anyone*, pronoun; *busy*, adjective

Exercise 1.B

1. *editor*, N; *followed*, V; *story*, N; *closely*, ADV
2. *I*, P; *found*, V; *great*, ADJ; *pair*, N; *of*, PRP; *boots*, N; *at*, PRP; *mall*, N
3. *He*, P; *has brought*, V; *two*, ADJ; *extra*, ADJ; *chairs*, N; *to*, PRP; *table*, N
4. *Eileen*, N; *is*, V; *talented*, ADJ; *photographer*, N
5. *Bad*, ADJ; *weather*, N; *led*, V; *to*, PRP; *cancelled*, ADJ; *flight*, N
6. *Ouch!*, INT; *that*, P; *was*, V; *my*, ADJ; *big*, ADJ; *toe*, N
7. *Books*, N; *and*, CON; *papers*, N; *were*, V; *everywhere*, ADV
8. *story*, N; *was read*, V; *aloud*, ADV; *by*, PRP; *teacher*, N
9. *He*, P; *wrote*, V; *letter*, N; *to*, PRP; *Attorney General*, N
10. *mysterious*, ADJ; *stranger*, N; *came*, V; *to*, PRP; *town*, N

Exercise 1.C

1. *proudly*, ADV; *top*, ADJ
2. *was crying*, V; *night*, N
3. *should have placed*, V; *icy*, ADJ
4. *they*, P; *appropriate*, ADJ
5. *By*, PRP; *among*, PRP
6. *Around*, PRP; *multi-coloured*, ADJ.
7. *includes*, V; *on*, PRP
8. *Look*, V; *are*, V
9. *troubles*, N; *him*, P
10. *felt*, V; *soft*, ADJ

Exercise 1.D

1. conjunction, noun
2. preposition, adjective
3. noun, noun
4. pronoun, noun
5. noun, verb
6. verb, noun
7. adjective, noun
8. adjective, adjective
9. adjective, adverb
10. pronoun, pronoun

Exercise 1.E

1. verb, verb
2. adjective, adjective
3. pronoun, preposition
4. verb (have made), adjective
5. adjective, noun
6. noun, verb
7. adjective, noun
8. adjective, verb
9. verb, preposition
10. noun, verb

Chapter 2

Exercise 2.1

Simple subject is underlined; *simple predicate* is in italics.

1. The young <u>woman</u> *suspected* her sources.
3. The little <u>boy</u> *has* a new tricycle painted bright red.
4. <u>He</u> *ran* to the house and *answered* the ringing phone.
5. <u>Wanda</u> *brought* the textbook to class.
6. <u>Soraya</u> *left* the class with all her books.
7. <u>She</u> *had taught* at colleges in England and Canada.
8. <u>Many</u> *avoided* the noisy demonstration.

9. He *put* the slides on the table beside the projector.
10. The audience *clapped* enthusiastically for the first number.
11. Pierre and I *ran* down the road and *waved* our hands.

Exercise 2.2

Simple subject is underlined; *simple predicate* is in italics.

1. The woman *set* the platter on the table and *sat* down.
2. My mother *entered* the room and *said* hello.
3. The darkest hour and the dawn *are* not far apart.
4. Karisa *stopped* the car and *rolled* down the window.
5. Boris and Natasha *went* into town for groceries.
6. She and I *have been* close friends for years.
7. They *travelled* to Europe and then *returned* home.
8. Germs and colds *travel* and *spread* like wildfire
9. The teacher and her students *eyed* the newcomer.
10. We *wrapped* the present and *mailed* it on Tuesday.

Exercise 2.3

Underlined answers refer to underlined words; italicized answers refer to italicized words.

1. He wanted *to become an expert* in the field. — *infinitive phrase*; prepositional
2. *After acing the exam,* Alain celebrated. — *gerund*
3. The flower beds *along the path* need watering. — *prepositional*
4. The teacher received an award *for her work.* — *prepositional*
5. *Helping the neighbours* was an all-day affair. — *gerund*
6. Three women stood *in the line* before me. — *prepositional*, prepositional
7. *Raising the phone* to her ear, she said hello. — *participial*; prepositional
8. We had fun *at the lake last weekend.* — *prepositional*
9. His favourite activity was *going cross-country skiing.* — *gerund*
10. Lisa drove *to the store* for milk, bread, and butter. — *prepositional*; prepositional
11. *Hoping for the best* helps to raise flagging spirits. — *gerund*; infinitive
12. We gave them a plaque *honouring their contribution.* — *participial*
13. *To learn a skill* requires consistent practice. — *infinitive*
14. *Holding her teddy bear,* Sarah entered the room. — *participial*
15. *The sun shining brightly,* she left the house without her umbrella. — *absolute*; prepositional

Exercise 2.4

1. Suzanne is the student whom I would choose. — *adjective clause*
2. Everyone knows how he can get to the arena quickly. — *noun clause*
3. Even though she dislikes crowds, Bena will attend the show. — *adverb clause*

4. Does anyone know if the coach is in his office? — *noun clause*
5. After I finished washing the dishes, I went out. — *adverb clause*
6. The gift that she returned was bought only a week ago. — *adjective clause*
7. Ask him where the school auditorium is located. — *noun clause*
8. They enjoyed the film that a friend had recommended. — *adjective clause*
9. They say that all six passengers were injured in the accident. — *noun clause*
10. She visited Mina in the hospital after she finished the shopping. — *adverb clause*
11. Tell your mother what happened in the mall today. — *noun clause*
12. He always went to Schwartz's when he visited Montreal. — *adverb clause*
13. The guitar was a Fender that had seen better days. — *adjective clause*
14. Emanuel had a clear idea of where he wanted to work. — *noun clause*
15. I was so nervous that my hands were trembling. — *adverb clause*

Chapter 2 Review Exercises

Exercise 2.A

1. They; discovered
2. We; decided
3. Mariana; collected, handed
4. We, could see
5. Glendon, went
6. Irene, Scott; have been
7. They; enjoy
8. Arianne; spent
9. Mother, father; attended
10. Donations, have been collected
11. Salad, rolls; were served
12. tree; grew
13. April; returned, locked
14. train; derailed, caused
15. He; ran, called
16. Carol; swept, emptied
17. manner; indicated
18. Patrice, Julie; stayed
19. I, found
20. She; got up, closed
21. Times; have changed
22. I; met
23. I; would have failed
24. Friends; invited
25. We; parked, went
26. Melissa, Vladimir; decided
27. couple; were planning
28. Claire; stopped, bought
29. half; end
30. I; like
31. She; folded, put
32. Penny, Zachary; attended
33. Hiroshi; distributed
34. Roses, lilacs; adorned
35. Jacqueline, Amir; have
36. Roxanne; is
37. bus, train; ran
38. boys; ran
39. Galatea; makes
40. I; urged
41. They; invited
42. She; went, picked
43. writers; cut, pasted
44. he; ran, lifted
45. I, work; I, get

Exercise 2.B

1. Prepositional phrase
2. Prepositional phrase
3. Subordinate clause
4. Participial phrase
5. Participial phrase
6. Independent clause
7. Prepositional phrase
8. Independent clause
9. Participial phrase
10. Subordinate clause

Exercise 2.C

1. Complex
2. Simple
3. Compound
4. Complex
5. Compound
6. Simple
7. Complex
8. Compound
9. Compound-complex
10. Complex
11. Simple
12. Complex
13. Simple
14. Complex
15. Simple
16. Simple
17. Compound
18. Simple
19. Compound
20. Compound-complex

Chapter 3 Review Exercises

Exercise 3.A

1. *held*, action verb; *end*, direct object; *watched*, action verb; *kite*, direct object
2. *felt*, linking verb; *good*, predicate adjective
3. *broke*, action verb; *machine*, direct object
4. *spent*, action verb; *dollars*, direct object
5. *seems*, linking verb; *content*, predicate adjective
6. *remained*, linking verb; *adviser*, predicate noun
7. *wrote*, action verb; *novel*, direct object
8. *was*, linking verb; *reporter*, predicate noun
9. *felt*, action verb; *grass*, direct object
10. *felt*, linking verb; *sad*, predicate adjective

Exercise 3.B

1. *found*, action
2. *seems*, linking
3. *looks*, linking
4. *became*, linking
5. *look*, action
6. *cooked*, action
7. *slowed*, action
8. *grew*, linking
9. *pass*, action
10. *avoided*, action
11. *grew*, action
12. *kept*, action
13. *looks*, linking
14. *are*, linking
15. *chased*, action
16. *are*, linking
17. *sat*, action
18. *sold*, action
19. *kept*, action
20. *remained*, linking

Exercise 3.C

1. *married*, verb; *moved*, verb
2. *me*, indirect object; *bowl*, direct object
3. *owners*, subject noun; *friendly*, predicate adjective
4. *Frannie*, subject noun; *dance*, direct object
5. *became*, (linking) verb; *artist*, predicate noun
6. *have put*, verb phrase; *packages*, direct object
7. *calls*, verb; *me*, direct object
8. *me*, indirect object; *article*, direct object
9. *It*, subject pronoun; *interesting*, predicate adjective
10. *eyes*, direct object; *ears*, direct object
11. *friend*, predicate noun; *colleague*, predicate noun
12. *won*, verb; *award*, direct object
13. *Zachary*, indirect object; *puppy*, direct object
14. *They*, subject pronoun; *arrive*, verb
15. *appeared*, (linking) verb; *irritable*, predicate adjective
16. *helped*, verb; *Danielle*, direct object
17. *Dinner*, subject noun; *pizza*, predicate noun
18. *have been*, verb phrase; *friends*, predicate noun
19. *Hafiz*, subject noun; *book*, direct object
20. *Three*, subject noun; *scholarships*, direct object

Exercise 3.D

1. *rare*, predicate adjective
2. *results*, direct object
3. *her*, indirect object; *book*, direct object
4. *professionals*, predicate noun
5. *cheesecake*, direct object
6. *presents*, direct object
7. *adequate*, predicate adjective
8. *letter*, direct object
9. *groceries*, direct object
10. *tires*, direct object; *oil*, direct object
11. *she*, predicate pronoun
12. *Jamie*, indirect object; *ball*, direct object
13. *biceps*, direct object
14. *flowers*, direct object
15. *Marybeth*, indirect object; *present*, direct object
16. *unusual*, predicate adjective
17. *dishes*, direct object
18. *quiet*, predicate adjective
19. *she*, predicate pronoun
20. *cups*, direct object; *saucers*, direct object

Exercise 3.E

1. *looks*, linking verb; *terrific*, predicate adjective
2. *meet*, action verb; *me*, direct object
3. *bought*, action verb; *tickets*, direct object
4. *is*, linking verb; *dancer*, predicate noun
5. *smell*, linking verb; *wonderful*, predicate adjective
6. *are*, linking verb; *theirs*, predicate (possessive) pronoun
7. *plays*, action verb; *pool*, direct object
8. *proved*, linking verb; *intelligent*, *creative*, predicate adjectives
9. *was*, linking verb; *they*, predicate pronoun
10. *could be*, linking verb; *she*, predicate pronoun
11. *became*, linking verb; *doctor*, predicate noun
12. *was*, linking verb; *pale*, *weak*, predicate adjectives
13. *could be*, linking verb; *they*, predicate pronoun
14. *investigated*, action verb; *rumour*, direct object
15. *redecorated*, action verb; *apartment*, direct object
16. *looks*, linking verb; *colourful*, predicate adjective
17. *asked*, action verb; *them*, direct object
18. *seemed*, linking verb; *excited*, predicate adjective
19. *wore*, action verb; *cardigan*, direct object
20. *was*, linking verb; *she*, predicate pronoun

Chapter 4 Review Exercises

Exercise 4.A

1. Kinga and Auren **discuss** their favourite issues often.
2. The teacher, along with her students **hopes** to make the trip.
3. The students, along with the teacher **are**) taking notes.
4. The reading club **is** unanimously in favour of reading that novel.
5. The number of requests **is** growing by the hour.
6. His pants **were** clearly second-hand.
7. The radio news **says** the storm is approaching.
8. The various media **were** present at the event.
9. **Do** they know the answers to the exam questions?
10. A number of reporters **are** asking for interviews.
11. Fifty dollars **is** the cost of admission.
12. **Was** either of the girls elected to the council?
13. They all want cookies but no one **wants** to drive to the store.
14. The action of the supervisor **was** deemed inappropriate.
15. Part of the roof **has** collapsed.
16. Half of the food **was** consumed in the first half-hour.
17. In the yard **are** several linden trees.
18. A number of cases of beer **were** delivered.

19. Part of the segments **have** been re-worked.
20. Half of the rink **was** flooded.

Exercise 4.B

 1. Some of the cupcakes **have** icing on them.
 2. Twenty years **seems** like a long time to hold a grudge.
 3. That group **was** late in getting started.
 4. Part of the arena **was** being renovated.
 5. Some of the people **are** going by plane.
 6. Everything **has** been taken care of in advance.
 7. Many a town in this region **has** seen better days.
 8. There **are** a hundred people lined up to get in.
 9. All of the cookies **are** baked.
10. Some of the ice cream **is** left.
11. The weather or upcoming exams **are** the probable reason for his absence.
12. My cousin and my friend **have** already arrived.
13. There **was** a great deal of food laid out on the table.
14. His aunt, along with her husband, **is** coming for a visit.
15. **Are** any of the crayons on the floor?
16. Every cup and saucer **was** dirty.
17. Regular work habits **make** for success.
18. The team **is** ready to board the bus for home.
19. The only flower available now **is** tulips.
20. Tulips **are** the only flower available now.

Exercise 4.C

 1. Semantics **is** a pretty heady discipline.
 2. A poll taken by the agencies **seems** to indicate the election will be close.
 3. There **are** too many cooks working on the main course.
 4. Neither Eloise nor Carl **knows** what happened at the scene of the accident.
 5. Both of the cars in the garage **need** washing.
 6. Everyone from first and second years **is** welcome to attend the show.
 7. News of world events **travels** fast over the Internet.
 8. Here **are** some books for you to peruse.
 9. One of my two dogs **is** sick.
10. Nuclear physics **has** addressed the mysteries of the universe.
11. Neither of you **is** willing to help.
12. Neither of your reasons **is** acceptable.
13. Only one of these class projects **is** first-rate.
14. Either Jared or Jessie **is** eligible for the scholarship competition.
15. Neither Robert nor his colleagues **are** ready to leave.

16. Neither my parents nor my aunt **is** at home now.
17. There **are** several students waiting to speak with you.
18. Bill, Lailani, and Neco **were** present at the ceremony.
19. I didn't think you **were** going to be able to make it.
20. Where **are** your friend and your cousin?
21. There **are** fifty ways, the song says, to leave your lover.
22. Greed, as well as incompetence, **is** to blame.
23. The consequences of the new bylaw **were** obvious to all concerned.
24. I will be happy to be one of the women who **are** chosen to represent the group.
25. The problem of high tuition fees **commands** our compassion.
26. All of us **were** partly responsible for the accident.
27. All of the cake **was** gone.
28. Some of the members **have** already left town.
29. Every man and woman in the club **was** required to help pay for the trip.
30. Where **are** the scissors?
31. Mathematics **is** my worst subject.
32. Neither my sister nor my brothers **are** eager for me to leave the country.
33. The leader, as well as the entire team, **is** unable to make the game.
34. The main part of the intestines **was** removed.
35. Neither you nor she **is** one-hundred-per-cent correct.
36. The entire class **is** present for the important lesson on parts of speech.
37. Six per cent **is** a fairly usual rate of interest for mortgages.
38. The supporters of the new bylaw **are** in the minority.
39. All of the food **was** consumed by the hungry children.
40. He volunteered to be one of the persons who **were** building the new gym.
41. All of us **were** right there when you made that promise to the kids.
42. The young woman's dreams **were** in the process of coming true.
43. Who **are** the bride and groom at this wedding?
44. Either you or I **am** eligible for this scholarship.
45. None of us knew that the results of the election **were** on our side.
46. Frederica will attend, and her mother and father **are** coming too.
47. Not a single one of the movies **was** cited for an award.
48. The question of ground rules **was** discussed by the debating team.
49. The young woman soon learned that there **were** many obstacles facing her.
50. Some of my closest female friends **are** quite a bit older than I.
51. His appearance, as well as his personality, **is** charming.
52. The nature of ambition—its joys and its perils—quickly **becomes** apparent.

53. She's one of the ablest musicians who **have** attempted this piece.
54. My girlfriend is one of those people who **are** always late.
55. None of us **is** without limitation.
56. Everybody thinks **he has** the ability to write well.
57. Although both juicers work, neither **works** very well.
58. The rose and the tulip **share** a garden bed.
59. Every plate, glass and ashtray **was** smashed.
60. Some of the cupcakes **are** missing; all of the cherry pie **is** gone too.

Chapter 5 Review Exercises

Exercise 5.A

Several solutions are presented below for each sentence; they do not, of course, exhaust the possibilities. Go ahead and improve on them.

1. Although she gave me a gift on my birthday, the gift wasn't that nice. / Although she gave me a gift on my birthday, my birthday wasn't that nice.
2. Whenever Carol was in town, she visited Marg. / Whenever Marg was in town, she visited Carol.
3. The large dog in the shed always barks at me. / The dog in the large shed always barks at me.
4. When my sisters visited Montreal, they met your sisters. / When your sisters visited Montreal, they met my sisters.
5. Hafiz and Narayan went to Hafiz's brother's place for Christmas./ Hafiz and Narayan went to Narayan's brother's place for Christmas.
6. That artisan has sketch I'd like to buy of an antique samovar. / I'd like to buy an antique samovar, like the one that artisan has sketched.
7. Idell picked up Theresa at Idell's office. / Idell picked up Theresa at Theresa's office.
8. When the truck hit it, the van was nearly totalled. / When it hit the van, the truck was nearly totalled.
9. When she plays duets with Joi, Frannie always plays too fast. / When she plays duets with Frannie, Joi always plays too fast.
10. Parents with young children should ensure the children get proper nutrition. / Parents with young children should ensure they themselves get proper nutrition. / Parents should ensure proper nutrition for both themselves and their young children.

Exercise 5.B

1. *his or her.* In Israel, all citizens must do army duty at a young age.
2. *himself or herself.* All who pass the final exam can consider themselves off to a good start. / If you pass the final exam, you can consider yourself off to a good start.
3. *his or her.* All were considered insufficiently skilled to adapt their scripts to the existing audience.

4. *him or her.* If you object, think up a better scheme. / Anyone who objects should think up a better scheme. / Let anyone who objects think up a better scheme.
5. *his or her.* All citizens in a free country must regard it their duty to vote.
6. *his or her.* All were asked to do their best to sell tickets.
7. *his or her.* Joan was worried that someone had not received an invitation. / Joan was worried that some had not received their invitations.
8. *himself or herself.* Let all try to make themselves a market niche.
9. *her.* Women who hate children should re-examine their values.
10. *his or her.* Each one of us had to present a piece of ID at the door. / We all had to present a piece of ID at the door.

Exercise 5.C
Choose the correct form from the two in parentheses.
1. Each of the articles sat on **its** own shelf.
2. The city had memorials designed to honour **its** heroes.
3. Every one of the women has done **her** part.
4. Either one or the other must pay for **his** ticket.
5. If Kara or Anne calls, tell **her** I'll call back.
6. Neither man wants to commit **himself**.
7. Each of the candidates had to provide the committee with **her** portfolio.
8. All the students paid **their** fees.
9. Neither man presented **his** case with any conviction.
10. Both boys ordered textbooks through **their** local bookstore.
11. Everything was in **its** own place.
12. Each girl who competes will receive a questionnaire that **she** must answer.
13. Neither of the tomcats will touch that new food in **his** bowl.
14. The company holds the annual general meeting in **its** boardroom.
15. All the new students know how to get to **their** classes.

Exercise 5.D
1. If either student finishes the work, **he or she** may leave.
2. One may pay online if **one** prefers.
3. Her girlfriend and colleague contributed **her** time.
4. Barbara's mother got re-married when **Barbara** was six years old.
5. Anyone can apply by sending **a** résumé.
6. One does well to meet **one's** obligations.
7. Each of the items had **its** special place on the shelf.
8. Either Jim or Ira will give **his** presentation.
9. The teacher and the student gave **their** opinions.

10. The company usually hires **its** new employees in January.
11. Each of the contestants wrote down **his or her** phone number.
12. If anyone wants a ticket, **he or she** should call Janine. / Anyone who wants a ticket should call Janine.
13. Before you leap, **you** should look.
14. Some law firms do **their** recruiting in May.
15. A volunteer is usually motivated to do **his or her** part.

Exercise 5.E

1. The family received **their** passports yesterday.
2. The firm sent a memo to **its** staff about the new health plan.
3. If anyone else objects, let **him or her** speak up now.
4. If a student works hard, **he or she** will probably ace the exam.
5. The team is continuing on to **its** third competition.
6. Everybody has to deal with **his or her** own problems.
7. The band took out **their** instruments.
8. Each girl expected **her** essay to receive an A.
9. When you are in error, **you** should be ready to admit it.
10. Some of the teams had **their** various colours displayed.
11. I love **this** kind of apple but not **that** kind of orange. / I love these kinds of **apples** but not those kinds of **oranges**.
12. Harry's father became a doctor when **Harry** was born. / When Harry was born, his father became a doctor.
13. Some of the material has lost **its** shape.
14. The company has already moved to **its** new offices.
15. The school has planned **its** first semester.
16. Who wants to take **his or her** own car?
17. Each of the programs will have **its** own writers.
18. My friends Allie and Sandy have **their** own way of doing things.
19. Every single chair in the place had a reserve sign on **its** seat.
20. The faculty has been informed of **their** vacation dates.
21. One shouldn't leave home without **one's** wallet.
22. Every girlfriend she knew had invited her to **her** wedding.
23. None signed **his or her** name to the petition.
24. **These** kinds of poems leave me cold.
25. The singers turned to the audience and took **their** bows.
26. Many a man owes **his** success to the right education.
27. Both the winner and the guy who placed second had **their** good points.
28. A performer in top form can do **his or her** best with ease.
29. The members of the orchestra rose from **their** seats.
30. When one is in a glass house, **one** shouldn't throw stones.

Exercise 5.F

1. Come swimming with **us** this afternoon.
2. I am sure that the winner will be **she**.
3. **We** writers find ingenious reasons to avoid the blank page.
4. **He** and **I** have been colleagues for years now.
5. Did you think the young musician was **he**?
6. I'm certain of it; I have no doubt it was **she** who complained.
7. It was **they** who told me the story about the rabbit.
8. Let **us** take care of the children.
9. Did you phone **him** and **me**?
10. Please wait for Alex and **me**.
11. Between you and **me**, I wouldn't believe that story.
12. Everyone has gone but **her**.
13. You and **I** can be relied upon to do a good job.
14. I intend to invite Cynthia, Gail and **him** to the performance.
15. **Whom** are you going to see?

Exercise 5.G

1. The women **who** fought for the right to vote were called suffragettes.
2. I'll introduce you to my sister, **whom** you have yet to meet.
3. I've never known a man **who** is as kind as Ehud.
4. **Who** will I say is calling?
5. **Who** do you wish you were?
6. The architect, **whom** we hired to renovate our house, did a good job.
7. You can invite **whomever** you like to the party.
8. I wonder **whom** you saw walking down the street.
9. To **whom** would you like to speak?
10. There was a bully in my neighbourhood **who** made my life difficult.
11. Will Jack or **she** be hired, do you think?
12. After the games were over, the most valuable player turned out to be **he**.
13. Following a heavy meal, **we** health nuts would rather walk than ride.
14. **Who** is knocking on the door?
15. Give these free clothes to **whoever** asks for them.
16. Professor Gagnon is the one **who** we think will win.
17. Doctor Cantley is the one **whom** we hope to elect.
18. Sunanda bakes better bread than **I**.
19. The novelist offered Sara and **me** some kindly advice.
20. They came to meet the teachers and **us**.
21. I would rather talk it over privately, just between you and **me**.
22. **Whom** should I ask for directions?
23. A group of **us** students protested the new regime.
24. I thought Carla and **he** brought the refreshments.

25. My parents disapproved of **our** driving on the dangerously icy Coquihalla.
26. **We** instructors have just as much fun as you students do.
27. Frannie and **I** planted an apple tree in the front yard.
28. It wasn't **I** who called the police.
29. It was **she** who said that **we** boys were being too rough.
30. **She** and the three boys went swimming in the lake.

Chapter 6 Review Exercises

Exercise 6.A

1. You will receive **complimentary** tickets to the show in the mail.
2. She has three **dependants** under the age of six.
3. I am **averse** to travelling in these **adverse** conditions.
4. A **breech** birth is one in which the baby is born buttocks first.
5. She hesitated to **broach** the topic.
6. With her blinding migraine headache, she found the **tortuous** country road a **torturous** and harrowing experience.
7. The convicted man was **hanged**.
8. Even though she was confident of her speaking abilities, she was glad to hear the professor say that he would not include **oral** components in the final exams.
9. The crime scene presented a **grisly** sight.
10. Lying about the matter can only **aggravate** an already bad scene.
11. I had just **lain** down when the phone rang.
12. Chaim was **beside** himself with joy after winning first place in the violin competition.
13. The profits were obtained by **illicit** means.
14. I'd prefer to discuss this **further** at another time.
15. The captain forbade the troops **to go ashore** but did not prohibit them **from drinking**.
16. A salesperson or **pedlar peddles**; a cyclist or **pedaller pedals**.
17. Sunanda had **already** left by the time Sarah and the children were **all ready** to go.
18. One thing **precedes** another when it comes before it.
19. Colds are **contagious**; AIDS is **a contagious** disease.
20. The reason I didn't attend the party is **that** I wasn't feeling well.
21. She appealed to him to **try to** understand.
22. I have already stated my **principal** objections in the letter.
23. She hoped her **capacity** for restraint would not desert her as she watched him try to fill the suitcase beyond its **capacity**.
24. He taught in the slums and saw every day the **effects** of poverty.
25. By cutting behind the football field, she hoped to **elude** her tormentors.

26. **among** the three friends, there were few secrets.
27. With a huge bang, the balloon **burst**.
28. The collage was **composed** of dozens of tiny images that **constituted** an impressionistic whole.
29. With Beren's **excepted**, all the job hunters' applications were **accepted** for review.
30. The teacher said that **continual** interruptions would not be allowed.
31. Anyone who believes the witnesses are **credible** must be **credulous**.
32. The odour of sulphur was more **diffuse** now.
33. Looking after someone else's children is different **from** having your own.
34. As the years passed, **fewer** former students came to see the professor.
35. How can I **persuade** you to join us?
36. Margot had a certain **flair** for the arts.
37. If you want to win at a game, you can't **flout** the rules.
38. The fate of the ship was sealed; it **foundered**.
39. Patrick hated to **forgo** reading the book reviews.
40. The **formerly** plump child was now thin and pale.
41. Of the three dresses you tried on, the **first** suits you best.
42. It was only by a **fortuitous** meeting that she learned the truth.
43. The faculty members decided to have a **fuller** discussion later.
44. Athletes of both **sexes** will compete in the event.
45. Considering the circumstances, his decision was **judicious**.
46. From the information on this graph, we can **infer** that things are improving.
47. Mark walked right **into** the room and handed his application **in to** the boss.
48. She was **reluctant** to accept the assignment.
49. Bill devised an **ingenious** method for moving tools to the shed.
50. The letter rambled on for several pages; its meaning was barely **intelligible**.
51. They flatly **denied** the allegations.
52. He asked his parents if they would **lend** him the money.
53. When the books arrived, the boy **virtually** devoured them.
54. Cigarettes taste bad, **as** you might expect.
55. He tried to **advise** them of their rights, but his **advice** was ignored.
56. Police confirmed that the store had been **robbed** and the thieves had **stolen** thousands of dollars.
57. It was **almost** midnight when **most** of the guests went home after **a most** enjoyable party.
58. She narrowed her eyes as she tried to remember the **quotation**.
59. Students began to feel **nauseous** and were sent home even before the reason—**noxious** fumes—was discovered.
60. Most people are **loath** to admit when they are wrong.

61. It's **all right** with us if you want to **bring** your dogs when you come to the cottage.
62. A large **number** of these kinds of errors can be attributed to lack of experience.
63. I **can** drive there but I **may** not drive there this weekend because my father needs the car.
64. **Because of** car trouble, we postponed our trip.
65. Given what they'd had to overcome, they did an **altogether** fine job.
66. The decision to **censor** the film followed the **censure** of critics.
67. Intelligent discussion can act as a **stimulus** to positive change.
68. She didn't mind the **comprehensive** nature of the 20-page exam, but she found some of the essay questions barely **comprehensible**.
69. The **noisy** machinery gave Sonja a headache and the **noisome** fumes made it worse.
70. The elected municipal **councillors** decided to **counsel** caution.

Exercise 6.B

1. This summer Roxanne went swimming almost every day.
2. I jumped out of bed in my bare feet as the radio alarm went off.
3. The portable laptop computer helped my grandfather, unable to walk because of a stroke, recover his will to live.
4. Speaking slowly, the guest lecturer ensured the class could hear every word he said.
5. Last week I found a beautifully carved mahogany box containing an old healthcare card.
6. Alone, she felt more scared in the abandoned lot than she had felt earlier that day there with friends.
7. In the pet store, each of the budgie birds has a really weird name, like Kissing Cousin, Captain Courageous, or Blue Blogger.
8. Barely daring to breathe for fear of waking the baby, we passed her room as she slept peacefully.
9. Flying south for the winter, exotic birds from more northern climes fill the sky.
10. While waiting for the fibreglass shower unit to arrive from Vancouver, the whole family often used the bath tub.
11. I watched the black stallion, nostrils flaring, speed away.
12. Kate and Beth were laughing wildly at the top of their lungs as they walked across campus.
13. We bought only a few gifts to take home for the children.
14. In a busy airport, she first fell for the man who would become her lover.
15. They dumped in the recycle bin the bags that Anne-Marie had prepared the day before.

16. A woman who tries to be only as good as a man is said to lack ambition.
17. Gail took care of the wonderful artwork she had bought from an artist and hung on the walls in the den.
18. Please sit down either on the sofa or in the armchair.
19. He begged her to meet him behind the weighing station at the border crossing later, when night fell.
20. We all know that the human child at birth is utterly vulnerable, and would in fact die without parental care.
21. While she was out jogging, her dog followed her into the woods and chased a bear.
22. Alan put the roast, which they planned to eat later, in the freezer.
23. Vivian says she remembers only part of the novel's plot.
24. I think that we hardly ever go out dancing anymore.
25. Surveying the scene with interest, we saw a beautiful house standing on a distant hill.
26. We decided to believe completely what the actor said.
27. Never give to a baby food that hasn't been cut into small pieces.
28. The housekeeper bent down, and groaning loudly, picked up the umpteenth pair of socks.
29. An author of two books, with a third coming out soon, he found his office was always full of printed material.
30. Swearing profusely, he put the dog out after it bit a visitor.
31. While giving a lecture outside on a beautiful spring day, the professor saw a giant panda bear round the corner from the direction of the clock-tower.
32. To understand Canadian literature, students should carefully study seminal figures such as Timothy Findley and Margaret Atwood.
33. Since I was the youngest child in the family, Father and Mother relaxed the rules for me.
34. When Sandy was five, her father decided to marry again.
35. If one studies correctly, one can learn a lot from the literature of fiction.
36. Looking over her shoulder at her pursuer, she thought home seemed distant.
37. Entering the foyer, a visitor sees through the window a large park.
38. Being a big city, it allowed stores to stay open day and night, including Sunday.
39. Fritz almost caught the flying plate just before it crashed into a thousand pieces on the floor.
40. Having never before lived in Kamloops, she found the organic food co-op a delightful surprise.
41. When writing articles, you should have several good reference texts close at hand.

42. Flies are easier to catch with honey than with vinegar.
43. As if in a dream, we watched the first snow of the season falling lightly.
44. The teacher called an ambulance for her ailing student who had lost consciousness.
45. As a reward for getting top grades, I got the use of the family car for the whole of Saturday evening.
46. Feeling sick and tired, I found the work was difficult.
47. Rounding the corner, he could see the house.
48. Marsha hoped to find a private teacher with a PhD. for her two-year-old.
49. While washing dishes, she broke her favourite wineglass.
50. Returning from his linguistics seminar, he finally heard his pet parrot speak.

Chapter 7 Review Exercises

Exercise 7.A

1. Shawnee is a young wolf dog with a thick black coat, beautiful amber eyes, and a bark much worse than his bite.
2. The entire Grade 6 class was worried, but also happy, about the move to the new location.
3. In the glove compartment, they found several items: a book of bus tickets, a half-eaten orange, and the keys to the house.
4. It is normal to have greater muscle content in a newborn male than in a newborn female.
5. Lainey grabbed the megaphone, climbed on top of the car, and began to speak.
6. My mother always has ironed and always will iron towels.
7. Either you must hand in your final exam before the end of class, or I must dock you ten points.
8. We decided that we should stay the night in Cache Creek and leave early the next morning for Kamloops.
9. Timothy Findley's novel *The Wars* is as good as, if not better than, other novels written by Canadian authors about the First World War.
10. The piano movers were built like tanks, with massive chests and shoulders, and strong arms, hands, and backs.
11. Dana's favourite desserts were chocolate ice cream, chocolate donuts, and baklava.
12. Eating, drinking, and smoking are not allowed in the classroom.
13. Lulu couldn't make up her mind whether she wanted to eat, clean her paws, or go outside.
14. I have neither the time nor the inclination to help you.
15. They agreed they would re-convene at 9:00 the next morning and settle the dispute.

16. Kelly's essay was well written and quite a bit longer than Kara's.
17. This digital watch is pretty, reliable, and accurate.
18. The exercises were not only lengthy, but also quite hard.
19. Planning to exercise does not provide the same benefit as actually exercising.
20. Marcel is a writer and an athlete.
21. I have always liked sewing and cooking.
22. The Canadian Charter of Rights and Freedoms calls for freedom of expression, communication, and assembly.
23. She wrote that she would leave in August, travel to Montreal by plane, and stay for several weeks.
24. Anne is a woman with leadership qualities who therefore should be elected chair.
25. Professor O'Regan is intelligent, creative, and hardworking.
26. I hope to spend my vacation in either Mexico or Cuba.
27. The chair of the department must advise students who undertake a degree and must also take part in committee work.
28. The drama coach wants to meet with people who enjoy theatre; he hopes to stage an amateur production at the high school.
29. He thought that weather conditions were improving and that the wildfires crisis was nearly over.
30. A plumber's earnings are often as hefty as a professor's.
31. He is as short as if not shorter than his brother.
32. I never have abided and never will abide fools gladly.
33. I was fairly impressed, but most of my students were wildly unimpressed.
34. We gave him an orange and a pear.
35. I was distressed by and anxious about his near-disaster in Asia.

Exercise 7.B

1. That she'd been looking for her raincoat was Penny's excuse for keeping us all waiting.
2. The grammatical error called a dangling modifier occurs when a participial phrase has no grammatical subject.
3. I always believed that if I did the work, I would become a professional.
4. The reason is that she had a toothache.
5. She had always thought that white is a good colour with adobe.
6. After he started exercising and eating right, he no longer thought of his body as his worst enemy.
7. We are as tall as if not taller than they.
8. After he finished the last novel of the trilogy, George finally took a holiday.
9. The new school lab has flat-screen computers, which are harder to hide behind.

10. Success in university appears to be a matter of luck.
11. I remember that day as hot and humid.
12. One way to better society is to follow the golden rule.
13. In order to have the wedding in August, hundreds of details had to be attended to and dozens of purchases made.
14. A bias is an established preference or a pre-formed judgment, often arrived at without careful consideration of the facts.
15. Her need to earn a living eventually led to Penelope's receiving an offer to work at the National Film Board.
16. Landing your first reporting job at a big-city daily makes you feel bold.
17. Though she showed signs of tiredness, she won the race.
18. Though he loved her, he had to leave.
19. I read in the paper that the Strawberry Hill fire is completely contained.
20. Although they are not perfect, they certainly have merit.
21. Although she was extremely tired, she managed to finish her homework.
22. Because he was a great believer in learning by doing, he never gave long lectures.
23. I wanted to bake a cake, but I had no flour or sugar in the house.
24. Cristine tried hard and paid attention in class, but she didn't get the A she wanted.
25. Although the event was well-planned, the turnout was low.
26. Because no one else showed up, we decided to leave.
27. Because she was the only one in the office at the time, she took the call.
28. Wanting to impress him, she put on her best clothes.
29. Because it was getting late and they couldn't decide who should drive, they took a cab.
30. Although Sunny says she wants to meet someone, she doesn't go out much.
31. Because he got to know her better, he no longer judges her harshly.
32. After they finished the rehearsal and closed the studio, they went for coffee.
33. Because I was busy with the baby, I asked Jeremy to prepare dinner.
34. An example of their stubbornness is their refusal to engage in teamwork.
35. The article on video games explains why the games grew popular.

Exercise 7.C

1. Language may be partially defined as sounds made with the tongue; indeed, the English word "language" comes from the Latin word *lingua*, which means "tongue."

2. Nevertheless, not all sounds made by humans qualify as "language," even though speech is the basic and most widely used form of human communication, with a much longer history than writing.

3. Animals clearly produce sounds that communicate meaning to others of their species, albeit in a limited range.

4. Any definition of language would have to include the concept of "meaning" and the means of expressing meaning, including gesture, sound, and the complex symbolic system of written language.

5. It would seem that humans are set apart from other mammals not so much by their ability to communicate with spoken sounds as by their invention of writing, an invention that has allowed them to expand their knowledge and understanding of the world.

Chapter 8 Review Exercises

Exercise 8.A

1. He believes he won the essay contest because he chose an excellent topic and wrote well.

2. The girl standing beside Janine is my sister.

3. The disorganization was, to put it mildly, rather disconcerting.

4. Before she could enter the swimsuit contest, she had to convince her mother it was a good idea.

5. All students, without exception, are welcome to attend the senior prom.

6. Please pass the sugar, Naomi; it's right beside you. / Please pass the sugar, Naomi. It's right beside you.

7. On reading his letter, I learned he had finished graduate school, married, and moved to Los Angeles.

8. Many people know Noam Chomsky, the brilliant linguist, only by his political writings.

9. My sister, who lives in Big Trout Lake in Northern Ontario, is coming to visit me.

10. No, John, you shouldn't send cash through the mail.

11. Professor Belshaw won an award for his book and plans to celebrate with his colleagues.

12. I give you my word that I will treat your application confidentially; please let me know if I can be of further assistance. / I give you my word that I will treat your application confidentially. Please let me know if I can be of further assistance.

13. She felt truly grateful for all the information and help that her teachers had provided over the course of her job hunt.

14. I am most concerned about her progress in English, mathematics, science, and social studies.

15. When I sat down, she stood up.

16. After I sat down, she stood up.
17. She stood up after I sat down.
18. He was writing in response to their letter of February 5, 2002, from Montreal, Quebec, to say he would accept the job in Vancouver, B.C.
19. Some people seek to fix the blame; others, in my opinion more intelligent, seek to fix the problem. / Some people seek to fix the blame. Others, in my opinion more intelligent, seek to fix the problem.
20. Despite our desire to see the program flourish, we possessed insufficient funds to continue the work.
21. "Please pass the sugar," he said.
22. "Where did I put the car keys?" he asked.
23. "I don't know where you put your keys," she said.
24. Would you mind holding open the door for me, Jack.
25. "Sandy," she said, "where did you get those shoes?"
26. She's planning a trip to Europe with friends; however, she has yet to inform her mother. / She's planning a trip to Europe with friends. She has, however, yet to inform her mother.
27. My older brother lives in Los Angeles, California, and my younger brother in Montreal, Quebec.
28. Jessica, the bride's cousin, sang the Simon and Garfunkel song, "Like a Bridge over Troubled Water."
29. The word "accommodate" is often misspelled; remember to double the "c" and the "m." / The word "accommodate" is often misspelled. Remember to double the "c" and the "m."
30. The provost said, "I'd like to announce that all faculty members with more than ten years service at Thompson Rivers University will receive raises of ten per cent or more; that is, at least ten per cent."

Exercise 8.B

1. We now have more than 50 tomato plants ready to harvest, Fritz. Don't you think we should begin? / We now have more than 50 tomato plants ready to harvest, Fritz; don't you think we should begin?
2. Who was it who said: "Ask not what your country can do for you; ask what you can do for your country"?
3. Even the committee chair, Vivian's strongest supporter, had to admit that when Vivian said "stuff it" to the director, her chances of getting funding evaporated.
4. Professor Edge's latest article, "The Press We Deserve," appeared in an academic journal called *Textual Studies in Canada*, where it provoked much interest.
5. "It's such a lovely day, Harold," she said. "Let's hop in the car and take the kids for a country outing."
6. Did you say you would pick me up at the train station at 6:15?

7. "Hey Bugsy," said Kevin, "show Adam how you wiggle your eyebrows like Groucho Marx."

8. "Warren, please help your sister with the dishes, as you promised to do." "I'm too tired," Warren said. "And anyway, she didn't help me last week, when it was my turn."

9. "Sorry," he said. "I've got to split." In the sixties, the word "split" meant "leave."

10. She seemed to think everything would work out if we all just agreed never to discuss the problem, to keep it a secret.

11. "Would you like a cup of coffee, Eloise?" he asked kindly.
    "Thanks, no," said Eloise. "I've already had too much coffee and it's barely noon."

12. Sit down and be quiet. If I want your opinion, I'll ask for it. / Sit down and be quiet; if I want your opinion, I'll ask for it.

13. Martin turned to Mikelle and made a motion toward the far end of the table. "Please pass the wine," he said coolly, avoiding her eyes. "Why certainly," she answered, her voice dripping ice.

14. "Open your mouth and say, 'Ah,'" the nurse said. She peered down into Tom's mouth and frowned. "Looks like a bad infection," she half whispered. "I'll prescribe antibiotics."
    "Are you sure they're absolutely necessary?" Tom asked.

15. The word "*bienvenue*" means "welcome" in French, Canada's other official language.

16. Pointing to a large evergreen in the distance, Paula said, "That evergreen marks the northern boundary of our property." Then her eyes clouded over as she thought about the fires that still threatened to consume the B.C. Interior. Almost to herself, she added, "Pray for rain."

17. The house was a small stucco bungalow that she fell in love with at first sight. "It's small," she said to her guests, "but it's the perfect size for us. We love it."

18. "To remember the parts of speech and the way they work, use mnemonic and organizational aids," she said. "For example, take the word 'grammar' itself."

19. It will be a long time before I forget the look on his face when you said, "We should have some guts and show some leadership here." I think it took him a full minute to regain his composure before he responded, "I agree, but I can, nevertheless, do nothing to change management's decision."

20. The old Blackfoot elder told his grandson the story about how every human has two wolves battling for control of the human soul, the good wolf and the bad wolf. "Which wolf wins in the end?" the grandson asked. "The one you feed," the elder answered.

Glossary of Grammatical Terms

absolute construction   An absolute construction or phrase is one that modifies a sentence or main clause (rather than particular words within the clause) but that is not joined to the sentence by means of a preposition or subordinating conjunction. An absolute phrase usually contains a noun and a participle. Here are two examples:
  - An hour having passed, we decided to make enquiries.
  - The rain having stopped, we decided to venture outdoors.

abstract nouns   Nouns that refer to ideas and relationships such as beauty and truth are abstract. Concrete nouns name specific things that can be apprehended with the senses (seen or touched, for example). It's not possible, or even advisable, to try to avoid all abstract nouns, especially in expository writing. On the other hand, the most reliable way to suck the life out of any piece of writing is to use abstract nouns excessively. Stay specific and concrete.

active voice   See VOICE.

adjective   One of the eight parts of speech, the adjective modifies a noun or pronoun. The various kinds of adjectives include descriptive adjectives (*blue sky, great work*); demonstrative adjectives (*this, that, these, those*); indefinite adjectives (*many, some,* etc.); interrogative and relative adjectives (*which, what, whose,* etc.); possessive adjectives (*my, her, their,* etc.); and numerical adjectives (*one, two, three,* etc.). The definite and indefinite articles (*the, a, an*) are also considered adjectives and are often referred to as "noun markers" or "noun determiners," because they show that a noun will follow. A predicate adjective is one that comes after a linking verb, modifying the subject (*she was energetic*). Phrases (*the woman wearing a red dress*) and clauses (*the woman who ran with wolves*) can also be used as adjectives to modify nouns and pronouns.

adjectival   An adjectival is a word that can serve as an adjective but that generally functions as another part of speech. In *dish towel*, for instance, the word *dish*—usually a noun—functions as an adjective, modifying *towel*. Some grammarians classify possessive nouns and pronouns as adjectivals.

adverb   One of the eight parts of speech, the adverb can be used to modify a verb, an adjective, or another adverb. Adverbs can also be used to modify verbals (gerunds, infinitives, and participles), phrases, clauses, and whole sentences. When adverbs are used to modify verbs, they show when, where, why, or how something happened or was experienced. Used to modify adjectives or other adverbs, they show degree (*a very large dog, contributed fairly often*).

adverbial clause   An adverbial clause is a subordinate clause (also called a dependent clause) that functions as an adverb.

> ◦ I was attending university *while my sister worked in a law office.*
> ◦ The children were happy *until they moved.*
> ◦ Martin works faster *than David does.*

agreement   Correct grammar requires two kinds of agreement or correspondence: that between subjects and verbs on the one hand, and that between pronouns and their antecedents on the other. Subject-verb agreement requires that the verb agree with the subject in person and number. (*I go,* but *he goes. She goes,* but *they go.*) Pronoun-antecedent agreement dictates that pronouns must agree with their antecedents in person, number, and gender.

> ◦ Each girl must write her name on the list.
> ◦ Each boy must write his name on the list.
> ◦ Every student must write his or her name on the list.
> ◦ All students must write their names on the list.

antecedent   Pronouns have antecedents. The antecedent of a pronoun is the word (noun, pronoun, or other substantive) that the pronoun substitutes for or refers to. In the sentence, *I gave the pen to Lailani, and she gave it back to me,* the antecedent of *she* is *Lailani;* the antecedent of *it* is *pen;* the antecedent of *me* is another pronoun, *I.*) The antecedent usually comes before the noun or pronoun it refers to, but it can also come after, as in: *When she confessed, the woman began to cry.* The antecedent, *woman,* comes after the pronoun *she.*

appositive   An appositive is a word or group of words that follows another word or group of words, and that identifies, describes, or explains the first. The second noun or pronoun (or other substantive) is said to be "in apposition" with the first.

> ◦ We sent along roses, her favourite flower.

(*Her favourite flower* is here in apposition with *roses.*) The appositive is essentially a clause shortened into a phrase. Without the option of appositives, we would have to write this:

> ◦ We sent along roses, which were her favourite flower.

article   See ADJECTIVE.

auxiliary verb   An auxiliary verb is a "helping" verb used to conjugate other verbs. The verbs *be* and *have* are commonly used as auxiliaries. Examples:

> ◦ You were watching TV when she called.

(The auxiliary verb *were*—the second person, past tense form of the verb *to be*—is used to form the past progressive tense of the verb *watch.*)

◦ They have gone away for the Christmas break.

(The auxiliary verb *have* is used to form the present perfect tense of the verb *go*, in third person plural.) Modal auxiliaries are a special group of auxiliaries that don't change form for a third-person-singular subject; they include must, ought to, used to, can and could, shall and should, will and would, and may and might. (See MOOD.) The auxiliary verb *be* is also used to form the passive voice. (*I held the pen*; active voice. *The pen was held by me*; passive voice.)

case   Case is a quality of nouns and pronouns that indicates the "place" of the noun or pronoun in relation to the rest of the sentence. There are three cases: the subjective (also called nominative); the objective (also called accusative); and the possessive (also called genitive). Nouns use the same spelling for subjective and objective cases, but pronouns have different forms for each case. The following sentence indicates the three cases respectively of the third person plural pronoun *we*: <u>We</u> (subjective) *put the items they gave <u>us</u>* (objective) *in <u>our</u>* (possessive) *car*.

clause   A clause is a group of related words that contains both a subject and a predicate. Clauses are either independent (also called main) or subordinate (also called dependent). An independent clause makes sense by itself and can stand alone as a sentence. Independent clauses may be joined by co-ordinating conjunctions, such as *and*.

◦ She took a bath and then she made a pot of tea.

A subordinate clause cannot make sense by itself; it needs to be attached to an independent clause. Subordinate clauses are joined to independent ones by subordinating conjunctions, such as *because*, and relative pronouns, such as *who*.

◦ *Because she was tired,* she declined the invitation.

◦ They invited the new girl, *who declined the invitation.*

Subordinate clauses can function as nouns, adjectives, or adverbs:

◦ Noun: *What I dreamt about* surprised me.

◦ Adjective: I liked the girl *who had lovely red hair.*

◦ Adverb: *While I was cooking dinner,* the phone rang.

comparison   Adjectives and adverbs have three degrees of comparison: positive (*the large dog barked <u>loudly</u>*); comparative (*the larger dog barked <u>more loudly</u>*); and superlative (*the largest dog barked <u>most loudly</u>*).

complement   Broadly defined, grammatical complements are words that complete the meanings expressed by verbs. There are three kinds of complements:

1)   the direct and indirect objects that complete action verbs by receiving the action of the verb,

2)   the predicate complements—nouns, pronouns, and adjectives—that complete linking verbs by referring to the subject, and

3)   the objective complements that follow direct objects and complete the meaning of the verb by referring to the object.

The indirect and direct objects of action verbs are substantives—nouns, pronouns, and phrases and clauses that act like nouns. (*She gave _him_ a gift*.) The predicate complements (also called subjective complements) of linking verbs are either predicate nouns or pronouns (*she is a _professor_; this is _she_*) or predicate adjectives (*she is _tall_*). The objective complement (also called the object complement) following a direct object is a noun or an adjective. (*They named the dog _Blue_. They painted the wall _red_*.) Notice that objective complements can occur only in sentences or clauses with transitive action verbs (action verbs that take direct objects).

complex sentence   A sentence is classified as complex when it contains one independent clause and one or more subordinate clauses.

compound sentence   A sentence is classified as compound when it contains two or more independent clauses joined by co-ordinate conjunctions.

compound-complex sentence   When a sentence contains two or more independent clauses and one or more subordinate clauses, it is classified as compound-complex.

concrete   Concrete words can be roughly defined as words that are definite and specific and tend to evoke sense impressions. In your writing, generally prefer the concrete to the abstract.

conjugation   Conjugation refers to changes in the form or spelling of verbs to indicate tense, person, number, and so on. The verb *be* is conjugated as follows: *I am, you are, he, she or it is, we are, you are, they are.*

conjunction   One of the eight parts of speech, the conjunction connects words or groups of words in a sentence. Co-ordinating conjunctions join equal elements (words to words, phrases to phrases, clauses to clauses); the most common is the word *and*. Subordinating conjunctions join subordinate clauses to independent clauses, e.g. *When I was a child, I spoke as a child.*

conjunctive adverb   A conjunctive adverb is a special kind of adverb that does double duty as an adverb and as a conjunction. Conjunctive adverbs include *nevertheless, besides, however, while, therefore, moreover, thus,* and *then.*

> ○ I can attend today's class; *however*, I will have to miss the one tomorrow.

As an adverb, the word *however* signifies a particular logical relationship; as a conjunction, it joins two independent clauses. The conjunctive adverb is often preceded by a semi-colon.

connectives   A connective is any word or phrase used to signify a relationship between two other elements (words, phrases, clauses, sentences, or paragraphs). Connectives thus include certain parts of speech (prepositions, conjunctions, and sometimes pronouns) as well as conjunctive adverbs and various connective phrases (such as *of course* or *for instance*). It's crucial to use connectives precisely, since they express logical relations (contradiction, addition, cause and effect, etc.).

co-ordinate clauses   When two independent clauses are joined together, either by a co-ordinate conjunction or by a semi-colon, they are said to be co-ordinate.

declension   Declension refers to changes in the form or spelling of nouns and pronouns to show their person, number, and case. To decline a pronoun means to give the various forms; for example, here is the declension of the first person pronoun, showing subjective, objective, and possessive cases in singular and plural: *I, me, mine; we, us, ours.*

determiner   A determiner is a noun marker; it is an adjectival word that signals a noun will follow. The determiner may be a possessive adjective (*my, his, their,* etc.), a demonstrative adjective (*this, that, these, those*), an indefinite adjective (*some, all, many,* etc.), or an article, either the definite article (*the*) or the indefinite article (*a/an*). Determiners indicate the approach of a noun or noun phrase, but not all nouns are preceded by determiners. Proper nouns and some abstract nouns, for example, are not preceded by determiners. Other kinds of words besides nouns can have "markers": auxiliary verbs (such as *have* and *are*) can act as markers, signalling the approach of verbs; adverbs (such as *very* and *mostly*) can signal the approach of modifiers; and subordinating conjunctions (such as *because* and *when*) can signal the approach of subordinate clauses. To recap, a grammatical marker is a word that shows a noun, verb, modifier, or subordinate clause will follow. When the marker indicates a noun will follow, the marker is called a determiner.

ellipsis   An ellipsis consists of three periods in a row and indicates that words have been omitted from a quoted passage. When the ellipsis is used to indicate words omitted from within a quoted passage, use three periods in a row; when the omission comes at the end of the passage, use four periods (three for the ellipsis and one to indicate the end of the sentence).

expletive   In common parlance, an expletive is a swear word or exclamation. In grammar, an expletive is a word unrelated grammatically to the rest of the sentence; it is added to a sentence to fill in for the subject and render the sentence more natural sounding. The words most commonly used as grammatical expletives are *it* and *there*.

  ○ *There* were at least a hundred people attending the ceremony. The subject of the sentence is *people*, not *there*. Expletives are sometimes useful, but more often they weaken a sentence.

finite verb   A finite verb is one that has person and number and so can serve as the predicate of a sentence. Its opposite is the non-finite verb form, which cannot serve as a predicate because it has no person or number. See also "non-finite verb."

flow The word *flow* is variously used in writing circles. Informally, flow refers to the forward movement of a piece of writing, to how smoothly the words, images, and ideas fit and flow in the context of the whole. More technically, flow can be defined as the overall coherence and continuity within and among the parts of a piece of writing (the coherence of words in a sentence, of sentences in a paragraph, of paragraphs in an essay), a coherence based on and created by various means such as the repetition in successive sentences of key words and grammatical constructions, the use of a pronoun to recall an antecedent from the preceding sentence or paragraph, and the skilful (read impeccably logical) use of connectives.

gender Gender refers to the classing of nouns or pronouns according to sex. Grammatical genders number four: feminine (*girl, she*), masculine (*boy, he*), neuter (*computer, it*), and common (*professionals, they*).

gerund A gerund is a verbal noun. Like the present participle, it ends in *ing* but it functions as a noun instead of a verb. The present participle in the following sentence is a gerund.

> ○ My colleagues appreciated her *speaking* frankly.

Compare this to the present participle, used, with its auxiliary, as a finite verb form:

> ○ She *was speaking* frankly.

The perfect participle may also be used as a gerund:

> ○ My colleagues appreciated her *having spoken* frankly.

Compare this to the use of the past participle, spoken, with its auxiliary, as a finite verb form:

> ○ I *have spoken* to you about this.

grammar Strictly speaking, grammar is the study of the rules governing the use of a given language. Once you master the vocabulary, the study of English grammar can reveal, like a series of linguistic X-rays, the language's structure and inner workings. Thus traditional (or "school") grammar is both prescriptive (laying down the rules) and descriptive (describing how the language works). When, on the other hand, we discuss the arts of clear, effective, and expressive speech and writing, we're discussing rhetoric. The more you read, write, study, and come to love the language, the more clearly you can see why grammar and rhetoric ought to be studied together (the way they were in Ancient Greece).

idiom Non-literal constructions and expressions that are characteristic of a given language are called idiomatic expressions, or idioms. Examples: *over the top, off the wall, out of sight, don't throw the baby out with the bathwater.*

impersonal construction An impersonal construction uses expletives (such as *it* or *there*) for expressions in which no noun or pronoun is stated as the subject of the verb. For example: *It* is raining.

indirect object   An indirect object follows the preposition *to* or *for*. When the indirect object follows a direct object, the preposition needs to be stated. (*She gave a gift to him*.) When the indirect object precedes the direct object, the preposition does not need to be stated; it is understood. (*She gave him a gift*.)

indirect question   An indirect question restates a question as a declarative sentence. Here is a direct question: *When will they arrive?* Here is an indirect question: *Niki asked when they would arrive*. (Notice that an indirect question is not, strictly speaking, a question at all, and so takes no question mark.)

indirect quotation   An indirect quotation is a restatement of another's original words (either spoken or written). A direct quotation restates the original words, exactly as spoken or written. The following is a direct quotation: He said, "I hope to see you at the game on Saturday." Here is the same information, second-hand, in an indirect quotation: He said he hopes to see me at the game on Saturday.

infinitive   An infinitive is a verbal that can be used as a noun, an adjective, or a pronoun, and it is often preceded by the word *to* (the sign of the infinitive). When used in a sentence, the *to* of the infinitive may be omitted, its meaning being understood. Here are examples of the infinitive functioning as three parts of speech: a noun (*to err* is human; *to forgive* is divine); an adjective (she brought a stack of books *to read*); and an adverb (he worked *to earn* his keep). The infinitive is also the first of the three principal parts of a verb, and it retains some of the characteristics of a verb: it can take objects and modifiers. If I write "to speak sincerely is a virtue," *to speak* is a verbal (an infinitive) acting as a noun. But the word *sincerely* is still an adverbial modifier (not an adjectival one).

inflection   Inflection means a change in the form (or spelling) of a word to show a change in its use or meaning. The inflection of adjectives and adverbs is called comparison (for example, *loud, louder, loudest,* or *quickly, more quickly, most quickly*). The inflection of nouns and pronouns is called declension (*I, me,* and *mine*). The inflection of verbs is called conjugation (*I have, you have, he has; we have, you have, they have*).

interjection   One of the eight parts of speech, an interjection exclaims; it is grammatically independent of the rest of the sentence and usually expresses an interruption, a surprise, or a strong feeling. (*Ouch! Hey you!*)

intransitive verb   An intransitive verb is an action verb without a direct object. In *The cat meowed*, the cat did not "meow" anyone or anything—the verb is intransitive.

irregular verb   Irregular verbs, sometimes called strong verbs, are those whose various forms don't follow a regular pattern. The inflection of irregular verbs often involves a change of vowel in the stem of the verb (rather than a change of spelling at the end of the word), as exemplified by the principal parts of the verb *see*: *see* (infinitive); *saw* (simple past tense); and *seen* (past participle).

linking verb   The linking verb expresses a condition or state of being (as opposed to the action verb, which expresses an action, though not necessarily a physical one). While an action verb may have its meaning completed with direct and indirect objects, a linking verb has its meaning completed with predicate complements (also called subject or subjective complements). The predicate complement is either a predicate noun or pronoun, in some way identifying the subject, or a predicate adjective, describing or modifying the subject.

marker   A marker is a word that signals the approach of a noun, verb, modifier, or subordinate clause. The articles are noun markers (*a hat, an apple, the opera*); auxiliary verbs are verb markers (*is going, has gone, may not come*); adverbs are markers for adjectives and other adverbs (*very nice, too funny, most happily*); relative pronouns and subordinating conjunctions are subordinate-clause markers (*the kid who lives next door, when she's good, she's great*).

modal auxiliaries   See AUXILIARIES.

modify   To modify means to describe, limit, or further define or describe a word. The two parts of speech that modify are adjectives and adverbs. Adjectives modify nouns or pronouns; adverbs modify verbs, adjectives, or other adverbs. Adjectives are often classed as one of three main types: proper (*a Dickensian scene, a Canadian writer*); limiting (*five women, the tallest man*); and descriptive (*blue skies, fluffy clouds*).

mood   Mood is a characteristic of verbs. There are three moods: indicative, for statements of fact (*the doorbell rang*); subjunctive, for a possibility, a wish, or something else contrary to fact (*if I were queen*); and imperative, for commands and requests (*stop yelling; please open the door*).

nominal   A nominal is a substantive or noun substitute (the word literally means "like a noun"). See also SUBSTANTIVE. In the following sentence, the substantive phrase is underlined: *I love swimming in the lake*.

non-finite verb   A non-finite verb is another name for a verbal, a verb form that functions as another part of speech. A verbal cannot serve as a predicate or sentence verb because it isn't conjugated; it shows no person or number. There are three kinds of non-finite verb forms or verbals: the gerund (the present participle used as a noun); the participle (the present, past, or perfect participle used as an adjective); and the infinitive (the first principal part of the verb, often preceded by the word *to*, used as a noun, adjective, or adverb).

noun   One of the eight parts of speech, a noun names. Nouns name people, places, and things, including concrete things, such as spoons and forks, and abstract things, such as ideas and qualities.

number   In grammar, number—singular or plural—applies to nouns and pronouns, and to verbs. A difference in number can mean a difference in form or spelling. For substantives, the issue is the spelling of plurals (*one cat, two cats; one goose, two geese*) and the spelling of plural possessives (*one cat's meow; two cats' meows*). For verbs, the issue is subject/verb agreement: singular subjects take singular verbs (*he goes*); plural subjects take plural verbs (*they go*).

object   There are three types of objects in English grammar: the object of a preposition, the direct object of a verb, and the indirect object of a verb. An object is always a SUBSTANTIVE, and follows either a preposition or a transitive verb. The simple object is the substantive itself; the complete object includes any modifiers. See also INDIRECT OBJECT.

objective (or object) complement   An objective complement is a word (noun, pronoun, or adjective) that follows the direct object of a verb, and completes the meaning of the clause.

- They elected John *dean*.
- We named the baby *Lienne*.
- She coloured her hair *auburn*.
- He painted the room *yellow*.

parallel construction   Attention to parallel construction can help improve your writing style dramatically. Grammatical constructions are parallel when they join elements of equal rank: words to words, phrases to phrases, and clauses to clauses.

- Unparallel: She loved reading, hiking, and to play the guitar.
- Correction: She loved reading, hiking, and playing the guitar.

parse   To parse a sentence is to analyze the grammatical forms and functions of its words, to break it down into its constituent parts.

participle   Participles are derived from verbs. There are three: the present participle (*e.g. talking*), the past participle (*talked*), and the perfect participle (*having talked*). When a participle isn't used as the main verb in a verb phrase (*I am talking; I have talked*), it is a verbal, functioning as an adjective (e.g. *the singing telegram; a done deed*). Note that the perfect participle does not function as a finite (or sentence) verb.

parts of speech   Parts of speech categorize words by function and form the basis of traditional English grammar. Every word in every sentence can be classed as one of these eight parts of speech: noun, pronoun, verb, adjective, adverb, preposition, conjunction, and interjection. Nouns name; pronouns substitute for nouns; verbs assert; adjectives and adverbs modify; prepositions and conjunctions link; interjections interrupt.

passive voice   See VOICE.

person   English grammar allows for first, second, and third persons, each of which may be singular or plural. First person is the person speaking (*I*, singular; *we*, plural). Second person is the person spoken to (*you*, singular and plural). Third person, usually used for expository writing, is the person or thing spoken about (*he, she, or it*, singular; *they*, plural).

phrase   A phrase is a group of related words that does not contain a subject and a predicate. A phrase serves as a single part of speech, functioning as a noun, an adjective, or an adverb. (In terms of form, rather than function, there are five basic kinds of phrases: prepositional, participial, gerund, infinitive, and absolute.)

plural   Plural means more than one. In English grammar, the term is applied to nouns (*one goose, two geese*) and pronouns (*I alone, we together*), as well as to subjects and predicates. For example, two subjects joined by the co-ordinating conjunction *and* form a plural subject.

point of view   The common sense meaning of point of view is the physical vantage point, or the mental attitude or approach of a given individual to something. In English grammar, however, the term relates to whether the writer relies on statements made in the first person, second person, or third person. For example, a first-person singular point of view looks out on the world from the perspective of an "I"; it is used in autobiography, letters, essays, and some narratives. If I decide to write in second person, I will use the pronoun *you* and probably focus on the perspective of the reader. This is the point of view used for many articles in popular magazines, especially "how-to" articles. The third-person point of view, because of its greater detachment and its almost limitless applicability, is the one most commonly used in expository writing. Compare the examples below:
First person point of view:
  o I think travel broadens the mind; that's certainly been my experience.
Second person point of view:
  o You travel, and discover that it broadens your mind.
Third person point of view:
  o Travel broadens the mind. (That has certainly been their experience.)
  o Whales are mammals.
  o History is written by the winners.

post position   Adjectives usually come before the nouns they modify; when they come after the noun, they are said to be in post position.
  o From her window seat, she surveyed the sky, *blue* and *cloudless*.

predicate   A predicate is that part of a sentence that asserts something about the subject and contains the main verb or verb phrase of the sentence. The simple predicate is the verb or verb phrase alone; the complete predicate is the simple predicate along with any objects or modifiers. A predicate can be compound, just as a subject can be compound.

○ Jack and Jill went up the hill to fetch a pail of water and fool around.

predicate adjectives, predicate nouns, and **predicate pronouns** See PREDICATE COMPLEMENTS.

predicate complements   Linking verbs do not take objects; they take predicate complements (also called subject or subjective complements). These predicate complements—predicate nouns, predicate pronouns, and predicate adjectives—complete the meaning of the verb by saying something about the subject. The predicate noun or pronoun identifies the subject. (*He is the groom. This is she*). The predicate adjective describes or modifies the subject. (*She was happy to be home. He felt good about the trip.*)

preposition   A preposition is a word that introduces an object, and shows the relation of the object to other words in the clause or sentence. Examples include *to, from, of, for, into* and *under*.

principal parts   Verbs are said to have three principal parts: the infinitive (to *eat*); the past tense (he *ate*); and the past participle (the one used with *have* to form the perfect tenses: he has *eaten*). All other forms and uses of the verb are derived from these three principal parts. To remember the three principal parts of any verb, substitute any verb for *walk* in the following sentences:

○ I walk today
○ I walked yesterday
○ I have walked a lot in the last two days.

pronoun   A pronoun substitutes for a noun; the noun it substitutes for is called its antecedent. Like nouns, pronouns are in one of three cases: subjective, objective, or possessive. Unlike nouns, pronouns change form to indicate each case. (Nouns change form for the possessive case only.)

regular verbs   Regular verbs (also called weak verbs) form their past tense and past participles by adding *-ed* to the infinitive form: *I move, I moved, I have moved; I walk, I walked, I have walked*. For regular verbs, the past tense and past participle (used to form the perfect tenses) are identical. This is not the case for irregular verbs. For the irregular verb *show*, for instance, the past tense is *showed*, but the past participle is *shown*.

sentence fragment   A sentence fragment, considered a grammatical error, is a group of related words without a subject and predicate, punctuated nonetheless as a sentence.

○ Men with brooms at the ready.
○ Women putting their feet up, lighting cigars.

Of course, professional writers use fragments routinely, in dialogue and for emphasis or effect. So go ahead and use them; you'll be in excellent company. Just make sure you know what you're doing and why.

sign of the infinitive The sign of the infinitive is the word *to* that often precedes the infinitive (*to go, to see, to arrive,* etc.). In certain expressions, especially with certain auxiliary verbs, the *to* is only implied: "He can [to] go." "I do [to] see."

singular Singular means only one (as distinguished from plural, meaning more than one) in the number classification of nouns or pronouns, and of subjects and predicates.

subject The grammatical subject of a sentence verb is the noun, pronoun, or other substantive about which something is asserted or by which some action is performed. The simple subject is the substantive itself; the complete subject includes the simple subject and any modifiers. A compound subject consists of two or more substantives linked by the conjunction *and*. (*Jack and Jill went up the hill.*)

subordinate clause A subordinate (or dependent) clause is a group of related words containing both a subject and a predicate. While an independent clause can stand by itself as a sentence, a subordinate clause needs to be attached to an independent clause to have meaning.
   ○ *Even though she wasn't feeling very well,* she won the race.

substantive A substantive is a noun or pronoun, or any group of words that acts as a noun (that functions as a subject or an object). A gerund, for example, is a substantive; like the present participle, it ends in *–ing*, but it is employed as a noun, not as an adjective. An infinitive can also function as a noun. Phrases and clauses that function as nouns are substantives. In the following sentence, the italicized phrase is a substantive because the whole phrase acts as the subject of the sentence:
   ○ *From Kamloops to Nelson* is about a day's ride.
The italicized words in the clause of the next example also form a substantive, acting as the object of the verb:
   ○ I hope *that they will arrive tomorrow.*

syntax For practical purposes, syntax is sentence structure. Most dictionaries and grammarians define the term rather more broadly as the way in which words are arranged to form phrases and sentences, along with the grammatical rules governing such arrangement.

tense Tense is that quality of verbs that tells the time of the action or condition expressed by the verb. There are six main tenses in English, the three simple or primary tenses (present, past, and future), and the three compound or secondary tenses (present perfect, past perfect, and future perfect). In addition are the progressive tenses (which use the auxiliary verb *be* and the present participle) and the perfect–progressive tenses (which use both *have* and *be* as auxiliaries).

transitive verb   A transitive verb is an action verb that has a direct object. (*We gather rosebuds. Lightning struck the tree.*) Most verbs can be used both transitively or intransitively.

verb   One of the eight parts of speech, the verb asserts something. Action verbs show the subject doing something (though not necessarily something physical or even visible); linking verbs show the subject being or experiencing something.

verb phrase   A verb phrase includes a main verb and any auxiliaries (*is going, was finished, will have taken,* etc.). When a verb phrase includes more than one auxiliary verb, the last verb is the main verb, and the first auxiliary sets the tense. Do not confuse a verb phrase with a VERBAL.

verbal   A verbal is a non-finite verb form; it functions not as a verb but as some other part of speech—as a noun, an adjective, or an adverb. There are three kinds of verbals: participles, which act as adjectives; gerunds, which act as nouns; and infinitives, which can act as nouns, adjectives, or adverbs. A verbal cannot function as a sentence verb, but like a verb, it can take objects and modifiers.

voice   Voice—active or passive—is a quality of action verbs. A verb is in active voice when the subject performs the action indicated. A verb is in passive voice when the subject is acted upon, when it receives the action of the verb. The passive voice is formed using the past participle with the appropriate form of the verb *be*.

   ◦ Active voice: I shot the sheriff.

   ◦ Passive voice: The sheriff was shot by me.

(Incidentally, the term "voice" has another, more literary meaning, to wit: the personality projected in a piece of writing, the sense of a real human speaking.)

Resources

Grammar, Usage, and Style

In addition to the *Canadian Oxford English Dictionary*, I have found the following sources especially helpful:

Cook, Claire Kehrwald. *The MLA's Line by Line: How to Edit Your Own Writing*. Boston: Modern Language Association of America, 1985.

Editing Canadian English. Prepared for the Editors' Association of Canada/ Association canadienne des réviseurs. Catherine Cragg, et al., eds. 2nd ed. Toronto: McClelland & Stewart, 2003.

Fowler, H. W. *A Dictionary of Modern English Usage*. 2nd ed. Revised by Sir Ernest Gowers. New York: Oxford University Press, 1983.

Gordon, Karen Elizabeth. *The Deluxe Transitive Vampire: A Handbook of Grammar for the Innocent, the Eager, and the Doomed*. New York: Pantheon, 1993.

Jespersen, Otto. *Essentials of English Grammar*. University: University of Alabama Press, 1964.

O'Connor, Patricia. *Woe Is I*. New York: Grosset/Putnam, 1996.

Pinckert, Robert C. *Pinckert's Practical Grammar: A Lively, Unintimidating Guide to Usage, Punctuation, and Style*. Cincinnati, OH: Writer's Digest Books, 1986.

Plotnik, Arthur. *The Elements of Editing*. New York: Macmillan, 1982.

Strunk, William and E. B. White. *The Elements of Style*. 3rd ed. New York: Macmillan Publishing Co., Inc., 1979.

Truss, Lynne. *Eats, Shoots and Leaves: The Zero Tolerance Approach to Punctuation*. New York: Penguin, 2003.

Writing

Barzun, Jacques. *Simple and Direct: A Rhetoric for Writers*. New York: Harper and Row, 1975.

Bates, Jefferson D. *Writing With Precision: How to Write So That You Cannot Possibly Be Misunderstood*. 3rd ed. Washington, DC: Acropolis Books Ltd., 1980.

Brande, Dorothea. *Becoming a Writer*. Los Angeles: Jeremy P. Tarcher, 1981. Reprint. (First published in 1934.)

Cameron, Julia. *The Right to Write*. New York: Jeremy P. Tarcher/Putman, 1998.

———. *The Sound of Paper*. New York: Jeremy P. Tarcher/Penguin, 2004.

Cappon, Rene J. *Associated Press Guide to News Writing*. New York: Macmillan, 1991.

Elbow, Peter. *Writing with Power: Techniques for Mastering the Writing Process*. Toronto: Oxford University Press, 1981.

Flesch, Rudolf, and A. H. Lass. *A New Guide to Better Writing*. New York: Harper and Row, 1949.

Goldberg, Natalie. *Writing Down the Bones*. Boston: Shambhala Publications, Inc., 1986.

Hale, Constance. *Sin and Syntax: How to Craft Wickedly Effective Prose*. New York: Broadway Books, 1999.

Howard, V. A., and J. H. Barton. *Thinking on Paper*. New York: William Morrow and Company Inc., 1986.

Kaye, Sanford. *Writing Under Pressure: The Quick Writing Process*. New York: Oxford University Press, 1989.

Lamott, Anne. *Bird by Bird*. New York: Bantam Doubleday Dell, 1994.

Nafisi, Azar. *Reading Lolita in Tehran: A Memoir in Books*. New York: Random House, 2003.

O'Connor, Patricia. *Words Fail Me: What Everyone Who Writes Should Know About Writing*. Orlando, FL: Harcourt, Inc., 1999.

Plotnik, Arthur. *The Elements of Expression*. New York: Henry Holt and Company, 1996.

Provost, Gary. *100 Ways to Improve Your Writing*. New York: New American Library, 1985.

Rico, Gabriele Lusser. *Writing the Natural Way*. Los Angeles: Jeremy P. Tarcher, Inc., 1983.

Robertson, Heather. *Writing From Life*. Toronto: McClelland & Stewart, 1998.

Rooke, Constance, ed. *Writing Home: A PEN Canada Anthology*. Toronto: McClelland & Stewart Inc., 1997.

Root, Robert L, Jr., and Michael Steinberg, eds. *The Fourth Genre: Contemporary Writers of/on Creative Nonfiction*. Needham Heights, MA: Allyn & Bacon, 1999.

Shaw, Harry. *20 Steps to Better Writing*. Totowa, NJ: Littlefield, Adams & Co., 1975.

Ueland, Brenda. *If You Want to Write*. St. Paul, MN: Schubert, 1983. (First published in 1938.)

Williams, Joseph M. *Style: Ten Lessons in Clarity & Grace*. 3rd ed. New York: HarperCollins, 1989.

Zinsser, William. *On Writing Well: An Informal Guide to Writing Nonfiction*. 5th ed. New York: HarperCollins, 1994.

Index